To:

Rulon Joh

A good

working to make a

good state better—

Don Wills

GEORGIA STUDIES

Donald T. Wells

VIEWPOINT PUBLICATIONS, INC.

Georgia Studies is the successor book to *This Is Your Georgia* which has been used in Georgia schools for the past quarter of a century. The author of *This is Your Georgia* was the late Bernice McCullar.

Viewpoint Publications, Inc.
P.O. Box 6
Woodville, AL 35776

Printed in the United States of America

Designed by Faith Nance
Production by Eleanor Cameron

Donald T. Wells is Professor of Political Science and Chairman of the Department of Political Science at West Georgia College. He has over thirty years experience in teaching.

Contents

INTRODUCTION

GEORGIA ON MY MIND

"History should tell a story," says historian Henry Steele Commager. From that story we should learn things about ourselves that enable us to enrich our lives and communities. Geography should give us a sense of place. An understanding of geography should enable us to live better in relation to our land and to make a better living from it. Government, in the words of Abraham Lincoln, should be "of the people, by the people and for the people." Understanding government should enable us to keep government representative and acting in the interest of the people. In a nutshell, these are the reasons why we study history, geography and government. We shall come back to these things many times throughout this book.

Why should we study history, geography and government?

Georgia's history, geography and government can teach us a lot. Georgia's history is a story full of triumphs and tragedies, of courage and cowardice, of great statesmen and self-serving politicians. But most of all it is the story of the daily enduring courage of ordinary men and women who have put their strength and their character into the state and made it great.

So Georgia's history is not just a list of dry-as-dust dates and facts. Dates are important because at that moment in history something happened to people. What happened? Why did it happen? What did they do about it? How does it affect us today? What can we learn from that experience?

How should we study history?

Georgia's geography is rich and varied. It is a land that helped shape our destiny. Mountains and plains, rivers and oceans, wind currents and land formations all have influenced where Georgians settled, how they lived, and what they became. How does our land affect us today? How can we be the best stewards of our natural heritage? What should we develop and what should we leave undeveloped? What can our past use of the land and its resources teach us about how we ought to use them now and in the future?

Georgia's government touches our lives each moment—while we sleep and while we are awake. It helps protect us against physical harm. For many, it provides essential services like water and sewage disposal. It does everyday things like disposing of garbage and extraordinary things like providing schools to educate our people. What kind of government do we have? How has it served our state in the past? How can we assure that it will serve the best interest of our state in the future?

How should we study government?

And, yes, in all of them—history, geography and government—there is both fact and fiction. In many ways, the facts are made more colorful by the folklore laced into them—the Barnsley Gardens where brothers dueled with poisoned wine, the ghosts of headless children who danced by the moonlit pool, the superstitions we still have, the fictitious stories of Georgia men and women. Separate fact from folklore but know and cherish both for what they can teach us about ourselves and our land.

Through it all, do not forget to look into your own community. What are the words on that monument or historical marker you pass every day? How do you explain the large round rocks stacked on one another at the edge of the woods? Who was the most famous person who ever lived in your community? Do you have a city manager and who is that person? What is the major economic activity in the place you call home?

The more you know about Georgia, the better you will be able to help solve its problems. Just think of the Georgia we could build if we learned from our past, used the talents we have in the present and invested our energies here. All of us are making history for Georgians to read tomorrow. What kind of history will it be? Can we handle wisely the swift changes bearing down upon us? No road leads back, as Alvin Toffler points out in *Future Shock.* We must learn to cope with change and to direct it toward goals that will make Georgia a better place to live and work. The best preparation for the future is to know the past, the land and its people and the way they lived their lives together in state and community.

Why study about Georgia?

It is wise and good to know distant lands and faraway planets. But it is unwise and bad for the human spirit to know those things and not know the place called home. Georgia is a remarkable place to know. It is your history, your land and your government.

CHAPTER 1

THE LAND AS LITERATURE

A study of the land can tell us much. It can certainly tell us much about the land itself—about natural features, mountains and rivers, and natural resources. But it can also tell us a great deal about ourselves. A study of the land can indicate why immigrants settled where they did, why they planted the crops they grew and established the businesses and industries that they did. Mankind has been described as an "earthbound creature." Only recently has man gone into space and even now astronauts come back home to the Earth. The study of the land, then, is one of the most basic factors in understanding who we are and why we developed the way we did.

Why study geography?

GEORGIA BEFORE MAN
A Varied and Rich Land

History is the systematic record of the experience of mankind. But the land existed before man. Robert Frost made this point famous in his poem entitled *The Gift Outright.* Reading the poem at President Kennedy's inauguration, Frost said "this land was ours before we were the land's." We call the time when the land existed before man **prehistory**. There was a time when the land called Georgia was without human inhabitants.

What is prehistory?

One of the most useful ways available for social scientists to understand things is the thought experiment. A thought experiment is thinking carefully and logically about an event or topic. We will ask you to do several thought experiments throughout the book. To think carefully and logically is one of the most important things we can learn to do.

What was Georgia like before man?

So engage in a thought experiment. What was Georgia like before man? A good place to start thinking about that question is to say that anything man-made would not exist. Products created or made by man are called **artifacts**. Artifacts tell scientists important things. We can learn where people lived, what they did, and even some of what they believed from artifacts. Now think of all the things that are man-made and take them out of your view of what Georgia in prehistory was like. There would be no roads, not even trails. There would be no buildings, no fields cleared for farming, no lakes created by dams. There simply would be no artifacts. How many artifacts can you think of that would not have existed in prehistory?

Now with all the artifacts gone, think of what Georgia was like before man. If you thought back far enough in prehistory, you would find that much of what is now Georgia was under the sea. There was a narrow band of land along what is known as the **fall line** today. Interestingly, that narrow band

Representative Artifacts Courtesy: Archaeological Lab, West Georgia College

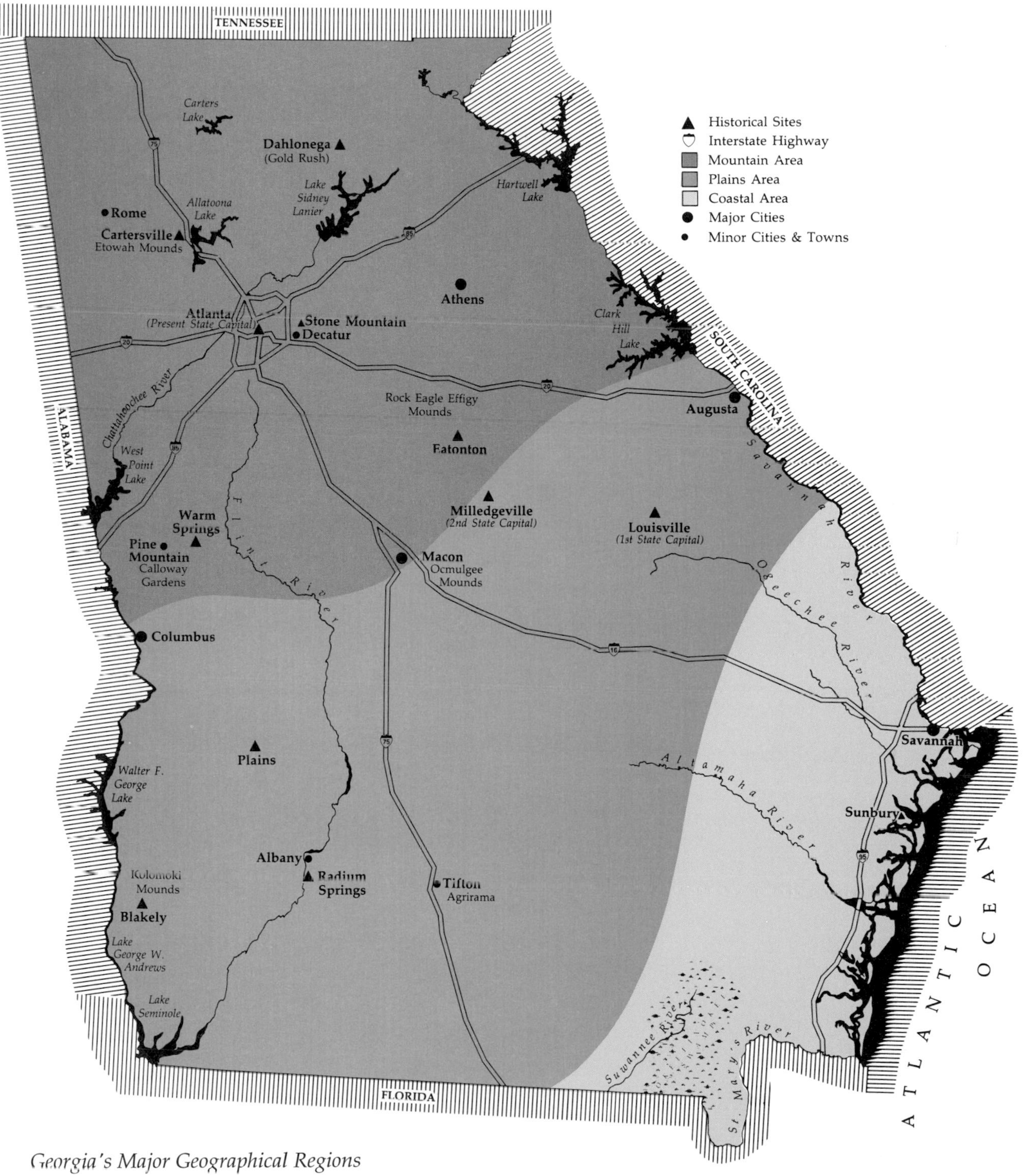

Georgia's Major Geographical Regions

What factors influenced land formation?

of land was dotted with volcanos. Two events were most important in explaining how the present land mass of Georgia was formed. The first is called **uplift** and involves mountain formation. The second was the movement of the **continental ice sheet** which caused sea level to change by several hundred feet. It was that change in the level of the sea that most determined the shape of Georgia's sea islands. Also, some geologists think that the Okefenokee Swamp was formed when a bay was cut off from the ocean by the emergence of a **barrier island**. As the sea level dropped, the island served as a dam holding water in the swamp.

Georgia's land mass in its present form is rich and varied. Georgia is divided into three distinct geographical regions. Across the northern part of the state are the mountains. Georgia's mountains, a part of the Appalachian range, are older than the Rockies, the Alps, or the Himalayas. The Appalachian system runs 1,600 miles from Canada's Gaspe Peninsula down through Georgia to Alabama. The Appalachian Trail, the longest continuous hiking trail in the world, starts at Springer Mountain in north Georgia and runs 2,065 miles to Mt. Katahdin in Maine. Much of the old mountain area of the Cherokee Indians is now the Chattahoochee National Forest. This beautiful area spreads over some 20 counties and contains nearly two million acres.

What are the regions?

South of the mountains, Georgia consists of the gently rolling plateau. The southern boundary of this region, the **fall line**, is an imaginary line from Columbus through Macon to Augusta. At the fall line, rivers used to fall from the plateau. The falls created water power and power plants were first established in this area. Although the falls have now been eroded away, many of Georgia's cities developed in this region because of the early availability of water power.

Moving to the southeast, the plateau drops off the fall line to a great **coastal plain**. The plain is rich, flat land ending with

126 miles of coastline. The Georgia coast is unique in several ways. It is a complex system of salt marshes and sounds. Georgia hosts one-third of all the salt marshes on the entire Atlantic coast. Along with the marshes, there are the eight great barrier islands. Unlike many other islands along the Atlantic coast, Georgia's islands are largely undeveloped even today. About two-thirds of the land mass of the barrier islands is in the form of parks, refuges, or preserves. These islands are important features of Georgia's geography.

How is the coastal plain unique?

Georgia and her neighbors

IMPORTANT GEOGRAPHICAL FEATURES OF TODAY'S GEORGIA

Let's move beyond prehistory to think about important features of Georgia's geography today. As you read about these geographical features, try to imagine how they affected people—how people settled the state, what type of farming and manufacturing they did, even how these geographical features affected their art and literature. We will give you some indication of these things.

Size and Location

Georgia is the largest state east of the Mississippi River. It has a total land area of 58,910 square miles. If you were traveling from north to south, the state is 315 miles in length. From east to west, Georgia is 250 miles wide. The geographical center of the state, appropriately marked, is 17 miles southeast of Macon. The highest point in the state is Brasstown Bald with an elevation of 4,784 feet above sea level. And, of course, the Georgia coast is at sea level.

How big is Georgia?

Georgia is located in the southeastern region of the United States. This area is part of a larger region referred to as the

In what region of the U.S. is Georgia located?

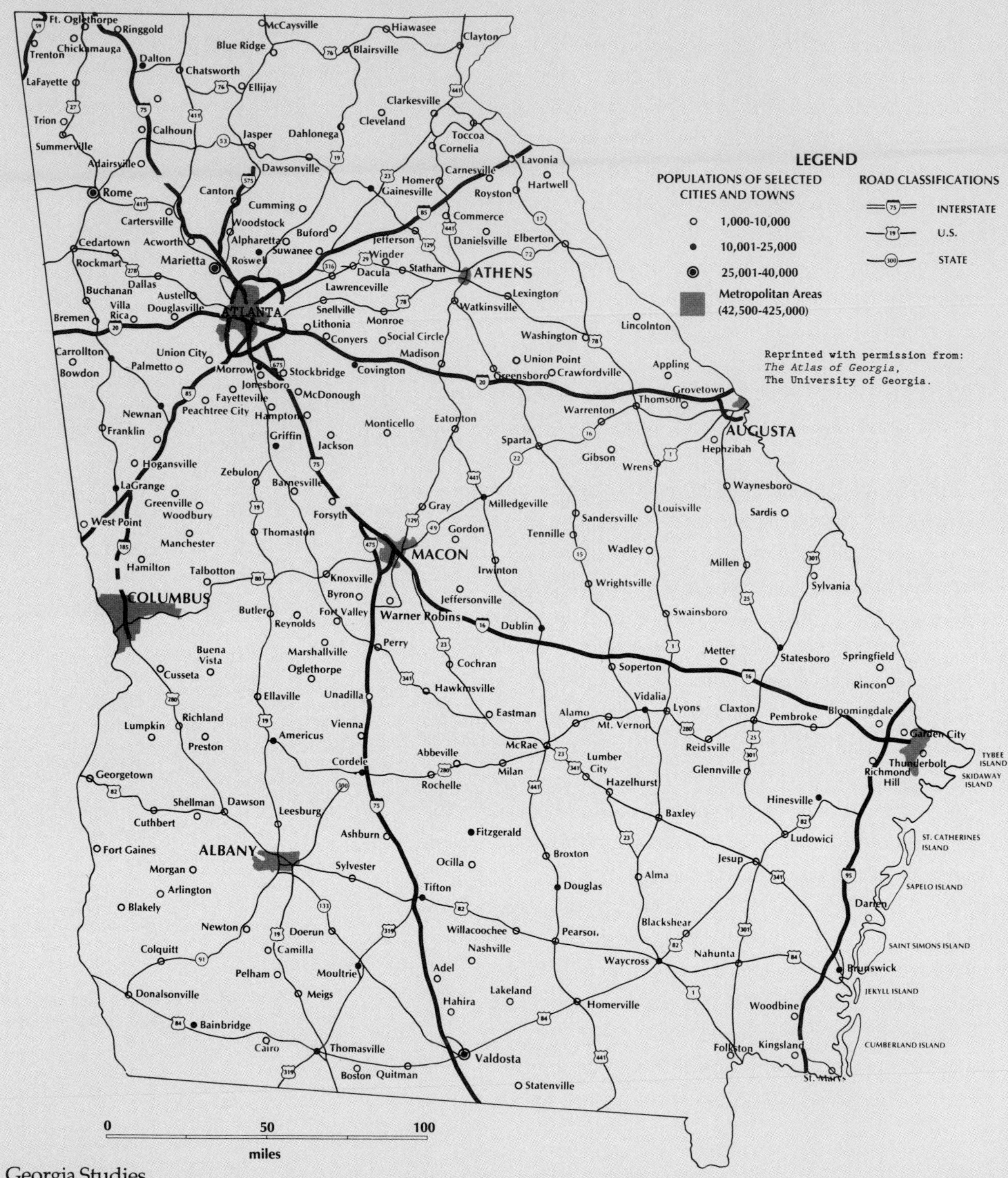

Reprinted with permission from:
The Atlas of Georgia,
The University of Georgia.

Sunbelt. The region is called the **Sunbelt** because of its temperate climate and many days of sunshine. The Sunbelt is generally viewed as containing a number of important resources for economic growth. As a result, the entire region is growing at a more rapid rate than the nation as a whole. Georgia was one of the fastest growing states in the nation in population in the 1990 census.

Within the Sunbelt, Georgia shares its boundaries with five other states. It shares much more than a boundary with them. Georgia and its neighbors have a common geography. Additionally, there are scholars who say that the southeastern region is the only one in the nation with a distinctive culture. Most of us are familiar with the "southern drawl" that is the unique feature of the region's language. There have also been many common elements in the economic development of the states in the southeast.

How is the southeast distinct?

When you look at a globe, the oceans make distances look vast. But actually Georgia is close to many areas of the world. For example, the state is closer to the Yucatan peninsula in Mexico than it is to Denver, Colorado. Air travel has "shrunk the globe." From Atlanta it is only six hours by air to Western Europe, nine hours to Argentina and twenty hours to Japan. You can get a good sense of Georgia's relationship with the rest of the nation and the world by looking at the map with its projection centered on Atlanta. This projection is very useful in understanding where Georgia is in relation to Japan, Africa and other important places in the world.

Where is Georgia in the world?

Climate

There are two major climate zones in Georgia. One of them is very small and includes the most northern part of the state. This mountainous area is in the cool temperate zone. Most of the state is in the warm **temperate subtropical zone**. This

What are the climate zones?

Georgia's Global Relationship

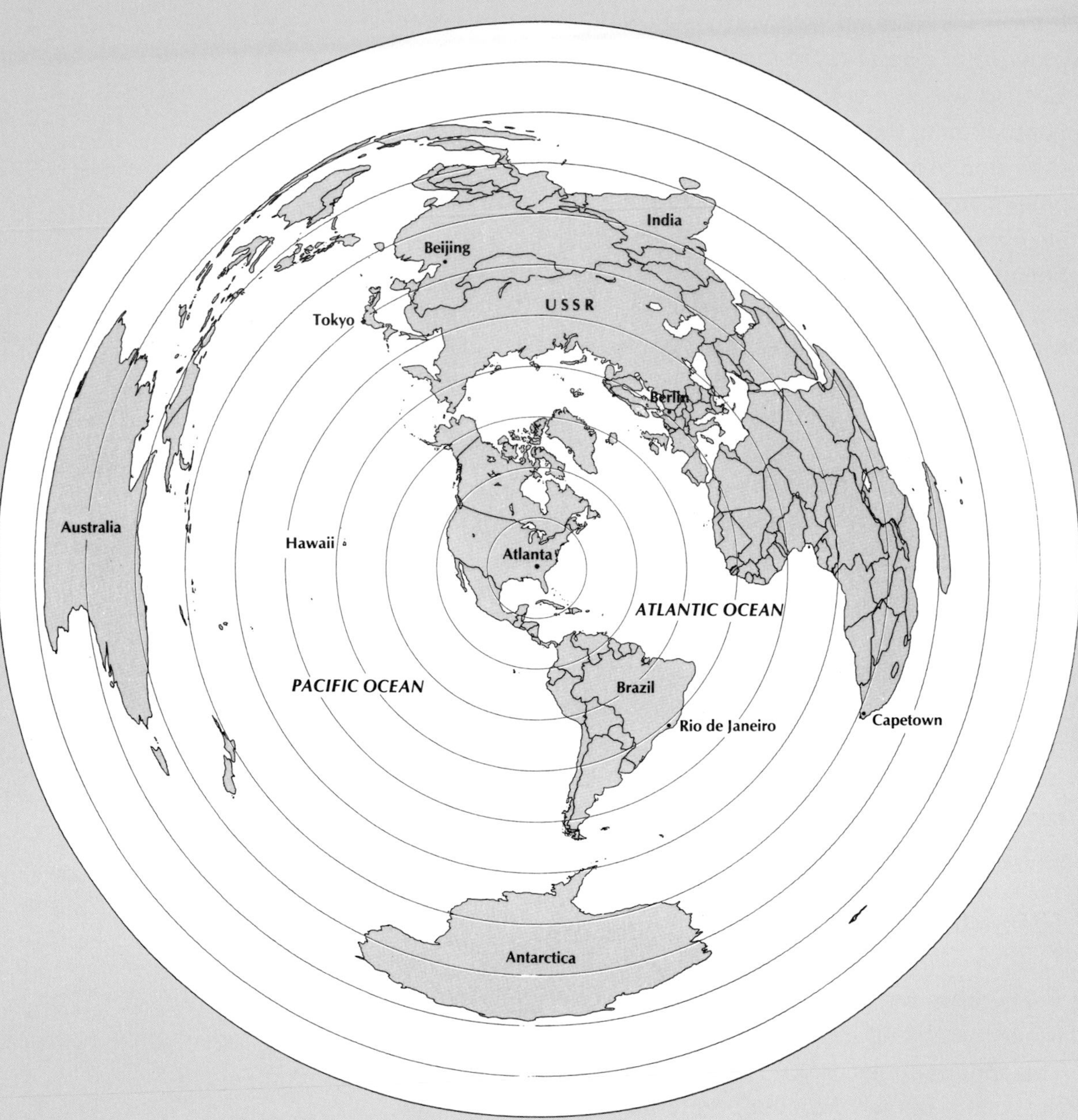

Source: The Atlas of Georgia

means that it has a moist climate year-round. There are no long dry periods in the state. It also means that Georgia's summers are hot and have sizable amounts of rainfall. Early settlers in Georgia, for example, complained about the hot climate since they were accustomed to the cooler areas of Europe.

Temperature and rainfall amounts vary between years. So figures on them are generally expressed by averages. To illustrate Georgia's subtropical climate, Atlanta has an average January temperature of 42.4 degrees and an average July temperature of 78.0 degrees. Atlanta receives an average of 48.34 inches of rain a year. Its average relative humidity in January is 66 per cent and in July, 70 per cent. All of these factors make up what is known as **the comfort index**. As implied in the term sunbelt, Georgia's climate is attractive in that regard.

What is Georgia's temperature and rainfall?

Natural Resources

Georgia has several different types of soil. Along the coastal plain, the primary soil type is **alapaha**. This is a very sandy soil that is best suited for timber production. With the nearly level nature of the coastal plain, this soil does not drain well. After the coastal plain, there is a wide band of soil of the **faceville** type. This consists of a sandy clay and is well suited to many agricultural purposes. Much of Georgia's farming occurs in this area. In the southwest corner of the state, the **tifton** soil pattern occurs. This is also a sandy clay and is the most adaptive soil type in the state. The **cecil** soil type is found across the center of the state, roughly from the fall line to the mountains. This is the well-known "red clay" soil that many people associate with Georgia. It is also very good for farming. The northeastern part of the state is dominated by the **fannin** soil type. This has a sandy loam surface and a

What types of soils are found in Georgia?

sandy clay subsoil. It is best suited for forest and pasture. In the northwest area **townley** soil is found. This type has a lot of shale and sandstone content and can be useful for crops and pastures.

What minerals are located in Georgia?

Minerals are another of Georgia's valuable natural resources. Georgia is one of the nation's leading mineral producers. The state ranks first in production of kaolin, fuller's earth (clay), granite, marble and crushed slate. It ranks second in the production of crushed marble, kyanite, and iron oxide pigments. There is major production of feldspar, bauxite, barite, and mica. The world's largest open pit quarry is at Tate in Pickens County. The value of Georgia's mineral production in 1983 was $850,224,000. Minerals are very important to Georgia's economy.

How much commercial forests does Georgia have?

Georgia has more acres of commercial forest than any other state in the nation. In 1982, there were 24 million acres in commercial forest. That means that there were other forest lands as well. The state's climate and soils are best suited to the southern pine. This tree is a fast grower, reaching pulpwood size in 15 years and timber size in 35 years. The value of Georgia's forest industry products is $6 billion a year. That makes the forest industry the second largest in the state. The textile industry is the largest.

Water

What is an aquifer?

Georgia has great surface and groundwater resources. Groundwater is found in underground systems known as **aquifers**. As a source of water, aquifers tend to be more important south of the fall line. They provide water for both home consumption and irrigation. To farmers, the depth of the water table is an important consideration

North of the fall line, most of the water used comes from surface water. Georgia has more than 75 rivers. Not all of them flow into the Atlantic. Three, the Chattahoochee, the Flint, and the Suwannee, flow into the Gulf of Mexico. Since early immigrants tended to settle along the rivers, much of Georgia's early history happened on the rivers. As we describe some of the most important rivers, remember to think about how they affected people—the way they settled, what they did and how they felt.

What are Georgia's most important rivers?

The Savannah River is one of the most important rivers historically. It is 314 miles long, forming the boundary between Georgia and South Carolina. It drains 10,000 square miles of the state and has the second highest annual discharge of any Georgia river. It is tidal for 50 miles above its mouth.

De Soto was probably the first white man to see the Savannah. He crossed it in the spring of 1540. The Savannah is the site of Oglethorpe's settlement at what is now the city of Savannah. A century after Oglethorpe, Florence Martus, Georgia's famous *Waving Girl,* began waving to passing ships, a handkerchief by day and a lantern by night. Sailors from all over the world learned to watch for her friendly wave.

The Savannah River forms the boundary between Georgia and South Carolina.

The Chattahoochee River was made famous by Sidney Lanier, Georgia's first great poet, in *The Song of the Chattahoochee.* The river begins with a trickle of water near Horse Trough Mountain in Union County. From there, it flows 436 miles to the Gulf of Mexico. After it gets to West Point, it forms the Georgia-Alabama boundary. In the southwest corner of the state it joins the Flint to form the Apalachicola.

The Indian name Chattahoochee means painted rock. Somewhere along its banks, never revealed, the Indians found their materials for war paint.

The Suwannee River is thought to rise somewhere in the soft, weird depths of Georgia's Okefenokee Swamp. It flows through Florida and on to the Gulf of Mexico. Suwannee means "the river of the deer" and the river may be named for an Indian Princess.

Stephen Foster

Stephen Foster, the man who set the world singing about the river, never laid eyes upon its black waters. He had written a song about a river for Christy's Minstrels in New York and he needed a name for the river. He considered the Pee Dee, which South Carolina calls, "the mighty Pee Dee." Then he thought of the Yazoo River in Mississippi. This name means "river of death" and is not very musical. Finally, putting his finger on the map, he came upon the Suwannee River. When he published the song, he found that nobody had ever heard of the Suwannee, so he called the song *Old Folks at Home.*

The Suwannee River has a ghost, Hannah, said to have been a pretty girl deserted by her lover, a British soldier. Legend says she stands on the banks of Hannah's Island, in the river, and calls to boatmen, "Throw me your rope and I'll tie it." And then she screams!

Georgia shares the 285-mile Coosa River with Alabama. It is formed at Rome by the 99-mile Etowah and the swift 45-mile Oostanaula. The name Etowah means "place of the dead wood," and Oostanaula means "rock that bars your way."

The Altamaha River was, until 1763, the southern boundary of Georgia. In that year, at the end of the French and Indian War, England acquired the land below the Altamaha and Georgia's territory was doubled. The Altamaha drains a basin of 965,000 Georgia acres, much of it in forests. Two seaports, Darien and Brunswick, are at its mouth.

The Ogeechee River is a 250-mile tidal river which flows parallel to the Savannah. It rises in Greene County in the Piedmont Plateau, flows by Louisville, the old state capital, and enters the Atlantic by way of Ossabaw Sound.

Early in the 20th century, Henry Ford bought 80,000 acres in Bryan and Chatham counties. He hired 1,000 men to landscape the site and build a beautiful home overlooking the Ogeechee. Once a month his master mechanic would come down from Michigan to dust his $60,000 chandelier. Ford and his wife gave money for several buildings on the Berry School campus at Rome.

The Flint River is 330 miles long. It starts near Atlanta and flows to the Gulf. Once boats carried cargo and passengers on it—boats with odd names: *The Joke, Hard Times, The Flint Bride,* and *Flint Fanny*. Bainbridge was once an Indian trading village run by an Englishman married to an Indian girl. Now it is Georgia's chief inland port, with a million dollar dock and the great Jim Woodruff Dam, which forms Lake Seminole.

One of the most crooked rivers in the world is the St. Mary's on Georgia's southern boundary. Of its 180 miles, 175 meander between two points only 65 miles apart. It may start at Billy's Lake in the Okefenokee Swamp. Classed as a tidal river, it is one of the deepest rivers for its width in the United States.

Once ports and trading posts were all along the river. It was also a favorite site for pirates and smugglers. At St. Mary's once, smugglers lifted a horse into the church tower to distract attention while they unloaded smuggled cargoes of gin and rum before they sped out to sea.

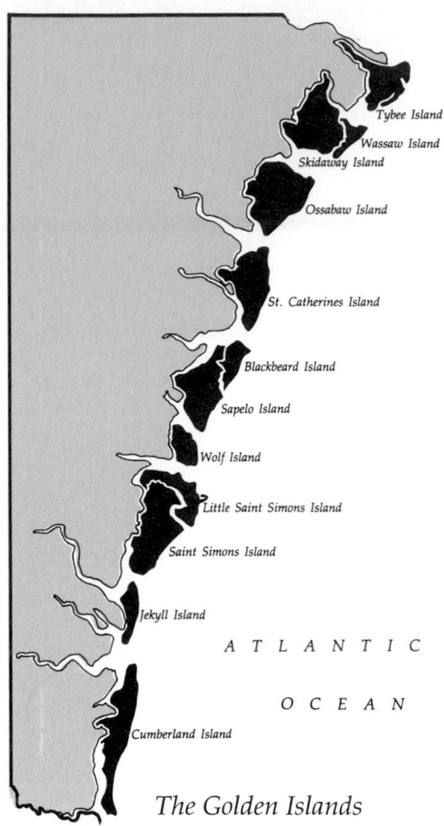

The Golden Islands

Why are the Golden Islands important to Georgia?

What is important about each of the Golden Islands?

The Indian name for this river was Thathlothlaguphka. It means "rotten fish." However, old river hands remember that sailing ships came from afar to get casks of St. Mary's river water because it lasted, sweet and fresh, through long voyages. The town of St. Mary's was founded before the Revolution by wealthy Englishmen on a 1,672-acre tract bought for $38.

The Golden Islands

Past and future bump into each other on the Golden Islands along the Georgia coast. Famous in history and legend, these sun-splashed islands are prosperous because of sea-related industries and tourism. But the problem is to keep a balance between development and conservation. There is strong disagreement about the future of the islands. Some believe the islands should be developed commercially. Others believe they should be left in their natural state. An official from the National Park Service has said, "Georgia's islands are the greatest recreation resource in America." We will describe some of the best known of the Golden Islands.

Wassaw Island will be kept forever wild. In 1866 George Parsons bought the island for $2,500 and dropped the deed into his wife's lap while they were honeymooning there. In 1969 the Nature Conservancy, Inc., bought the island from the Parsons Trust for $1 million and gave it to the federal government to be kept for birdwatching and nature study. There are no plans to build a bridge to connect it to the mainland. Sometimes called the smallest, wildest and best of all Georgia's islands, Wassaw is a natural museum for nature study. None of its trees—some over 250 years old—have been cut for over a century.

Ossabaw Island, 20 miles below Savannah, is the northernmost of the chain of barrier islands. In its 40,000 acres are jungles, dunes, highlands, marshes, forests and rivers—all teeming with wildlife. There is an Institute of Human Ecology where students from many colleges come for study and research, sometimes living off the resources of the island alone. Trees grow to strange shapes on Ossabaw, twisted by winds and storms. One with a grotesque form was called the "Gnome Tree." On this and all the islands turtles crawl up to lay their eggs in the sand. It is not unusual for 100 turtles to come in one night. Each lays from 85 to 150 eggs, weeping all the while. Nobody knows why.

St. Catherines Island contains 25,000 acres and is 16 miles long. It was the home of Button Gwinnett, one of Georgia's three signers of the Declaration of Independence. The house thought to be Gwinnett's was renovated in 1929 and the old slave cabins made into guest cottages. In 1943, the island was bought by E.J. Noble who had made a fortune with LifeSavers. His daughter set up the Noble Foundation and designated the University of Georgia to determine the use to be made of the island.

Blackbeard Island, tucked into the side of Sapelo, was once the haunt of Blackbeard the pirate, an 18th-century rascal who may have hidden his loot here. Blackbeard's name was Edward Teach. He was plundering coastal ships from Nova Scotia to the West Indies in his ship *Queen Anne's Revenge* about 1702. A picture now in the main house on the island shows a fierce-looking man with a heavy black beard tied with tiny bows, each bow said to represent a wife he had along the seaboard. He used to stick slow-burning ropes into his braids, and with knives shining and guns blazing, terrified the passengers of the ships he plundered. If they were slow to give rings, he chopped off their fingers. Many other pirates hid treasures along the shore. Robert Louis Stevenson drew the character of Long John Silver in *Treasure Island* from one of them.

Blackbeard

In 1914 Woodrow Wilson had the island made into a refuge for water fowl. About 20,000 ducks spend the winter here. Deer roam through the sun and the silver fog. There are also curlews, sandpipers, raccoons, hoot owls, bald eagles, ospreys, red-tailed hawks, turtledoves, rabbits, snakes and many other forms of wildlife.

The story of **Sapelo Island** is entangled with the French Revolution. In 1789 a number of French noblemen took refuge on Sapelo from the Reign of Terror and its busy guillotine. The noblemen planned to raise and sell slaves but they quarreled and the scheme was not successful.

The last private owner of Sapelo was Richard J. Reynolds, heir to the tobacco fortune. In 1954 he made possible the establishment on the island of the University of Georgia's Marine Institute. The work of the Institute contributes greatly to the knowledge of the sea and its promise for mankind's future.

After Reynolds died, the State of Georgia acquired ownership of the entire island except for 400 acres reserved for the residents of Hog Hammock, a black community. Sapelo is a National Estuarine Sanctuary.

Sea Island is the location of Retreat Plantation, home of Thomas Butler King and his wife. John James Audubon had been in Savannah taking orders for his book, *Birds of America*, at $1,000 a copy. He wrote his wife Lucy of a chance visit with the Kings:

> Our boat was passing the island when a sudden storm drove it on to land. I made for the shore, and met a gentleman named King on the beach. I presented him my card and was immediately invited to dinner. I visited his garden and got into such agreeable conversation and quarters that I was fain to think that I had landed on one of those fairy islands said to have existed in the golden age.

The Cloisters, a world-famed resort, was opened in 1928 on the site of Retreat Plantation.

St. Simons Island was the site of Oglethorpe's only home in Georgia, Orange Hall, near the village and fort of Frederica.

Frederica has been excavated and established as a national park.

A way of life grew up on St. Simons that has now vanished. The plantation owners sent to Europe for their clothes, books, and furniture. Tutors from Harvard and Yale and governesses from England were obtained for their children. Guests from all over the world were entertained lavishly. The life of the island centered about Christ Church, established under the Church of England in 1736.

St. Simons, like the other islands, has its ghosts. Two headless children are said to dance about a pool on moonlit nights. At Ebo Landing a group of chained Africans from the Ibo country of Biafra dashed into the water and drowned rather than become slaves. It is said that their tribal death chant can still be heard on dark nights. The gray, ghostly moss and the eternally lonely sound of the sea make St. Simons a good place for telling shivery tales.

Christ Church on St. Simons Island

An old lighthouse on St. Simons Island.

The Shrady James Mansion on Jekyll Island

Jekyll Island was once one of the most famous resorts in the world. It was acquired in 1791 by Christopher Dubignon, an aristocratic French refugee from the Terror. In 1886, his heirs sold it to 100 millionaires who together were said to control one-sixth of all the money in the world. One of them was blind Joseph Pulitzer, the legendary newspaperman who set up the famed Pulitzer Prizes. Pulitzer was so sensitive to noise that he paid a boat captain $100 a day not to blow his boat whistle when he passed the island. "Indian Mound," the Rockefeller cottage, with 25 rooms and 15 baths, is now the Georgia history museum.

A telephone with an old-fashioned crank stands in a case on Riverview Drive. It commemorates the first transcontinental telephone call made in the United States, on Jan. 25, 1915. Why was Jekyll Island involved? Because Theodore N. Vail, then president of the American Telephone and Telegraph

Company, was there with an injured ankle. A thousand miles of copper wire was strung so that Vail could get in on the conversation with Dr. Alexander Graham Bell, inventor of the telephone, who was in New York; Bell's assistant, Thomas Watson, who was in San Francisco; and President Woodrow Wilson, the former Georgian, who was at the White House.

The millionaires finally gave up their retreat. In 1947, Georgia bought the island for a playground resort and convention center. With its 10 miles of beach and its beautiful buildings, it is now a show place.

Cumberland Island was called "Missoe" by the Indians. Oglethorpe changed that to Cumberland at the request of an Indian boy who went to England with him in 1734 and had been given a gold watch by the young Duke of Cumberland.

In 1970, the National Park Service acquired 27,000 acres on the island, assuring its preservation as a National Seashore in its wilderness state. Cumberland, 22 miles long, is the largest, southernmost, and best preserved of the Golden Isles of Georgia. It is possibly the last truly untouched such landmark off the Atlantic coast. In 1981, the Candler family of Atlanta, known for its early connection with the Coca-Cola Company, made an agreement to sell its 1,350 acres of land on Cumberland to the National Park Service. The sale price was $9.8 million, far below the appraised value. It assures that Cumberland can be preserved as a wilderness area.

The Skidaway Institute of Science, the research arm of the Ocean Science Center of the Atlantic, is located on **Skidaway Island**. The institute conducts vast research, largely financed by the federal government, into the almost limitless resources found in the sea.

A high percentage of Earth's creatures live in the sea. Ecologists now believe it is a scientific necessity to save the estuaries and their rich marsh grasses. These areas produce more protein per acre than the most fertile land.

GEORGIA'S SEVEN WONDERS

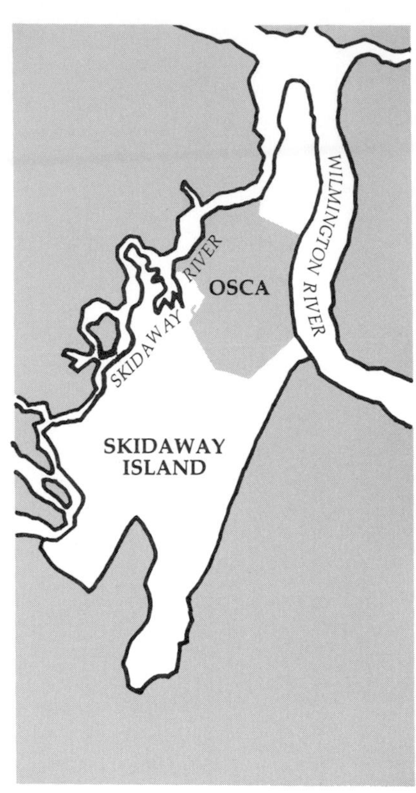

How was the swamp formed?

The ancients had their seven wonders of the world, all man-made, but Georgia has many natural wonders. Seven of them are the Okefenokee Swamp, Warm Springs, Amicalola Falls, Providence Canyons, Radium Springs, Tallulah Gorge, and Stone Mountain. These great natural wonders have affected Georgia's people and history in important ways.

The Okefenokee Swamp

This mysterious, weirdly beautiful swamp of 412,000 acres is the second largest freshwater swamp in the United States. The Indian name for it was O-wa-qua-phenoga. It means "the land of the trembling earth," because of the peculiar sponge-like quality of the soil and the water under it. William Bartram wrote about its gloomy beauty in 1774. In 1889, the Suwannee Canal Company bought the swamp from Georgia and spent over a million dollars trying to drain it for rich farming land. The venture failed. In 1937 President Franklin D. Roosevelt designated it as a wildlife refuge.

Once part of the ocean, the swamp was cut off by Trail Ridge when the rest of Georgia rose out of the sea. This 130-mile ridge still separates the swamp from the Atlantic. The swamp is at the head of the St. Mary's River. Oddly, no river flows into the swamp.

Its wildlife includes alligators and colorful birds. Among the starkly beautiful growing things are cypress, black gum, and bay trees draped with old Spanish moss. There are 40 kinds of frogs that live in the swamp. One of them, the "carpenter frog," makes a sound like a man hammering nails. There are also tiny mice of a strangely golden color, with bright brown eyes.

Vereen Bell, Georgia novelist who died in World War II, based his novel *Swamp Water* on life in the Okefenokee.

The Okefenokee Swamp.

Warm Springs

Why is Warm Springs world-famous?

The Creek Indians often brought their wounded from the wars to Warm Springs to be healed by the gentle waters. The place became world-famous when Franklin D. Roosevelt came to the spring in search of treatment for polio. The temperature of the water is about 87 degrees Fahrenheit. Patients crippled with polio can exercise their limbs in it. The Warm Springs Foundation was established by him and his friends.

Amicalola Falls

The Indian name means "tumbling waters." The falls are near the Georgia end of the Appalachian Trail in northwest Georgia. Seven waterfalls cascade over Amicalola Ridge, dropping over 700 feet into the Amicalola River.

Providence Canyons

How were the canyons formed?

Sometimes called "the little Grand Canyons," they are in a state park eight miles west of Lumpkin, near the Chattahoochee River. They are a phenomenon of terrible land erosion started only about 150 years ago. Some of the chasms are now 200 to 300 feet deep and cover a thousand acres.

Like a great hungry monster out of mythology, the canyons have devoured half the county's farming fields, part of the forest, and even houses. One family saw the canyon take its fields, then its barn and yard, the family home, and last of all, a fig tree by the door.

The area has 43 different soils. The cliffs shade from dazzling white through bright red, candy pinks, fudge brown, sky blue, sunset yellow, and purple like far-off mountain peaks.

The canyons get their name from the Providence Methodist Church in the vicinity.

Radium Springs

Four miles below Albany, Radium Springs are now the center of a resort hotel. Their cool blue waters, 68 degrees Fahrenheit, were considered by the Creek Indians to have healing powers like the waters of Warm Springs. The Indians thought their blue color dropped from the blue skies. The main spring is the largest in Georgia, flowing 70,000 gallons per minute. The source, as well as the name, is a mystery.

Radium Springs

Tallulah Gorge

Habersham County's Tallulah Gorge is a dramatic sight—a canyon with thick, swamp-like growth on its sides. For many years, Tallulah Falls was one of the state's tourist attractions. People came to see the spectacular gorge and to visit nearby Tallulah Falls School, known as the "Light in the Mountains."

Legends hover around Tallulah. The Indian word Tallulah means "terrible." Adding to the mystery, no Indian artifacts have been found in the gorge, even though Indians lived in the vicinity.

Stone Mountain

Georgia's oldest and newest scenic attraction is Stone Mountain, a great granite monolith. It is the largest exposed granite rock in the world. It covers 563 acres, is 650 feet high, two miles long, and seven miles around.

The Indians called it Crystal Mountain and held councils on its summit. The first white man to see it was probably the Spaniard Juan Pardo who was sent to Georgia in 1567 to build some forts. He noted that rubies and diamonds could be found lying around Crystal Mountain. (Geologists today say that the "rubies and diamonds" were most likely garnets and quartz crystals.)

Why was Stone Mountain important to the Indians?

Early in the 20th century the United Daughters of the Confederacy set up plans for the carving of a gigantic memorial on the mountain, with figures of Lee, Davis and Jackson. The sculptor Gutzon Borglum, well into the work, entertained 40 guests at breakfast on the shoulder of Lee. The completed figure was to be 130 feet high, including Lee's horse Traveller. But the money ran out, disagreements set in, and the memorial remained unfinished.

What is the history of the sculpture?

However, on May 9, 1970, after 60 years, the Confederate Memorial at Stone Mountain, completed by Walter Hancock,

Stone Mountain is the world's largest monolith with the world's largest work of sculptured art.

was dedicated. Bigger than a football field, it is the largest carving in the world except for the Buddha carved by the Chinese in 700 A.D.

The Memorial is the highlight of the great 3,800-acre Stone Mountain Park. More than four million people come each year to see the carving, ride the sky lift, walk the 1.3 miles to the top, go through the typical plantation houses, see antebellum enterprises or sit on the porch of the hotel and look at the giant gray mountain. It has been rated by some as the outstanding tourist attraction in the southeast.

Some plants grow on Stone Mountain that grow nowhere else in the world. One is *Hypericum splendens*. These gnarled and twisted trees, survivors of many storms, may be from 500 to 800 years old.

SYMBOLS AND NAMES

Georgia's symbol features the words "Wisdom, Justice and Moderation" from Plato's *Republic*. Authorized by the legislature in 1799, it was designed by Daniel Scruggs, who was paid $30 for his work. It appears in many places.

The Georgia Flag

Adopted in 1956, Georgia's present flag is red, white and blue. It has at the left a vertical blue broad stripe with the Georgia seal in blue and white. The right side features the Stars and Bars of the Confederacy on a red background with 13 white stars. Some groups object to the Confederate symbol while others consider it an important part of Georgia's history.

The Georgia Flower

The Georgia flower came from China but was named after an Indian tribe. It is the Cherokee rose and it came to Georgia by way of England in the 1750s. Its botanical name is *Rosa laevigata* Michaux, named by Andre Michaux, a Charleston botanist who was born in France. Adopted by the legislature in 1916, the Cherokee rose grows in many parts of the state, often wild.

The Georgia Tree

The state tree is the live oak, one of some 250 native trees found in Georgia. The oaks live to a great age, grow to 40 to 50 feet in height and spread sometimes up to 100 feet. There are many famous oaks in Georgia. One at Thomasville is 55 feet high, 170 feet across and 25 feet around the trunk. It is enrolled as the 24th member of the National Live Oak Association.

Georgia's Two State Birds

A governor's proclamation in 1935 made the brown thrasher Georgia's state bird. In 1970 the legislature named the bob-white quail the state game bird.

The brown thrasher is brown with white breast stripes, has a big beak and a long tail. It measures from 10 to 12 inches, nests on or near the ground, is short-tempered and doesn't sing too well. De Soto's crew wrote about the quail, the first record of bird life in the state.

The Georgia Song

Georgia was made the official song of the state by the General Assembly in 1922, but Georgia's state song is now *Georgia On My Mind*. It was adopted by the legislature in the late 1970s, an occasion highlighted when Ray Charles played and sang it for the legislators.

Names and Places

Georgia's 159 counties are dotted with unusual names. There are cities and counties named in memory of great Georgians and Americans. There is one north Georgia place that has a name connecting it with Tennessee and Georgia—Plum Nelly. The saying goes it's "plum outa Tennessee and nelly outa Georgia."

An interesting project would be to look around your area and find out where your county and community got their names. Why were nearby creeks, rivers, and lakes given the names they have? It's all a part of the history of a most interesting state—your state of Georgia.

For Extended Thinking

1. Visualize how Georgia looked when it was under the sea. Draw the landmass on a map.
2. What can a clay pot made in 800 B.C. tell about the people who made and used it?
3. What impacts did the continental ice sheet have on Georgia? Think of the great power the movement of an ice sheet would have.
4. How did the barrier islands influence the settlement of Georgia?
5. What is the importance of rivers to Georgia?
6. Why would a noted scientist say that he would rather Georgia be rich in water than in oil?

Names, Terms and Concepts

prehistory	fall line
Trail Ridge	Cherokee rose
continental ice sheet	aquifer
artifacts	sunbelt
tidal basin	uplift
kaolin	alapaha
barrier islands	Brasstown Bald
plateau	cecil soil type
UGA's Marine Institute	missoe

To Help You Study

1. Why is geography important?
2. Why should we study and understand history?
3. What does government do that affects our lives?
4. How was the land mass of Georgia formed?
5. What is an artifact and why is it important?
6. What is meant by prehistory?
7. How was the Okefenokee Swamp formed?
8. Where is Georgia in relation to the nation and the rest of the world?
9. What river was the original southern boundary of Georgia?
10. What river does Georgia and Alabama share?
11. Name the island that is known for bird watching and nature study.
12. What is another name for Edward Teach and on which island is it possible that he buried treasure?
13. Why are minerals important to Georgia?
14. How important are Georgia's forests?
15. Who started the carving on Stone Mountain? Name the three people on it.

16. What is the state flower? The state song? The state tree? The state bird?
17. What is the state's motto and what is its source?
18. What difference is there between the Seven Wonders of the World from ancient man and Georgia's Seven Wonders?
19. What did the Indians believe about Warm Springs and how did the white man use it?
20. Why is the Okefenokee Swamp called the Land of the Trembling Earth?
21. How were the Providence Canyons formed?
22. What does the wordTallulah mean in the Indian language?

CHAPTER 2

THE PEOPLE COME

INDIANS, SPANISH AND ENGLISH

Whose feet first touched the earth that is now Georgia after the Atlantic Ocean no longer washed up beyond Macon and Augusta?

The answer is lost in the mists of time. But more than 10,000 years ago there were people of mystery in Georgia who left important artifacts. The **Mound Builders** built mounds that still exist at Kolomoki near Blakely, at Ocmulgee near Macon and at Etowah near Cartersville. In addition, there are effigy mounds, made in the shape of creatures like the Rock Eagle Mound in Putnam County. And there are mysterious markings left by people of long ago, such as the curious scribblings at Track Rock Gap near Blairsville and the Yuchi stone found near Columbus.

EVIDENCE OF MYSTERIOUS PEOPLE LONG AGO

Who were the Mound Builders?

Nobody really knows who the Mound Builders were, where they came from, how they disappeared, or why they built the mounds. Historians are inclined to think they were early Indians. But the Indians who were here when the first white men came knew no more about the Mound Builders than the white men did. The Creeks especially held the mounds in superstitious awe and would not disturb them. Many people, including Thomas Jefferson, have tried to solve the mystery of the mounds.

How did they build?

The Mound Builders had no wheels and no domesticated animals. They built the mounds by carrying millions of basketfuls of earth. They did not have even a wheelbarrow. It was

The Ocmulgee Mounds near Macon.

Two grotesque figures from the Etowah Mounds near Cartersville.

labor as long and hard as that of the Egyptians who built the pyramids or the Chinese who built the Great Wall. These mysterous people evidently used the mounds for holding councils, for religious worship, for watch towers, for signal stations, for the chief's residence, and for burying their dead. Why did they stop building the mounds? Nobody knows.

Within Georgia are three of the four most important Indian mounds in the southeast. The fourth is near St. Louis, Mo. The largest mounds in Georgia are the Kolomoki Mounds, the Ocmulgee Mounds, and the Etowah Mounds.

Who built the Kolomoki Mounds?

The **Kolomoki Mounds** are near Blakely in the southwest corner of the state. They are on Kolomoki Creek about 15 miles east of the Chattahoochee River. Historians and archaeologists believe that these mound builders were wandering through this region in search of food more than 10,000 years ago. By 500 B.C., they were living in family groups and using a new weapon, the bow and arrow. It was more effective than the spear in getting food. There were certainly settlements in the area during the years 800 to 1200 B.C.

The **Ocmulgee Mounds** are near the banks of the Ocmulgee River just outside of Macon. While the mounds date back to at least 900 B.C., there is evidence that six different groups lived in the area over a period of 10,000 years. The Mayas, who later went on to Yucatan in Central America, could have been among them. Some archaeologists believe that the Ocmulgee Old Fields were an ancient council town set up by the Mayas. For example, a circular row of 50 seats could have been where the rulers sat. In all, the Ocmulgee Mounds extend 20 miles down the river and may have been important for other Indian settlements. Creek tradition holds that Ocmulgee was the first Creek settlement in the area.

Why were the Ocmulgee Mounds built?

The **Etowah Mounds** near Cartersville were the center of a vigorous Indian life. Objects were found there that were not native to the region. This suggests that people came from hundreds of miles away for festivals, assemblies and trading. The Mounds were the center for a hundred settlements throughout the Etowah River valley. They served as the political, economic and religious headquarters of the settlements. The people were highly skilled in weaving cloth and making baskets. They shaped fine objects from clay, bone, shell, wood and copper. They have been rightly praised for their magnificent achievements in architecture, painting, sculpture and agriculture.

Were the Etowah Mounds the center of Indian life?

The **Rock Eagle Effigy Mound** in Putnam County is different—a great rock eagle built by some people of long ago. Legend has it that the great mound was built by a chieftain whose little child was carried away by an immense eagle, but the fact is that eagles do not carry off children. The great bird's wingspread is 120 feet. It is 102 feet from top of head to tip of toe. Near the effigy is a marker with these words:

How is the Rock Eagle effigy different?

Tread softly here, white man,
For long ere you came strange races
Lived, fought and loved.

Rock Eagle Mound in Putnam County.

The Rock Eagle Mound is said to be the most perfect effigy mound in North America. It is the center of one of the world's largest youth camps.

Finally, there are two very important rocks with curious

A diorama of Indian Emporer Brim.

markings on them. On a large rock on the side of a mountain road near Blairsville at **Track Rock Gap** are strange markings on soapstones. The markings seem to be both animal and human footprints. There are also markings like bird tracks, and geometric squares, circles, and straight lines in no special order. Were they messages of meaning or just the doodlings of hunters or warriors as they rested? The Cherokee Indians said these marks were there when they first came to Georgia.

What do the Track Rock markings say?

A square, five-pound stone found near Columbus suggests that Yuchi Indians from Europe were in American 3000 years before Columbus discovered America. Markings on the stone were alphabetic writings from Minoan scripts used by people who lived on the island of Crete in the Mediterranean 3000-1000 B.C. Since the script disappeared about 3500 years ago, whoever brought a knowledge of it to America probably came from the Mediterranean around 1500 B.C.

How were the Yuchi Indians different?

The Yuchi Indians differed from other early Indians in Georgia. They claimed to have come from the south, somewhere near the Gulf of Mexico. Most authorities think all American Indians came from Asia, probably Siberia, by way of the Aleutian Islands. The Yuchis also had a sacred harvest dance that was almost identical with a Jewish religious observance described in Leviticus in the Bible. They may have learned this from Jewish people around the Mediterranean. The Yuchis were moved from Georgia to Oklahoma in 1836.

THE INDIANS THAT WERE HERE WHEN THE WHITE MAN CAME

Why are American Indians thought to be Asian?

The Indians that were here when the Europeans came are thought to have been Asiatics. This conclusion is derived from certain physical characteristics, including their black, straight hair, high cheekbones, and copper skin. It was this group who came to the American continent over the Bering Strait. Georgia's history is that of many tribes, sub-tribes, and bands that included Creeks, Cherokees, Hitchitees, Seminoles, Yuchis, Yamassees, Shawnees, Yamacraws, Chickasaws and many others. Among these groups three stand out as the most important to the history of Georgia. These are the Cherokees, who belong to the Iroquois linguistic family; the Creeks, who were Muscogeans; and the Seminoles, also Muskogeans, who lived along the lower border of Georgia and in upper Florida. The Cherokees lived above the Creeks in the mountains north of a line running roughly from Elberton to Atlanta to Cedartown. There may have been as many as 25,000 Indians in Georgia at one time, but no one knows since there is no way to count them. We will consider the history of these Indian tribes more fully later on in the book.

THE FIRST EUROPEAN SETTLERS IN GEORGIA

Three powerful nations, Spain, France and England, struggled to possess the New World, including the land that was to become Georgia. Spain claimed it first because the Italian, Christopher Columbus, had been sailing for Spain when he discovered America in 1492. Although he made four voyages in all Columbus died in 1506 without having set foot on the North American continent.

What Spaniards established Spain's claim?

It was a Spaniard who had sailed with Columbus who

Who was the first white man to come to Georgia?

discovered the continent itself. His name was Ponce de Leon. When he was young, he had been a page at the court of King Ferdinand and Queen Isabella. When he came to America, he was 32 years old and he did not want to grow old. De Leon had heard of a fabled fountain of youth and thought it was on the island of Bimini. He was searching for that island when he landed near the present site of St. Augustine, Florida, on Easter, March 13, 1513. He named the land he had discovered Florida, which means "the place of flowers."

Hernando de Soto

A band of slave-hunting Spaniards in 1526 may have stopped briefly near the mouth of the Savannah River. However, the best evidence suggests that a brave and cruel Spaniard named Hernando de Soto was, in 1539, the first white man to set foot in what is known today as Georgia. Hernando de Soto (called Ferdinand by Americans) had been a six-year-old boy in Spain when Columbus discovered America. When he grew up King Charles V of Spain appointed him governor for life of Cuba and Florida (Florida at the time meant the entire southeast and beyond!). But de Soto's life was not to be very long.

How did de Soto explore Georgia?

In 1538 he assembled men and ships for a venture into the north of the New World. He and his men left Cuba on May 18, 1539, leaving his wife to govern the island in his absence. There were about 600 soldiers and many other attendants of various kinds, including priests and writers. He brought a huge chair to sit on—for a throne when he dealt with the natives—and crucibles for refining the gold he expected to find. He also brought chains and leg irons for the prisoners he expected to take. De Soto and his men landed at Tampa Bay on May 30, 1539, and spent the following winter near the site of Tallahassee. They came into Georgia in the spring of 1540, near the site of Bainbridge. Their route up through the state carried them through what is now Leesburg, Hawkinsville, Cordele, Dublin, and on toward Silver Bluff below Augusta. Just below Cordele they erected a cross and observed the first Easter ever celebrated in Georgia.

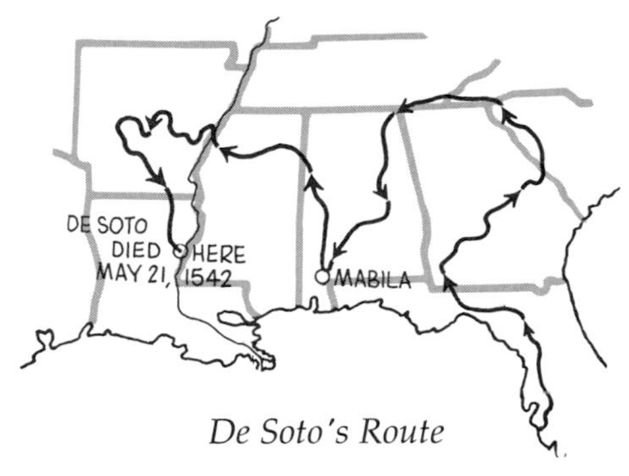

De Soto's Route

The Indians had never seen horses and at first they thought that horse and rider were one animal. Even later reaction to horses is interesting. The Creek word for horse, for example, is echothalako which means "big deer." Echo is the Creek word for deer.

These reactions give us the basis for another interesting thought experiment. What would have been your reactions had you been an Indian meeting the white man, or a white man meeting the Indians, for the first time? A good starting place is to remember that the European and the Indian had altogether different cultures. If there is such a thing as the clash of cultures it certainly would have occurred when the white man met the Indian and the Indian met the white man. Certainly a part of the reaction must have been wonderment. Wouldn't you have been a little puzzled by what you saw? Among the many questions both parties probably asked were these: Who are these people? Where did they come from? What do they want? Why do they dress that way? What language are they speaking? Use these kinds of specific questions and imagine yourself an Indian in 1540 meeting the white man for the first time. How would you have reacted? And imagine yourself as a member of de Soto's party and meeting the Indians for the first time. How would you have reacted?

How did European and Indian cultures differ?

There is evidence as to how the people involved actually responded to each other. Sometimes de Soto was kind and friendly to the Indians, giving them gifts and helping them in various ways. At other times, de Soto treated the Indians very cruelly. One of his own writers, known as "the gentleman of Elvas," noted this in his report: "The Governor is truly fond of the sport of shooting Indians." In addition, de Soto allowed his men to rob them, and sometimes even plunder the graves of their dead in search of gold.

How did Indians and white men respond to each other?

An example of this reaction involves an Indian princess who met de Soto near Silver Bluff. She was floating on a barge, like Cleopatra. She brought many pearls and skins. De Soto gave her a ruby ring from his own fingers. Despite her kindness, de Soto's own men thought he repaid her friendship cruelly. The reporter noted, "It was not so good usage as she deserved for the goodwill she showed and the entertainment she made him." But soon the princess escaped into the green swamps.

Indian reaction to the white man was also mixed. Sometimes the Indians were friendly and shared their food, giving the white men fish, turkey, and quail. The Indians knew how to roast meat slowly over glowing coals. The Spaniards called this meat barbecue. At other times, as was the case with some of the Cherokee warriors, Indian reaction to the white man was aggressive and warlike.

In the Mt. Yonah area, where some of de Soto's men were searching for gold in 1540, gold was actually found nearly 300 years later! In 1829 thousands came swarming to **Duke's Creek.** This was the nation's first gold rush. It occurred 20 years before the Forty-niners rushed to California to dig for gold at Sutter's Creek. But de Soto's men never found Georgia gold.

After two months in Georgia, they crossed the Savannah River into the Carolina country. Soon they turned westward. But what route did they take? Did de Soto re-enter Georgia after he had crossed the Savannah River in May 1540? Nobody really knows. The best evidence suggests that de Soto went from the Carolina country westward, then down the Tennessee River into Alabama. He pushed on west, camping near Tupelo, Miss., during the 1540-41 winter. He discovered the Mississippi, and went on beyond it into the future Arizona and Texas territory. Then he turned back toward the great river. Many of his men had died of fevers and some had been killed. About a hundred were left. De Soto himself became ill with fever. On May 21, 1542, two years after he had left Georgia, he died in Louisiana. His men, fearful that the Indians would at-tack their weak little band if they knew the leader was dead, buried him at night in the Mississippi River, weighting his hollowed-out oak-tree coffin with wet sand. Not more than 40

What happened to de Soto?

of de Soto's men got back to Cuba. They had trudged more than 4000 miles.

Spanish Missions: The Golden Age

The Spanish kings were enraged by attacks on Spanish ships bringing gold and other treasures out of Mexico. They began to set up settlements along the Gulf of Mexico, and later the coast of Georgia, for the protection of the Spanish fleet in Cuba. The first permanent Spanish colony in Florida was set up by Pedro Menendez, commander of the Spanish fleet in Cuba. He was also a religious fanatic. He came to the mainland because King Philip II of Spain was enraged that France had dared to set up a little settlement on the St. Johns River. This was Fort Caroline, a colony founded with the help of Capt. Jean Ribaut as a refuge for French Protestants fleeing religious persecutions. The King ordered Menendez to destroy it and drive the French off American shores. "Root out the Huguenots," ordered the Catholic king of Spain. Menendez said, "I come to hang and behead all Lutherans I can find . . ."

Why were the Spanish missions established?

How did Spain treat the French?

On Sept. 8, 1565, Menendez arrived near St. Augustine with 19 ships and 1,500 soldiers. He soon attacked the French colony, burning the village and shooting or hanging those who could not escape. Among these was Capt. Ribaut. Menendez reported to King Philip, "He was put to the knife for the glory of God and of your majesty."

What missions did Spain build in Georgia?

In 1566, Menendez sailed up the Georgia coast to talk with the Indians. He wanted to put forts on their islands to protect Spanish interests and to set up Catholic missions to convert the Indians. He landed on St. Catherines Island. He and Chief Guale sat on the beach and ate biscuit and honey. Chief Guale ruled over the territory known as Guale. Guale was the name by which Georgia first came to be known by the Spaniards, who regarded it as part of Florida.

The chief gave Menendez permission to put a fort on the island. The Spanish governor also put missions along the coast and some far inland, near Stone Mountain and on the Chattahoochee River. Georgia's Spanish missions are 20 years older than those in California and were the beginning of the Golden Age of Spanish missions. The Spanish conquistadors came for gold and glory; but the gentle priests came for the glory of God.

The Golden Age lasted about a hundred years. The Indians grew restive under the discipline of the church. Both In-dians and pirates attacked the missions at one time or another. Some of the priests died of malaria and yellow fever. By 1686 there were no Spanish settlements above the St. Mary's River and by 1700 the Spanish had been pushed backed to the St. Johns River.

The English Come Last, On Cabot's Claims

England based her claim to the New World on the explorations of John Cabot in 1497. After defeating the "invincible" Spanish Armada in 1588, the English sailed the seas of the world in search of power, glory and gold. Sir Francis Drake, in his ship *The Golden Hind*, had attacked and pillaged St. Augustine in 1586. He reported to Queen Elizabeth I this epi-sode about the Georgia coast: "We attacked the island [thought to be Jekyll], hung and burned the Spanish captain and 17 other Spaniards, but having in mind the merciful disposition of your Gracious Majesty, we did not kill the women and children, but having destroyed upon the island all their provisions and property and taken away all their weapons, we left them to starve."

How did the English establish their claim?

In 1629 King Charles I, the only king ever beheaded by the British, included the area that is now Georgia in a grant which he made to a friend, Sir Robert Heath, his attorney. The grant stretched from Virginia to Cumberland Island on the Georgia coast. Since it was never settled by Heath, the territory reverted to the crown.

In 1633 Charles II granted the same land to eight friends,

known as the Lords Proprietors. They named it *Carolina* in his honor. Two years later he extended the grant to include the Spanish colony of St. Augustine. Spain naturally objected. In 1670 a treaty between England and Spain returned the Georgia coast to Spain and recognized England's claim as far south as Charleston, S.C.

How did the Lords Proprietors get a claim to Georgia?

But the treaty settled nothing permanently. The Proprietors soon realized that they needed a **buffer** colony to protect them from the Spanish in Florida and from Indians who did not want any white men to settle on this continent.

Ft. King George and the Lonely Graves

Col. John Barnwell was an Irishman who had come to America and grown rich as a planter in South Carolina. He saw the increasing threat to British business from the encroaching Spaniards. The French, too, were proving troublesome. They had settled Biloxi in 1699 and Mobile in 1702. In 1718 they built a fort on the Apalachicola and were actually claiming the Altamaha. The Frenchman, Bienville, founded New Orleans in 1718.

About 1720 Barnwell got permission from London to set up a chain of protective forts. The first he established was Ft. King George at the mouth of the Altamaha, near Darien. This was the first actual English settlement in Georgia. Ft. King George lasted from 1721 to 1727. The Spanish protested its existence all the time. The soldiers lived in a small cypress blockhouse, about 26 feet square and 23 feet high, with four small rooms. They were attacked by Indians, and suffered from malaria and other diseases. During one year, two-thirds of them died. Many years later rows of skeletons were found at the location of the fort. They were buried in shallow graves that may have been dug hastily during an attack, but the graves were on row, in military precision. In 1727 the fort burned and was not rebuilt. It is now a designated historic site, open to the public.

What was the first English settlement in Georgia?

For Extended Thinking

1. What led the Mound Builders to build their structures?
2. What evidence suggests that the Yuchi Indians had Mediterranean connections?
3. Who led the Spanish exploration of the New World?
4. Why would the Spanish missions be called the Golden Age?
5. How did the English establish their claim in the New World?

Names, Terms and Concepts

effigy mounds
Etowah Mounds
Pedro Menendez
track rock
Ponce de Leon
Guale
Yuchi stone
Hernando de Soto
John Cabot
Kolomoki Mounds

Names, Terms and Concepts (continued)

echothalako
Ft. King George
Ocmulgee Mounds
Duke's Creek
John Barnwell

To Help You Study

1. Name the Indian mounds and their locations.
2. What was the purpose of the mounds?
3. Name the most unusual mound in Georgia. Where is it located?
4. What were the three most important tribes in Georgia?
5. Locate the part of Georgia where each tribe lived.
6. Which European nation first came to Georgia?
7. Who was the first Spanish explorer to come to Georgia?
8. What were the Spaniards seeking?
9. What area of the southeast did the French settle?

CHAPTER 3

GEORGIA BECOMES A COLONY

The events discussed in Chapter 2, along with many others, caused the British to consider the need for a colony in the area of Georgia. Some argued that such a colony was needed as a buffer between the British in the Carolinas and the Indians, Spanish and French who encircled them. South Carolina had been a British colony for over fifty years but the exact boundary between South Carolina and Spanish Florida was not known. There had been many disagreements between Britain and Spain over that boundary. Britain had gone so far as to build forts in the area which was to become Georgia, and Spain had occupied parts of the area from 1565 to 1686. In addition, South Carolina was in a long Indian War and needed a buffer between the colony and various Indian tribes. It was the need for a buffer between South Carolina and the Spanish and Indians that many historians think was the most important reason for establishing Georgia as a colony. For example, Randolph Anderson, writing in the Georgia Historical Quarterly, described Georgia as a military colony and reminded his readers that Oglethorpe was a soldier before he was a philanthropist.

Why was England interested in a colony in Georgia?

Others who favored establishing Georgia as a colony believed that such a colony would be a valuable region economically for Britain. Sir Robert Montgomery, who once had a grant from the King for the land now comprising Georgia, described Georgia as "the most favorable country of the universe" and called it a "future Eden." Listen to how he described Georgia to his fellow decision-makers in Britain: "Nature has not blessed the world with any tract which can be

How would Georgia serve Britain's economic interest?

Seal of Colonial Georgia

preferable to it; that Paradise with all her virgin beauties may be modestly supposed at most but equal to its native excellencies." This type of glowing report led a lot of people in England to believe that the raw materials in Georgia would be extremely important for England's economy. Thus they saw establishment of a colony in the area as a way to increase the trade and wealth of Britain.

The third reason for establishing a colony in Georgia—and the one that is popularly accepted as the most important—was to establish a refuge for England's "worthy poor." The condition of the debtor class in England had declined to a very low point. A number of debtors were sent to prison—one writer records that four thousand persons per year were sent to prison for debt in the city of London alone. And those prisons, as Oglethorpe was to find out when he investigated conditions in them, were a disgrace.

What did concern for the poor have to do with Georgia?

The establishment of a refuge for the worthy poor did enter into the planning for the establishment of a colony in Georgia. However, it probably was not a very strong motive in the decision to do so. Virtually no colonists for Georgia were recruited from the prisons of England. Additionally, only a handful of debtors chose to settle in Georgia—probably no more than in any of the other colonies. However, the concept of a refuge for the poor did serve to bring the complex military and economic motives into focus. This focus centered on Gen. James Edward Oglethorpe, who came to be known as the Father of Georgia.

OGLETHORPE AND THE TRUSTEES

What was Oglethorpe's background?

Sir James Edward Oglethorpe, born Dec. 22, 1696, was a member of a powerful and wealthy English family. He had come into his inheritance and had taken his place in Parliament. He learned that a friend had died of smallpox in a filthy

British debtors' prison. Oglethorpe was so shocked by the death of his friend that he demanded that Parliament investigate the prisons. He was made chairman of the committee. They brought in a blistering report that shocked England from end to end. Many jailers were fired and about 10,000 debtors were freed.

Gen. James Edward Oglethorpe

The publicity thus given to the condition of poor people brought to a focus the old talk about a new colony in the New World. Oglethorpe and his friends set about raising money and stirring up interest for such a colony. William Penn's son sent a hundred pounds from Pennsylvania. Parliament would invest a great amount of money in this 13th and youngest colony in America. Oglethorpe, rich and living in comfort in England, agreed that if such a colony could be started, he would come with the colonists and help them get established.

Now the problem of the new colony's Trustees was to persuade King George II to sign a charter. The Crown had some years earlier bought back the land previously sold to the Lords Proprietors. On June 9, 1732, the king finally signed the charter, providing for 21 trustees for 21 years. The Georgia charter specified "all those lands, countries, and territories situated, lying, and being in that part of South Carolina in America which lies from the northernmost part of a stream or river there, commonly called the Savannah, all along the sea coast to the southward into the Altamaha, and westerly, from the heads of the said rivers respectively, in direct line to the South Seas." Georgia was carved out of Carolina, and the charter stretched Georgia from sea to sea, Atlantic to Pacific.

How was a charter obtained for Georgia?

The charter clearly states the three purposes for establishing the colony. It begins like this:

> George the Second, by the grace of God, of Great Britain, France, and Ireland, King and Defender of the Faith, To All Whom These Presents Shall Come, Greeting: Whereas, we are credibly informed that many of our poor subjects are through

What were the purposes for establishing Georgia?

> misfortune and want of employment, reduced to great necessity inasmuch as by their labor they are not able to provide a maintenance for themselves and their families . . . wish to go to America . . . where they might gain a comfortable subsistence . . . and also strengthen our colonies and increase trade, navigation and wealth of these our realms. And whereas our provinces in North America have been frequently ravaged by Indian enemies . . . laid waste by fire and sword and great numbers of English inhabitants miserably massacred . . . We think it highly becoming our crown and royal dignity to protect all our loving subjects, be they ever so distant from us.

A copy of the original charter is on display in a glass case in the Archives Building in Atlanta.

King George II

The Trustees and Their Actions

Who did the Trustees select to come?

The Trustees decided to take only people of good character, to let each man have 50 acres (those who paid their own way could get 500) and to supply them with provisions for a year. No debtor was accepted without the consent of the creditor and few debtors came. Each man had to plant a portion of his land in mulberry trees (to feed silkworms). The ones who paid their own way could bring as many as 10 servants.

The Trustees tried to select younger men, insofar as possible, who would be able to work hard in a new land. They also tried to get a variety of talents and abilities among the first comers. Curiously, they allowed no lawyers, whom they regarded as "the pest and scourge of mankind."

The Trustees had a seal made. On it was their motto, *Non Sibi Sed Aliis,* which means, "Not for Ourselves but for Others." No Trustee could hold office, own a foot of land in Georgia, or make a profit from the new colony.

Their official title was "The Trustees for Establishing the Colony of Georgia in America." They decided to allow men of all faiths except Catholic to come to Georgia but Oglethorpe paid no attention to the rule against Catholics. They made some rules that the colonists, as it turned out, did not like: no rum was to be allowed (only wine and beer); the colonists could not own slaves; and a man could not own his land outright. These regulations were finally changed but it took a long time.

What rules did the Trustees make?

The Trustees believed that wine could be made in the new colony. This was because Georgia was in about the same latitude as the Madeira Islands where fine grapes grew to make excellent wines. They especially wanted the colonists to produce silk, which cost the English too much from other sources. They were not the first to believe that silk could be produced in America. King James I had the same idea back in Shakespeare's time. He had insisted that the British colony of

What farm products did the Trustees encourage?

Virginia, founded in 1607, "instead of that noxious weed tobacco." The shipwreck depicted in *The Tempest* was actually the wreck of a ship carrying mulberry plants to Virginia to feed silkworms. The reason these beliefs were widely held is that Georgia's latitude and temperate climate are very similar to silk-producing and wine-producing areas. Latitude and climate did have a lot to do with interest in colonizing Georgia.

But eventually all of these expectations turned out to be impractical. The colonists turned to more profitable things like lumber, tobacco, corn, livestock, and later, cotton.

The Trustees were mindful of cultural things, too. They ordered, according to their minutes, "Plato's Works, Bibles, Catechisms, Greek and Latin, and his Republique bought for use of the Mission in Georgia." Many years later, Georgia's permanent motto, "Wisdom, Justice, and Moderation," was to come from Plato's *Republic.*

The First Colonists Are Picked

Hundreds of people wanted to come to the new colony. The Trustees interviewed more than 600 during the summer of 1732. They could take only 114. Five months after the charter had been signed, by Nov. 17, 1732, the Trustees had picked 35 families, and had chartered a ship. They were delighted that Oglethorpe and the Rev. Henry Herbert, a Church of England clergyman, were to come with the colonists.

THE COLONY IS SETTLED

How did the first settlers get to Georgia?

On Jan. 13, 1733, the ship *Anne,* with Georgia's first colonists, after a voyage of two months and one week came into the harbor at Charleston, S. C. It then went down the coast to Beaufort, S. C. The Georgia colonists were to stay there while Oglethorpe went further south to pick out a site within the boundaries of the charter.

The people of South Carolina were warm, gracious, and generous to the weary new colonists. In future years there would be bitter quarrels between the two states but there was no sign of it now. The Carolinians were glad to have another colony between them and the Spanish, the French, and the Indians. Gov. Robert Johnson gave Oglethorpe seven horses and offered him some men to go with him. One of them was William Bull, an engineer, for whom Bull Street in Savannah was named. In due course Oglethorpe named Johnson Square for the South Carolina governor. Oglethorpe and the South Carolinians with him rowed down the coast until they came to the Savannah River. Then they went up the river about 18 miles. There Oglethorpe saw a high bluff which would make it easy to defend the colony from any attack. The river was navigable for ships and there were trees with which to build houses and furniture. The soil was fertile and he thought it would grow good crops. He named the place Savannah.

Why did Oglethorpe pick Savannah?

The stone bench marks the site in Savannah where Oglethorpe pitched his tent in 1733.

Back in Beaufort the colonists boarded four ships, and on Feb. 12, 1733, they landed at Savannah. On the bluff they put up four tents to shelter them until they could build their homes. That first morning the colonists gathered in front of "Father Oglethorpe's" tent for prayers by Rev. Henry Herbert. Then everybody went to work. Oglethorpe wrote, "The very first house was started this afternoon."

What problems did the first settlers face?

The people were not used to this kind of work and the houses went up slowly. They were not accustomed to the hot, humid climate. Sand flies and mosquitoes annoyed them, too. They had to haul their supplies up the steep bluff and cut timber for their houses. Three weeks later, Oglethorpe wrote the Trustees, "Our people still live in tents, there being only three clapboard houses and three sawed houses framed. Our crane, our battery of cannon and our magazines are finished. This is all we have been able to do, by reason of the smallness of our number, of which many have been sick, and others unused to labor, though I thank God the sick are pretty well now and we have not lost one since our arrival."

The first baby was born on March 17, 1733, the daughter of Henry and Hannah Close. They named her Georgia. She lived only nine months.

Soon there was a store, a grist mill, a public bakery, a good water supply, and a sundial. Oglethorpe laid out Savannah by a design from the book *Villas of the Ancients,* by his friend, Robert Castell, whose misfortune and death hadhastenedGeorgia's founding. On a square tract of 15,360 acres, Oglethorpe planned homes for 240 families.

Tomochichi and Mary Musgrove Help

What was Oglethorpe's attitude toward the Indians?

Even though the king had granted a charter for the colony, Oglethorpe tactfully wanted to get the consent of the Indians. The British had already made an agreement with them that no more colonies would be located below the Carolina colony.

Three miles from the bluff, Oglethorpe found the only Indian tribe living within 50 miles of the place. Tomochichi, six feet tall and already 90 years old, was their chief. He was a man of mystery. He had been banished from the Yamacraw tribe and many other Indians had come with him. Nobody ever knew why he was exiled. He did not talk about it. He reflected no bitterness toward them, and they spoke well of him. Tomochichi had settled with his little group near Savannah. He greeted Oglethorpe with quiet kindness, even though these Indians were not happy to see more white men come.

They needed an interpreter. They sent for Mary Musgrove, the half-breed wife of John Musgrove, a white trader. Mary was a tiny woman, about five feet tall, and about 33 years old. She wore her hair in two long braids, with a band of beads across her forehead, and a feather stuck into the band. Oglethorpe hired her as his interpreter and agreed to pay her a hundred pounds, English money. For many years she was a good friend to Georgia, but after Oglethorpe left, she was to cause much trouble.

Empress Mary Musgrove

Tomochichi, however, was a staunch friend all of his life. He told Oglethorpe that his tribe would come to welcome the whites as soon as they were settled. He advised the general to talk with the chiefs of the other tribes and get their permission to make a settlement here. Oglethorpe thought this was good advice. Tomochichi promised to send runners to summon the other Creek chiefs. "You can have big talk. I will help you make them your friends." The old Indian was very much interested in Oglethorpe's gun, which he called a "fire stick." One morning the colonists heard strange shouts and the sound of drums. Looking down toward the swamps, they saw Indians approaching. They were frightened. They gathered around Oglethorpe's tent. The men had their guns.

What role did Mary Musgrove play?

Oglethorpe said, "Do not be alarmed. The Indians are coming to welcome us."

In front of the Indians was their medicine man, dressed with bright feathers and beads and clanging bells. He leaped and strutted grotesquely while the Indians chanted. There was a sudden silence. The medicine man came up to Oglethorpe, stroked him with a feather fan and said, "May there be always peace between our people and your people."

Then Tomochichi gave Oglethorpe a buffalo robe. The old chief said, "We have come to welcome you, as I promised. I have brought you a present. This is the skin of a buffalo, which is the strongest of all beasts. Inside, you see painted the head and feathers of an eagle, which is the swiftest of all birds and flies farthest. So the English are the strongest of all people and nothing can withstand them. They have a swift and far flight like the eagle. They have flown hither from the uttermost part of the earth over the vast seas. The eagle's feathers are warm and soft and signify love. The buffalo robe is warm and signifies protection. Therefore, love and protect our little families."

Oglethorpe made a speech, too, and for Tomochichi he had a special gift: a bright scarlet robe, with heavy fringe.

The Indians liked Oglethorpe. He was fair and friendly. Tomochichi was eager for Oglethorpe to talk with other Indians. "They are stronger than we are and we cannot defend you from them. You had better talk with them," he said.

Tomochichi sent runners to the other eight towns of the Creeks and asked the chiefs and their leaders to come to Savannah and talk with Oglethorpe. Some came in canoes down the river but most of them came on foot. Many walked over a hundred miles to get there. On May 21, 1733, there were 56 of them there, including eight chiefs. In the largest house in Savannah, the Indians sat cross-legged on the floor, the chiefs in front and the warriors in back of them.

Tomochichi's brother, a wrinkled old man known as Long King, chief of the Oconas, made a speech. He said, "We are glad you have come. The Great Spirit who dwells in heaven and all around and who has given breath to all men, has sent you here to help us. We need help. You must protect us from our powerful enemies. You may settle in our land anywhere you please, for we have more land than we can use. But you must not disturb our hunting grounds nor our homes. Do not let your traders cheat us. Do not trade with any Indians but us. Teach us wise things. Instruct our children. You must let us forever keep our islands." They granted Oglethorpe the other land between the Savannah and the Altamaha. The islands that they wanted to keep were St. Catherines, Ossabaw, Sapelo, and a strip between Savannah and Pipemaker's Bluff.

What agreement did Oglethorpe make with the Indians?

They all smoked together the peace pipe and on that day, May 21, 1733, the chiefs and Oglethorpe signed the treaty of friendship. It was ratified by the Trustees in London on Oct. 18, 1733.

An Indian peace pipe.

Oglethorpe could simply have moved in, but he had tact and honor and he recognized the rights of the Indians. This was one of the reasons why these Indians became the friends of England and remained loyal to that nation throughout the wars ahead.

Sickness Plagues the Little Colony

It was not easy to start a new home in the wilderness. The first colonists had many problems, among them simply to stay alive. Malaria and other diseases attacked them. About 30 of the colonists died that first summer, a fourth of those who had come over on the ship *Anne*. Mary Musgrove lost four sons and her husband, John. Their pastor, Rev. Henry Herbert, died as he started back to England. But by March 1734, they had built 91 log houses and by 1736 they had built the famous lighthouse—"of the best pine, with brickwork around the bottom"—in the upper end of Tybee Island to guide the ships in from the sea.

Unfair Laws Cause Dissatisfaction

What laws did the colonists not like?

Three of the Trustees' laws with which the colonists were most dissatisfied were those about land, slaves, and liquor. A law prohibited land from being sold, deeded away, mortgaged, or willed to daughters. If there were no sons to whom a man could leave his land, it went back to the Trustees. Also, Oglethorpe and the other trustees were emphatic about not allowing slaves. The Trustees thought that the raising of silkworms was light work but the colonists wanted slaves for the hard work in the hot fields. They pointed out that South Carolina had slaves. They tried to evade the law by hiring "for life" blacks who were slaves in South Carolina. To hire them, they paid the market value of the slaves.

The colonists also wanted rum and other liquors. The Trustees, on the other hand, had seen the trouble that drink had caused poor people in England. They forbade liquor in Georgia, although they allowed light drinks such as wine and ale. Later, all three of these laws were relaxed or changed.

The Trustees' Garden and the Curious Silkworm

What is the importance of the Trustees' Garden?

The Trustees ordered 10 acres set aside for a public garden. Oglethorpe laid it out as soon as he could, and it provided vegetables and fruits for the colonists to eat. Moreover, the colonists could get their mulberry trees and other plants from the garden—the first agricultural experiment station in Georgia. Each family was assigned 50 acres, divided into three sections—a 30' by 90' house lot in Savannah, five acres on the edge of town, and the rest in the countryside nearby. They got their little farms started, and went to the Trustees' Garden to get cuttings, plants and mulberry trees.

But not everything the colonists attempted was successful. An old record says, "Vine dressers from Portugal were employed, and choice cuttings of Malaga vines were planted, resulted in a few gallons." The vineyards were soon abandoned. The record continued, "The olive trees from Venice, the barilla seeds from Spain, the kale from Egypt, and other exotics, obtained at much expense, after a short season withered and died in the public garden. The hemp and flax . . . never warranted the charter of a single vessel . . . and indigo did not commend itself to general favor." The colonists had to battle to raise what the soil would yield. They had no time for costly experiments in agriculture.

The cocoon of a silkworm.

Mulberry trees on which silkworms feed could grow along the Savannah River. Thus Oglethorpe believed that a fine quality of silk could be made in Georgia. This could save England much money paid to foreign countries for silk.

The colonists tried hard to grow silk. Cocoons cost them three shillings a pound. They got their mulberry trees, upon whose leaves the silkworms were to feed, from the Trustees' Garden, and planted them on their land. Each man had to plant 10 of his 50 acres in mulberry trees. If he did not, his land could be forfeited. But the weather proved hostile to the cocoons and the trees. Fortunately for the colony, corn, beans, pumpkins, potatoes, peaches, figs, grapes, rice, watermelons, and other plants grew well.

What happened in the effort to grow silk?

Georgians grew cotton as early as 1738. Europeans were surprised when the first eight bags were shipped to England. They were held up by the customs officer. He thought they had come from some other source and that somebody was violating British trade laws.

Oglethorpe Takes Indians to England

When Oglethorpe left on a business trip to England on April 7, 1734, he took with him a group of Indians. He wanted them to see the power and wealth of England and he thought that the British would be more interested in his colony if they could see the Indians. Tomochichi, his wife Senauki, and their

Why did Oglethorpe take Indians to Britain?

Tomochichi and his nephew.

nephew and adopted son, Tooanahowi, were among them. They were a sensation in England, though other Indians had visited Britain. Crowds swarmed to get a sight of these strange red people. King George II and Queen Caroline entertained them at Kensington Palace. Senauki, who was a remarkable woman, made a speech at court just as her husband had done.

Tomochichi asked the British a question: "Why do men, who are on earth so short a time, build houses that last so long?" He made a speech to the king. This is what he said:

"This day I see the majesty of your face, the greatness of your house, and the number of your people . . . I am come for the good of the children of all nations of the Upper and Lower Creeks, that they may be instructed in the knowledge of the English.

"These are the feathers of the eagle which is the swiftest of birds, and who flieth all 'round our nations. These feathers are a sign of peace in our land . . . and we have brought them over to leave them with you, O Great King, as a sign of everlasting peace."

The British gave Tomochichi presents to take back to his people in Georgia and the Indians arrived back in Savannah in December. Oglethorpe was not with them. When he came back to Georgia in 1736, so many people came with him that the voyage was known as the Great Embarkation. Much of the interest of these newcomers had been stirred up by the visit of the Indians to England.

OTHER GROUPS JOIN THE FIRST COLONISTS

The Jews

What Jews settled in Georgia?

The first people of the Jewish faith who came to Georgia were 40 who arrived in Savannah in a chartered ship on July 11, 1733, during the very first year of the colony. They brought with them the *Torah,* or Book of the Law, and the Ark. The Trustees did not want them to remain, but Oglethorpe allowed them to stay. He wrote the Trustees, "We have not better citizens than they are." One, Samuel Nunez, almost single-handedly saved the colonists in an epidemic. The little town of Nunez in Emanuel County was named for him and the county itself for David Emanuel, a Jew who fought in the Revolution and became governor. The Jews were a great help to Oglethorpe, but the Trustees wrote, "Reward them suitably . . . but not with lands in Georgia."

The Moravians and Salzburgers

Moravians, like the Salzburgers a German-speaking group, came over from Bohemia in Europe on the same ship with Oglethorpe and John and Charles Wesley in 1736. A few Moravians had come in 1735. John Wesley was greatly impressed by their brave faith and often went to consult them about his problems.

The Moravians settled between New Ebenezer and Savannah. Wesley helped them with their school for Indian children, the first such school in Georgia. But the Moravians did not stay in Georgia long. They were pacifists, or conscientious objectors, and this made them unpopular with the other colonists. About 1740 the Moravians left their little settlement and went to Pennsylvania, repaying the Trustees the money advanced for their passage to Georgia. Later they sent missionaries back into north Georgia to help educate the Indian children. They were a compassionate people.

What was the experience of Moravians in Georgia?

The Salzburgers built Jerusalem Church, which still stands in Effingham County. It has a glistening golden swan from the coat-of-arms of Martin Luther on top of the steeple. The Salzburgers were one of the Protestant sects that had grown vigorous in Europe following the leadership of Martin Luther, the monk who began the Reformation. They had lived by the river Salza in Austria, in the region where the famous Salzburg music festivals were later held. Persecuted for their religion, they left Austria. Oglethorpe invited some of them to Georgia in 1733; others came later, until there were about 1,500 in all.

Why did the Salzburgers come?

Their pastor, John Martin Bolzius, wrote of the new land:

> We lay at anchor off our dear Georgia in a very lovely calm, and heard the birds singing sweetly. We were received with joy, friendship and civility. Even the Indians reached out their hands to us. A good dinner was prepared for us.

Oglethorpe told them they could have any place not reserved by the Indians. They wanted to live among the hills to remind them of home. Oglethorpe went with their leader to pick out a place on a creek about 25 miles above Savannah for their new home Ebenezer, which means "stone of help."

They worked hard, but the soil was not fertile, the location was unhealthy and many had malaria. The creek was so shallow that boats could not get up to them. They asked Oglethorpe for permission to move to a site on Red Bluff, directly on the Savannah River; and this they named New Ebenezer.

The Salzburgers began to produce silk. They grew more silkworms and produced more silk than any other group in Georgia. About 1738, they experimented with cotton. They also raised peaches. They were good farmers and began to diversify their crops. Pastor Bolzius studied agriculture and, on Sundays after the sermon, instructed the men.

They started their little church in 1767 with bricks brought from across the sea. During the Revolution the British used it first for a hospital and later as a stable. Jerusalem Church, where the ministers preached in German until 1824, still draws Salzburgers back to worship under its swan-topped steeple.

The Salzburgers suffered greatly during the Revolution, both physically and mentally. They felt a deep loyalty to England because the Trustees had befriended them and paid their passage over, but they wanted to be loyal to their patriot neighbors, too. Many early leaders considered them Georgia's best colonists.

The Scotch Highlanders

Why did Oglethorpe want the Scottish Highlanders?

When Oglethorpe needed more brave men and good soldiers to defend the struggling little colony from the threat of the Spaniards in Florida, he sent a messenger to the Highlands of Scotland. The Scots he brought back were interested in Oglethorpe's offer of a new home in a new land.

In January 1736, they came swirling into Savannah in their colorful kilts. They settled at Darien, first known as New Brunswick. The first road built in Georgia connected Darien with Savannah and was known as Oglethorpe's Road.

The Indians liked the colorful Highlanders and hunted and played games with them. The Scots played a form of golf in Georgia, the first in this state and perhaps in this country. Once when Oglethorpe went to Darien he, too, wore kilts to honor them. The clan chief offered the general his bed, but Oglethorpe slept by the campfire, and the Scot chiefs lay down beside him there.

Many of the Scotch leaders, with their jaunty courage, played valiant roles in the Battle of Bloody Marsh on St. Simons Island. In the quiet little town of Darien there is a pink marble monument to them. In stone, the Highlanders march forever across the top of it, and the inscription reads, "To the Highlanders of Scotland who founded New Inverness in 1736. Their valor defended the struggling colony from the Spanish invader. Their ideals, traditions, and culture enriched the land of their adoption."

On the monument is the Cherokee rose, Georgia's state flower, and the Scotch thistle, symbol of Scotland.

A DIVERSE AND CREATIVE PEOPLE

From its earliest history, Georgia was populated by people from many cultures and backgrounds. The influence of the Indians and their culture remained strong, nurtured as it was by Oglethorpe himself. The early European settlers were from several nations, and they were to be joined later by many other nationalities. All of this contributed to a healthy, diverse and creative mix of people.

As for Oglethorpe, the only real home he ever had in Georgia was in Frederica. He called it The Farm and built on it a one-and-a-half-story cottage. In the garden were oranges, figs, grapes, and other fruits. He could look out across the road and see the great oaks, sweet gums, and pines, the draped moss and the jasmine as yellow as sunshine. The bronze marshes stretched away into the distance.

The events in the lives of these earliest settlers of Georgia can be the basis for a number of thought experiments. You should think carefully about Oglethorpe. Here was a man of nobility, wealth and position leaving his native country for an undeveloped land. How do you think he reacted and felt? Did he feel a sense of adventure, of commitment to a worthy cause, of furthering the interest of his homeland? Think about the 35 families who first came with Oglethorpe to Georgia. They brought with them members of their immediate family. But that means they left many relatives behind—and they certainly left their old homes and familiar communities. What inspired and motivated them? How did they feel as they sailed away from England and how did they feel when they first set foot on that bluff overlooking the Savannah River? And you really should think about the two little Indian boys—Tomochichi's son and nephew—who went to England with Oglethorpe. Imagine their reaction to the trip, to the pomp and ceremony of England and to all the strange things they would encounter. What do you think they would have told their friends on their return to their own tribe?

All these are our people. They settled Georgia and established it as a colony.

For Extended Thinking

1. If you were advisor to the king, what arguments would you make for establishing a colony in Georgia?
2. Why do you think individual people wanted to immigrate to Georgia in the first group?
3. How did Oglethorpe relate to the Indians?
4. What crops did the colony try to raise and what problems did it have with them?
5. What other groups came to Georgia and why did they come?

Names,Terms and Concepts

Robert Montgomery
hiring "for life"
Salzburgers
the worthy poor
mulberry trees
King George II
Scotch Highlanders
Tomochichi
Moravians
Oglethorpe's Road
Frederica
Mary Musgrove
the Great Embarkation

To Help You Study

1. Who was the person responsible for settling Georgia?

To Help You Study (continued)

2. Who were the Trustees and what was their responsibility?
3. What were the main reasons why Georgia was settled?
4. What did each settler get in the colony?
5. Who helped the colonists to locate in Georgia?
6. Who was the Indian chief who helped Oglethorpe? Who was Oglethorpe's interpreter?
7. What crops did the settlers try to grow? With what success?
8. What were the rules passed by the Trustees that were unpopular with the colonists?
9. What are some of the problems the colonists faced?
10. What religious group did the Trustees try to prohibit from settling in Georgia? What was Oglethorpe's reaction?
11. Tell which group of Georgia colonists was associated with each of the following:
    (a) Darien
    (b) silk, cotton, peaches
    (c) Indian school
    (d) Bohemia
    (e) Jerusalem Church
    (f) pacifists
    (g) Nunez
    (h) *Torah*
    (i) stone of help
    (j) New Ebenezer

CHAPTER 4

COLONIAL GEORGIA

Oglethorpe knew that Georgia had to develop strength, not only to support its people, but also to resist the Spanish from Florida when the showdown came. He worked hard toward that end. Under his leadership, Georgia developed culturally, economically and militarily.

COLORFUL PEOPLE CAME TO PREACH AND TO TEACH

Who were Georgia's first teachers?

Georgians needed someone to educate their children and religious leaders to look after their spiritual welfare. Sometimes the teachers were also preachers. These included the Wesleys, George Whitefield, and his assistant James Habersham, who became a prosperous businessman too. Sometimes the teachers and preachers taught among the Indians as well as the colonists. The first regular school was in Savannah and was taught by Charles Delamotte. The Trustees paid Delamotte only his expenses.

John and Charles Wesley in Georgia

The two great Methodist leaders, John Wesley and his brother Charles, came with Oglethorpe (who had been a friend of theirs at Oxford) when he returned from England in 1736. John was 33 and Charles was 29.

Describe Charles Wesley.

Charles Wesley, who wrote over 6,000 hymns and came to be known as "the sweet singer of Methodism," went to Frederica to become secretary to General Oglethorpe. He also preached. He was very strict, and the colonists were compelled to attend daily services, summoned by the drums of the army. He and Oglethorpe had a few misunderstandings and Charles Wesley grew very unhappy. He wrote to friends in England, "It has become unpopular even to speak to me. Those who washed my clothes now send them back to me unwashed. Thank God it is not yet a capital offense to give me a morsel of bread."

John Wesley

Sick, neglected, and longing for home, he had a hard time finding a bed in which to sleep during the last weeks he was at Frederica. Oglethorpe was too busy about his many duties to comfort young Wesley, and besides, gossipy tongues had made trouble between the two. Wesley wrote, "I would not spend another six days like the last six for all of Georgia."

Finally, after five months, Oglethorpe sent Charles back to England to carry some papers. He and Oglethorpe remained friends, however.

John Wesley and His Unhappy Georgia Romance

John Wesley, who was older than his brother, had remained mostly in Savannah. He had been eager to preach to the Indians, and he went to talk with Tomochichi and other chiefs. But his doctrines were too strict for the Indians. He was a small man, only five feet, five inches tall. He had long hair, which he wore hanging over his shoulder, and bright blue eyes. He wore a long black coat, knee breeches, and a three-cornered hat such as most Englishmen then wore.

What was John Wesley's relationship with the Indians?

Wesley walked tirelessly from one village to another preaching to the Indians and trying to teach them. But they never understood him, nor he them. Tomochichi, who was very fond of Oglethorpe, never had much to say to John Wesley. But Wesley made many staunch friends in Georgia. He and Charles Delamotte, who had come with him, founded the world's first Sunday School. Once when boys laughed at a child who came barefooted to Sunday School, Wesley himself came barefooted the next Sunday.

Oglethorpe had tried to encourage a match between the young minister and a pretty girl named Sophie Hopkey, niece of the colony's storekeeper, Thomas Causton. The two young people seemed very much interested in each other. Once they were together on a boat bringing some people from St. Simons back to Savannah. A storm came up and the boat had to land on St. Catherines Island. The damp passengers built a campfire. Sophie later reported that during the entire evening there by the glow of the campfire, Wesley quoted scripture to her. But sometime during the week he said to her, "Miss Sophie, I would count myself happy if I could spend the rest of my life with you." Later she claimed that was a proposal.

What was Wesley's experience with his Georgia Girlfriend?

Wesley seriously thought of marrying the pretty Georgia girl. But first he asked the advice of the Moravians, whose opinion he deeply respected. They liked Sophie, but they advised against their marriage because they felt that she was too young and frivolous to be able to settle down to the serious role of a minister's wife.

Sophie married William Williamson and stopped attending church. When she finally went back, Wesley refused to allow her to take Holy Communion because of her absence. It was a rule of the church. But for a young matron in that time, it was considered an insult. She and her family, indignant, brought suit against Wesley. Others who had considered Wesley too strict joined in the hue and cry against him. He was arrested and taken into court. The summons read:

Georgia. Savannah. s.s.

> To all Constables, Tythingmen, and others whom these may concern:
>
> You and each of you are hereby required to take the body of John Wesley, Clerk: and bring him before one of the Bailiffs of the said Town to answer the complaint of William Williamson

and Sophie his wife, for defaming the said Sophie, and refusing to administer to her the Sacrament of the Lord's Supper in a public Congregation without cause, by which the said William Williamson is damaged One Thousand Pounds Sterling. And for so doing this is your Warrant, certifying what you are to do in the premises.

Given under my hand and seal of the 8th day of August: Anno. Dom: 1737.

TH CHRISTIE.

When Constable Jones arrested Wesley and took him to court, Sophie's husband, William Williamson, was waiting there. He demanded that the minister give bail (pay money to guarantee his appearance for trial). But the judge said, "Mr. Wesley's word alone is sufficient."

He was nevertheless indicted on 10 counts, such as having had only two witnesses for some rite when three were customary. Damages of a hundred pounds were assessed against him.

Wesley had already been planning to leave Georgia. After the trial, he saw his further presence would only cause turmoil. He quietly left on Dec. 2, 1737. In his remarkably candid and interesting diary, he wrote, "I saw clearly that the hour was come for leaving this place; and as soon as the evening prayers were over, about 8 o'clock in the evening, the tide then serving, I shook the dust of Georgia off my feet and left, having preached the gospel there not as I ought but as I was able for one year and nine months." This same journal relates his later unhappy marriage. It is likely that his personal unhappiness spurred him to greater efforts for his church. He became one of history's greatest preachers. Later, when they met in England, Oglethorpe bent to kiss John Wesley's hand.

Wesleyan College in Macon is named for this great man. At Emory University in Atlanta there is an excellent collection of things relating to his life. On Cockspur Island near Savannah, the site is marked where Wesley first landed on February 6,

1736, and knelt to thank God for a safe journey. On St. Simons Island is the Wesley Center, where Methodists gather for various meetings. A nine-foot bronze statue of the great preacher has been placed on Reynolds Square in Savannah, near the site of Wesley's former house and garden. The sculptor, Marshall Daughtery, said, "I have shown him as youthful, tentative, and earnest, looking up from his Bible to the congregation."

Whitefield Starts America's First Orphanage

Reverend George Whitefield

Rev. George Whitefield arrived in Georgia on May 7, 1738. John Wesley had invited him, believing that the young minister, who had been drawing crowds by his preaching since he was 23, was needed in this new land. But Wesley had fled Georgia before Whitefield arrived with James Habersham.

So the blue-eyed, 25-year-old Whitefield came. He and Habersham found so many orphans that they started an orphanage in Savannah. Later Habersham picked a site on the Isle of Hope, 10 miles from Savannah, for their permanent buildings, and moved the school and orphanage there. They called it Bethesda.

Whitefield went up and down the colonies and back to England, preaching to raise money for these poor boys. How successful he was is illustrated in a story told by Benjamin Franklin in his autobiography:

What important work did Whitefield do?

> I happened to attend one of his sermons. I perceived early that he meant to take up a collection. I silently resolved that he should get nothing from me. I had in my pocket a handful of copper money, three or four silver dollars and five pistoles of gold. As the sermon progressed, I began to soften and concluded to give the silver; and he finished so admirably that I emptied my pockets into the collection dish, gold and all.

The Union Society, organized by a Catholic, a Jew, and a Protestant 10 years after the orphanage was founded, bought it in 1854. Bethesda School operates there now.

OGLETHORPE STRENGTHENS HIS COLONY AND RETURNS TO ENGLAND

Oglethorpe was so busy in the new colony that he did not have time to write to the Trustees in London as often as they thought he should. The Earl of Egmont had heard of William Stephens, a former member of Parliament and colleague of Oglethorpe. Stephens had gone from England to Ireland and then to America, where he was hired to oversee some lands in South Carolina. A man who kept voluminous diaries and wrote many letters, he seemed just the man to send to Georgia. He was appointed secretary in April 1737, and he arrived in Georgia on Nov. 1, 1737. He wrote the Trustees about the crops, the weather, the people, how they worked and whether they went to church, and the problems. Some considered him a nosy busybody, but he had been hired to make detailed reports, and this he did. The diaries have been reprinted by the University of Georgia Press.

Why is Stephens sent to report to the Trustees?

Stephens was 66 when he came to Georgia. He did everything he could to help Oglethorpe. He was deeply apologetic to the general when his son Thomas Stephens, who joined a group of people complaining against Oglethorpe and the Trustees, went to London on April 30, 1742, to complain about Oglethorpe's strict discipline. In his diary, Stephens refers to his son as "a furious, rash young fellow," and he assured both Oglethorpe and the Trustees that Thomas's opinions were not his.

In London Thomas Stephens was forced to apologize on his knees for his antagonistic attitude toward Oglethorpe and the Trustees. The Earl of Egmont wrote in his diary, "Tomorrow

(June 29, 1742) Thomas Stephens is to be brought upon his Marrowbones and Reprimanded from the Chair."

Oglethorpe's Showdown With Spain

From the first, Oglethorpe had foreseen that sooner or later England and Spain would clash on the frontier in Georgia. The English had colonies all along the Atlantic seaboard. However, it was the Georgia colony that was next to the Spaniards and had been founded as a buffer between the Spaniards and the other English colonies.

Oglethorpe started as soon as he could to prepare for the coming war. He set up forts and settlements at Augusta and at Frederica on St. Simons Island. The Trustees did not want Oglethorpe to settle Frederica. They believed it was dangerously near the Spaniards and outside the boundary of the charter. As a result, they thought he should keep the colony focused around Savannah. Oglethorpe needed it as a base to use in the coming showdown so he built it anyhow. He laid out a fort and a village, following the plans of Vauban, France's great military genius who had revolutionized the science of fortification. It was star-shaped with thick walls and a moat. He left the great live oaks standing. Walls and buildings were made of tabby (a word of African origin meaning "wall of earth or masonry"). Tabby was a mixture of lime, seashells, sand, and water, and it dries rock hard. It was used often as a building material in colonial Georgia.

Oglethorpe also built a narrow military road from Frederica to another fort on the south end of St. Simons Island. It was just wide enough for two to walk abreast.

At its peak, Frederica had a thousand residents. Oglethorpe encouraged the soldiers to bring their families and some did. They built houses in the little village next to the fort.

In 1736 Oglethorpe initiated some contacts with the Spanish that in late summer led to the arrival from Cuba of General

This Celtic cross marks the site of Fort Augusta.

How did Oglethorpe prepare for war with the Spanish?

Arredondo, the Spanish military commander. Despite Oglethorpe's hospitality and the toasts that were drunk to both the British and Spanish kings, the Spanish soon afterward sent Oglethorpe a formal demand to get out of Georgia. The general reported to the Trustees that the danger was serious.

Oglethorpe's Dangerous Journey

How did Oglethorpe get the Indian's help?

It was important for Oglethorpe to keep the Indians on England's side in the coming war. Tomochichi had advised him to meet with the Indians at Coweta Town, across the Chattahoochee River where Phenix City, Alabama, is now. That was a long and dangerous journey. In spite of that, the general, with a party of Scotch Highlanders and Indians, started out from Frederica and made the hard trip across Georgia, finally approaching the Chattahoochee River. They were met by a welcoming party about 40 miles from Coweta Town, or Kawita, as the Indians called it. Indian boys and girls gave the visitors watermelons, muscadines, venison, and wild turkey meat. Oglethorpe's party brought many gifts for the Indians, too. He arrived at the council town on Aug. 21, 1739.

The general sat with the Indians on logs covered with bearskins, drank their black tea and smoked the peace pipe with them. Some of the chiefs had come from settlements as far as 200 miles away. Besides the Creeks, the Chickasaws, and the Choctaws, there were Cherokees, who were very angry with the British. Some English traders had gone among them, carrying rum and diseased with smallpox; the Indians caught the disease, and many died.

"They did much damage to us. A thousand of our people died. We could not harvest our crops," the Cherokees told Oglethorpe.

"Were these traders from the Colony of Georgia?" he asked. They said no. Oglethorpe promised to give them 15,000 bushels of corn to feed their hungry people. At this news, the

Indians whooped so loud it nearly deafened their white guests.

Oglethorpe felt that his long, hard journey had been worthwhile. In September, there was important news: Spain had declared war on England. Oglethorpe was not surprised. There was other, and still sadder, news. The aged Chief Tomochichi was dying.

Tomochichi's Death Handicaps Oglethorpe

Tomochichi, who had been past 90 when Oglethorpe first met him, died on Oct. 5, 1739, at 97. He had done so much to keep the Indians friendly and to help Oglethorpe get Georgia started that the general felt a severe loss at his death. He knew that he would grievously miss the staunch old Indian in the coming trouble with Spain.

How did Tomochichi's death handicap Oglethorpe?

Tomochichi had said to Oglethorpe, "You have never made a difference between our people and your people. You have never broken a promise to us. When I die, I want to be buried in the white man's town, and not in the forest." *The Gentleman's Magazine* reported it this way:

> He desired his Body might be buried among the English in the Town of Savannah, since it was he who prevailed with the Creek Indians to give the land and assisted in the founding of the Town.

A big stone marks Tomochichi's grave in Savannah today. On it are these words:

> In memory of Tomochichi, Mico of the Yamacraws, the companion of Oglethorpe and the friend and ally of the colony of Georgia.

After Oglethorpe had helped lay the body of his friend in the Georgia earth, he turned his attention to the coming war. He sent friendly Indians speeding to the tribes to summon warriors. Mary Musgrove was enlisted to rouse the chiefs to the aid of Georgia. Then he went home to St. Simons.

The Peculiar War of Jenkins' Ear

Georgia's troubles with Spain were a tiny part of a much larger struggle between English and Spanish trade interests. This struggle began to come to a showdown in The War of Jenkins' Ear (1739-41). This peculiar war got its name from a British seaman whose ear was cut off as an object lesson by Spaniards who had caught him smuggling.

Georgia was the only one of the English colonies in American in which there was actual fighting in this war. It started in November when Spaniards landed on Amelia Island and killed two unarmed Scotch Highlanders out cutting wood. Capt. Francis Brooks, in command of the British fort on the island, heard the shots, rounded up his soldiers and drove out the invading Spaniards. He reported the occurrence to Oglethorpe, who sent for reinforcements, chased the Spaniards upriver, burned their ships and forced them back to their headquarters at St. Augustine.

What was Georgia's role in the War of Jenkin's Ear?

Oglethorpe had so awed the Spaniards that they did not come to attack him in Georgia for another two years. He knew, however, that they would come, because the question had to be settled: who would control the land in the future—England or Spain?

The Decisive Battle of Bloody Marsh

On St. Simons Island is a white marble monument that marks the site of the Battle of Bloody Marsh where Oglethorpe and his men fought an important battle.

In June 1742, the General heard that 56 Spanish ships with 7,000 men had left Cuba headed for St. Augustine. He knew that this was the beginning of the final showdown with Spain. They had already threatened to "wipe the English off the Atlantic coast."

On June 28, 1742, just at sunset, 36 ships with more than 3,000 Spaniards aboard neared the shore of St. Simons Island. Oglethorpe at that time had only 600 soldiers at Frederica. Quickly he sent again to Savannah, Darien, and other settlements for help. At most, he could muster about 900 men, but he said:

> We are resolved not to suffer defeat. We will, rather, die like Leonidas and his Spartans in old Greece if we can but protect Georgia and Carolina and the rest of the American colonies from desolation.

As the Spanish approached St. Simons, Oglethorpe pulled his men out of Ft. St. Simon on the southern end of the island. He destroyed the equipment and ammunition he could not move and concentrated his forces at Ft. Frederica on the upper end.

What happened at Bloody Marsh?

The Spanish soldiers landed and started marching up his narrow road, as Oglethorpe had known they would. The general and his men marched out to meet the enemy. In the ensuing battle a hundred Spaniards were killed and Oglethorpe himself took two prisoners. The Spanish were driven back to their ships.

Expecting another attack, the Georgia officers hid their men all through the woods. Captain Mackay told them, "When I hold up my cap on the end of my gun, that will be the signal for you to attack." The Spaniards came back. Thinking that the Georgians had gone, they relaxed and started preparing for supper. Mackay then held up his cap. The Georgians, with their Indian allies, rushed to the attack. They caught the Spaniards by surprise, and the ground at the battle site was strewn with the wounded and the dead.

"What a bloody marsh!" somebody said, and thus the site became known as Bloody Marsh. Even though this battle was small, it was so important to the future of America that

Carlyle, the British historian, called it one of the most momentous battles in history. But Oglethorpe knew that the Spanish were still on the island. He thought that they would attack again and he was ill prepared to resist them. Through a trick he managed to persuade the Spanish commander that strong reinforcements might be on the way. This officer did not know whether to believe it or not but he took no chances. He sailed away from Georgia on July 14, 1742. The power of Spain in America was broken forever.

What strategy did Oglethorpe employ?

Frederica, its mission accomplished, would soon fall into decay, its cannon rusted, its soldiers gone. More than two centuries later, the Ft. Frederica Association bought 78 acres and gave them to the federal government to create a national park. It is one of the few historic shrines in America dating back beyond the revolution.

Thanksgiving in July

Oglethorpe, jubilant at the victory, proclaimed July 25, 1742, a day of thanksgiving to God. So the first Thanksgiving Day was observed in Georgia not in November, but in July. Oglethorpe worded the proclamation like this:

How did Oglethorpe react to the victory?

> Truly God has done great things for us. Our salvation comes from the Lord. He has rescued us from the power of a great foe, who boasted that they would conquer and dispossess us. It is highly fitting, therefore, that we render thanks in His name Who had been our Deliverer. In regard to these considerations and for this purpose, I do herefore appoint this, the 25th day of July, one thousand seven hundred and forty-two, as a day of special thanksgiving to God for His Great Deliverance and the end He has brought to the Spanish invasion. And I enjoin everyone to observe this festival in a Christian and godly manner, abstaining from intemperance and excess, and extravagant signs of rejoicing.

OGLETHORPE LEAVES GEORGIA FOREVER

Oglethorpe had been in Georgia for over 10 years. He had left his comfortable home in England and come out to help a handful of people start a new life. He had ended the Spanish threat. Now he could think of going home. His little colony was safe: his work was done. He recommended to the Trustees that William Stephens, who was already president of the Savannah area, be made president of all Georgia, and that Maj. William Horton, who had come over with him in 1736, take over the duties of military commander.

Oglethorpe bade his people goodbye. He took a ring from his finger and gave it to Mary Musgrove, unaware that she would later cause much trouble to the little colony. Then, on July 23, 1743, he boarded the ship *Success* and sailed for England. Nine years later he married Elizabeth Wright, heiress of Cranham Hall, where they lived quietly, occasionally going up to London where Oglethorpe had a town house.

He still served as an officer in the king's army and as a member of Parliament. He became a member of the circle that revolved around Dr. Samuel Johnson. This included David Garrick, the actor; Oliver Goldsmith, the writer (who sometimes sang for them songs from his play *She Stoops to Conquer*); and Joshua Reynolds, the artist. Oglethorpe helped Goldsmith establish the science collection and group that later became the British Academy of Science.

What was Oglethorpe's life like after Georgia?

Toward the end of his life there were many in England who loved and appreciated Oglethorpe and knew him for the great man that he was. One was the writer, Hannah More. She wrote to a friend,

> I have a new admirer. He is the famous General Oglethorpe, perhaps the most remarkable man of his time. He is past 90, and the finest figure of a man you ever saw.

His literature is great, his knowledge of the world is extensive and his faculties as bright as ever. We flirt outrageously.

Of course she was joking about the last, and she was wrong about his age, too. He was only 89 when he died on June 30, 1785. The *Georgia Gazette* waited a whole year to carry the news of his death, ran only three lines about it in the June 8, 1786 issue, and got the date and his age wrong: "General Oglethorpe died August last, aged 103." It had been a long time since the general had left Georgia.

Georgia has a county, a town, and a university named for him, besides many streets, hotels, and other things. In Savannah there is a monument to his memory. High on a north Georgia mountain, Grassy Knob in Pickens County, is a monument to him. Ft. Oglethorpe keeps his name alive, as does Mt. Oglethorpe. The finest portrait of him in Georgia hangs in Oglethorpe University.

THE GEORGIA COLONY AFTER OGLETHORPE

Three presidents served as heads of the government in Georgia between the time Oglethorpe left and the coming of the first of the royal governors.

Mary Musgrove and her third husband marched on Savannah and demanded pay.

William Stephens, Georgia's First President

William Stephens, the "man with the diary," had already been appointed president of the Savannah area. When Oglethorpe left he recommended that Stephens be made president of the entire colony and the Trustees so decreed.

What problem did Stephens face?

It was during his regime that Mary Musgrove and her third husband, Thomas Bosomworth, roused the Indians to demand that she be paid for services to the colony and for goods from her trading station. The Indians put on their war paint and marched menacingly on Savannah. Stephens talked calmly to them and the matter was quieted. The claims were not to be settled until almost a decade later.

Stephens was a well-educated man and had been a member of Parliament. It was he who presided at the first venture into self-government that the Trustees had allowed the colonists. It was a representative assembly of 16 members, which met in Savannah on Jan. 15, 1751. Shortly thereafter, feeble with age, he retired.

Henry Parker and His Purple Robe

Henry Parker, who had been Stephens' assistant, was made the second president of Georgia by the Trustees on April 8, 1751. It was during his regime that more Germans came and settled Bethany, five miles northwest of Ebenezer. Germans also settled Goshen, about 10 miles below Ebenezer on the road to Savannah. Parker wore a purple robe trimmed with fur on official occasions.

What new settlers came during Governor Parker's term?

Other new settlers were also moving in. The first group of Puritans arrived on May 16, 1752, and included 280 whites and 536 black slaves. Later, others came, increasing the total to 350, with 1,500 slaves. They had bought 22,500 acres of land in the vicinity of the Midway River, halfway between Savannah and Darien. Because of its location, the Puritan settlement became known as Midway. These Puritans were descendants of the first Puritans who came to America and settled in the village of Dorchester in Massachusetts.

About 12 miles down the road from the little Midway Church is old Sunbury. It is now a ghost town, but Sunbury was once the bustling, prosperous port of the Puritans. By 1772 it had become so prosperous that the people there owned a third of all the wealth of Georgia.

The Puritans were destined to lead Georgia into the Revolution. With the Liberty Boys of Savannah they wielded a powerful influence against the Tories.

Patrick Graham Was a Druggist

Patrick Graham, the third president, was a dealer in medicines. It was Graham who was in charge of the government of Georgia when the king sent the first of the three royal governors. Graham turned the affairs of Georgia over to the new governor's council.

Why did Georgia prosper in Patrick Graham's term?

Georgia was becoming prosperous again when Patrick Graham was president because many of the people who had moved away due to the Trustees' harsh laws came back again. It was a much more prosperous and happy place that Graham was able to turn over to the first royal governor.

The Trustees Give Up Their Georgia Charter

On June 23, 1752, a year before their 21-year charter was to have expired, the Trustees gave up the charter. They had found it hard to govern a colony 3,000 miles away because they did not always understand conditions on the frontier. Besides, Parliament had been more and more reluctant to provide money for the colony.

Why were the Trustees willing to give up the colony early?

King George II decided that until the appointment of a royal governor, the officials in Georgia already in office should continue to handle its affairs. At that time, Georgia had 2,381 white people and 1,066 blacks. Ironically, there were more German than English settlers. In addition to these, of course, there was a substantial Indian population.

The French and Indian War—A Coming Danger

Just as the government of Georgia was changing from the presidents to the royal governors, the French and Indian War broke out. Though it really affected Georgia very little, this was the last and most important of several global struggles between England and France for colonial empire. When it ended in 1763 France had lost Canada and every threatening foothold to the west of the British colonies. Her ally, Spain, had lost Florida. As a result the southern boundary of Georgia was extended to the St. Mary's River instead of the Altamaha, an action which doubled its territory.

What was the result of the French and Indian War for Georgia?

GEORGIA BECOMES A ROYAL PROVINCE

By 1754 King George II and his ministers were ready to send a royal governor to the province of Georgia. The plan was to have a 12-man advisory council, named by the king, to serve as the upper house of the Assembly. The lower house, similar to the British House of Commons, would be composed of delegates elected by the people. The Church of England (Episcopal) became the established church and the colonists were taxed to support it.

The First Royal Governor

The first of the three royal governors of Georgia was a navy captain named John Reynolds, who arrived in Savannah on

Oct. 19, 1754. President Patrick Graham turned the government over to him.

What kind of person was John Reynolds?

Reynolds was used to commanding men but not to working with them. Though Georgians welcomed him with bonfires and kindness, his fussy ways and his bossy attitude soon involved him in bitter quarrels with his council.

He did one very good thing, however. He set up a bicameral legislature which met for the first time in January 1755, in Savannah. Its first act was to pass a law to punish any citizen who questioned its decisions! The representatives elected to this body had to be over 21 and own 500 acres of land. While this seems restrictive, it was an immense improvement over the only other representative government Georgians had had before.

The Acadians came to Georgia while Reynolds was governor. The French Acadians who lived in Nova Scotia had been driven out by the British. About 400 of them came by boat to Georgia in January 1756. These people were Catholic, however, and Georgia law prohibited Catholics from becoming citizens. Governor Reynolds and his people generously cared for them at public expense through the winter and helped them to go, when spring came, to other places like South Carolina and the bayou country of Louisiana. There the Acadians eventually became known as Cajuns, and to this day form one of the most colorful groups in the nation. Nova Scotia had strange ties with Georgia. Some of its people came here and when the Revolution began many of the British in Georgia, including the governor, went to Nova Scotia.

Why did the Acadians come?

Reynolds finally became so unpopular in Georgia that the Council sent a representative to England to complain about him. Among other things, they charged that Reynolds even changed the minutes of the Assembly and Council when they did not suit him!

In 1756 Reynolds was summoned to England to answer 14 complaints against him. His defense was that he may have been "guilty of mistakes, but never of crimes." Nevertheless, he was finally dismissed from office, and his lieutenant governor, Henry Ellis, was appointed governor on May 17, 1757.

The new governor thought Georgia was the hottest place on earth and went about with a thermometer dangling from his umbrella so he could see exactly how hot it was at any minute. In spite of this peculiarity, he was a man of remarkable tact. He listened while Georgians told him their troubles. He got the quarreling factions together, asked them to forget their differences and to work in harmony for the good of Georgia. But he firmly took back into his grasp the governmental duties that Reynolds had given over to the Council in a vain effort to gain favor with them. It was important to keep the Indians friendly because the French and Indian War was going on, and though it had not yet affected Georgia, nobody knew when it might. He met with the Indian chiefs and said to them: "The French have told you that my arms are red with blood, up to the elbow. I will roll up my sleeve and you can see for yourself that my arm is white. The French have told you that anybody who shook my hand would be struck by disease and die. If you believe these foolish lies, do not touch me. If not, I am ready to embrace you."

Royal Governor Henry Ellis kept check on Georgia's hot weather.

What was Henry Ellis' great strength?

He won the Indians over, and they agreed to oppose the French and other Indians who were allied with the French.

The Mary Musgrove claims against Georgia were finally settled by Ellis, as authorized by the British government. He gave her a deed to St. Catherines Island (where she and her third husband and his second wife, who was her maid Sarah, are buried). He also paid her 2,100 pounds in cash, which he got from the sale of two other islands, Sapelo and Ossabaw, and the campsite near Pipemaker's Creek, which the Indians had always reserved near Savannah.

Ellis' health finally failed in the hot climate. In 1760 he was succeeded by a man who most historians agree was the ablest of the three royal governors, Sir James Wright.

The Third Royal Governor

How did Georgia farming change?

Georgians had by now turned to more practical crops than silk and indigo. They were selling lumber and growing livestock, rice, corn, tobacco, and wheat. They also grew cotton. And, since the strict land laws of the Trustees had been relaxed, the plantation system had begun to grow in Georgia. Wright himself acquired 11 plantations, with 25,578 acres, worked by 523 slaves. He shipped about 3,000 barrels of rice abroad each year. Many other Georgia planters were growing so prosperous that they lived in fine style, ordering handsome clothes and furniture from Europe. They sent abroad for gold and silver jewelry, ribbons, and silver buckles for their shoes. They had tutors for their children.

Wright worked hard at his duties. Even those who did not like royal government respected him. He tried to convince Georgians that since England had invested much money in the colony, it should stay loyal to the king. Besides, he said, it was exposed on a dangerous frontier, and needed the king's protection. Some listened; some did not.

John Bartram, the naturalist, who came with his son William from Philadelphia in September 1765, wrote, "Governor Wright is universally respected by all Georgians, and they can hardly say enough in his praise." Quakers who came to Georgia in 1768 named their town, located above Augusta, Wrightsboro in honor of him. The modern town of Wrightsville was named in memory of him.

The Mystery of the Lost Flower

The two Bartrams studied the flowers and the animals in Georgia swamps. They found growing in the wild forest a beautiful flower that resembled the magnolia or camellia, known as the Gordonia. Nobody has been able to find the flower growing in Georgia since. It is known as "the lost Gordonia."

William Bartram wrote a book about his travels that tells much about Georgia. It became a classic. Carlyle and Emerson liked to read it. The poet Coleridge is said to have found in it some of the beautiful imagery he used in his poems about Kubla Khan and the Ancient Mariner. He wrote of dark green swamps, deep red berries, pale gold fish, dark gray storm clouds, yellow corn, white birds flying, purple muscadines, and spreading live oaks.

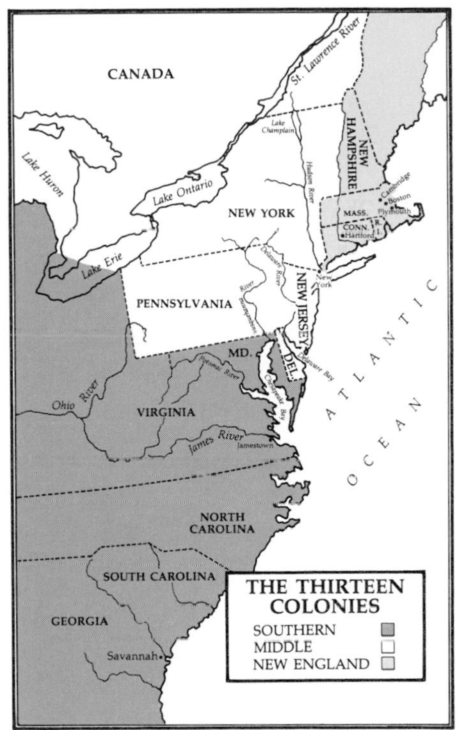

The Shadow of the Revolution

The little flower in the Georgia swamps was not the only thing lost in these years. A king far over the blue waters was soon to lose a whole new world, much to his surprise and sadness. For the American Revolution was gathering like a coming storm and would break in fury over Georgia and the other colonies soon. When it was over, the colonies would be free, and the king would be wandering in the darkness of insanity, like Shakespeare's troubled King Lear. But before that, there was a lot of fighting to be done, many would die, and battlefields would be bloody. Some of them would be in Georgia. A new nation was about to be born.

For Extended Thinking

1. What are some of the problems early preachers faced?
2. What was Oglethorpe's strategy in preparing for war with the Spanish?
3. How did the transition from Oglethorpe to the other governors take place?
4. What kind of men were the three royal governors?

Names, Terms and Concepts

Charles Delamotte
Coweta town
Patrick Graham
Battle of Bloody Marsh
Bethesda
John Reynolds
George Whitefield
Henry Parker
Acadians
William Stephens
Midway
James Wright
tabby
Sunbury
John Bartram

To Help You Study

1. What was John Wesley's experience in Georgia?
2. Who was appointed secretary of the colony?
3. What nations fought the War of Jenkins Ear? Why was it named that?
4. Oglethorpe made a dangerous journey. Where did he go and what was the result?
5. Who won the Battle of Bloody Marsh? Why was it named that?
6. When did Oglethorpe go back to England?
7. What was Oglethorpe's life like when he went back to England?
8. Who were the three presidents who headed Georgia's government before the royal governors came?
9. Why did the Trustees give up their charter earlier than necessary?
10. What was the effect of the French and Indian War on Georgia?
11. Who was the first royal governor and what did he do?
12. Who settled Mary Musgrove's claims and how?
13. Under which royal governor did Georgia prosper?
14. Tell something interesting about the Gordonia.

GEORGIA AND THE AMERICAN REVOLUTION

CHAPTER 5

The war of the American Revolution began with the skirmish at Concord, Massachusetts, on April 19, 1775. The situation that led to the fighting, however, had started 10 years earlier. John Adams, the dumpy little Boston lawyer who became the second president of the United States, said, "The Revolution was effected before the War commenced. The Revolution was in the hearts and minds of the people."

THE THIRTEEN COLONIES during The War for Independence

There were three million people in the 13 American colonies when the trouble with England began. In Georgia there were 20,000 white residents and 17,000 blacks. Those on the king's side were called **Tories** (the British called them **loyalists**) and those who sided with the patriots were called **Whigs**, or **Sons of Liberty.**

When did Georgia join the Revolution?

Georgia was late joining the other 12 colonies in the Revolution. Because of this, relations between Georgia and other colonies were somewhat strained. South Carolina actually passed a law decreeing death to any of its citizens who traded with Georgia. South Carolina became so picky that it refused to allow the Georgia Puritans to join with it to send delegates to Philadelphia.

Why was Georgia slow in joining the Revolution?

There were reasons for Georgia's being slow. It was the youngest of the 13 colonies. When Parliament passed the Stamp Act in 1765 it had been only 32 years since the first colonists had pitched their tents at the mouth of the Savannah. Its royal governor, when the trouble with England started, was Sir James Wright. He was able and well-liked and exerted a powerful influence in keeping Georgia loyal to the king. Additionally, most older and influential Georgians had grown up in England. It seemed to them disloyal to be against the king.

King George III

THE AMERICANS BEGIN TO REVOLT

The colonists' protest against the Stamp Tax surprised King George III. "I only want what is best for my people. Whoever opposes me is a scoundrel," he said. The little blue stamp was to be required for all documents, such as deeds, contracts, marriage licenses, newspapers, mortgages, pamphlets, and even diplomas. To add insult to injury, the tax had to be paid in silver or gold.

Why did America oppose the Stamp Act?

The Stamp Tax was not the first tax England had put on the colonies. But it was the first tax that would affect the daily lives of all the people. The colonists were not the only ones who objected. In England, the ailing William Pitt, Earl of Chatham, dragged himself before Parliament, waved his crutch, and said, "They will never stand for it. I might as well talk of driving them before me with this crutch. Let us retreat now while we can and not wait until we must!" Others spoke out with Pitt. The great Irishman Edmund Burke made an eloquent speech calling for compromise with the American colonies. Benjamin Franklin, then in London, warned the British: "I judge the other Americans by myself. I have many debts due me there, but I would rather they would never be paid than to submit to this tax." In 1768 Georgia hired Franklin as its agent in England.

How did the Liberty Boys oppose the Stamp Act?

In Georgia rumors flew. The **Liberty Boys**, the local organization of the Sons of Liberty, were stirring up sentiment against the British. They held meetings at Tondee's Tavern and paraded around Savannah shouting "Liberty, Property, and No Stamps!" They hanged the governor in effigy. Older residents called them Liberty Bawlers, Governor Wright called them Sons of Licentiousness, but the Liberty Boys had determined that no stamps would be sold in Georgia.

The governor was uneasy. The Liberty Boys were camped on the edge of Savannah and he did not know what they might do when the stamps came. For four days and nights Governor Wright did not take off his clothes.

The blue stamps finally arrived on Dec. 5 on board the ship *Speedwell*. The governor had them hidden until Jan. 6, 1766, when George Angus, the stampseller, arrived. Angus was frightened by the hostility he found. The governor took him to his home, which was guarded by British Rangers, and in a few days Angus left, unharmed. Only 70 stamps were ever sold in Georgia. Early in February Governor Wright returned the unsold stamps to the *Speedwell*.

Because of the Stamp Act Americans were boycotting British goods and British merchants campaigned for its repeal. In the cold gray London dawn of July 16, 1766, a Parliament that wrangled through the night voted 275 to 176 for repeal.

Georgia was as happy as the other colonies at the repeal. Like other colonies, it sent a thank-you note to the King: "Most Gracious Sire: Your majesty's loyal subjects of the Province of Georgia beg leave to thank you with hearts full of affection. May you long reign over us."

Savannah's Liberty Boys

"Champagne Charlie" Adds More Taxes

In 1767, Charles Townshend became Chancellor of the Exchequer in England. He did much to persuade Parliament and the King to put other taxes on America. He argued, "These colonies are children of the mother country. They were planted by our care and nurtured by us. They will not grudge us their mite to help with the heavy burden we bear." Col. John Barre scoffed, "Planted by our care indeed! They fled from our oppression, and thrive by our neglect!" James

What case did Townshend make for more taxes?

Habersham saw the coming trouble. He warned the British, "If you persist in your right to tax the colonists, you will drive them to rebellion."

In September 1769, the people of Savannah voted to boycott British goods. Other colonies were reacting in the same way—to such effect that finally England repealed all taxes except that on tea.

England wanted to keep one tax on the colonists as a sign that they were subject to English law. In his proclamation repealing the other taxes, King George said, "It is with the utmost astonishment that I find my subjects encouraging the rebellious disposition which unhappily exists in my colonies in America."

A British ship with tea on board was anchored in Boston harbor. On the night of Dec. 17, 1773, Paul Revere, John Hancock and others disguised themselves as Mohawk Indians, boarded the ship and dumped the tea into the water. The same thing was done in other ports. In Maryland, the patriots also burned the ships.

Eventually, on June 1, 1774, the furious British closed the port of Boston, saying that it would not reopen until the colonists had paid for the tea. They sent Gov. Thomas Gage as military governor to occupy the city with four regiments. People grew hungry because no ships could go in or out. One man wrote, "We eat pork and beans one day and beans and pork the next! And a fish when we can catch it." This is probably why Boston came to be known as Beantown. In any event, there was much suffering.

THE PATRIOTS TAKE OVER GEORGIA'S GOVERNMENT

Later in that eventful summer of 1774, two rival factions developed in Georgia. One was for the king and the other opposed to him.

Events during this important time are the basis for very fruitful thought experiments. First, put yourself in the position of an individual who supported the king. What case would you make for loyalty? Certainly, you would say that colonies should support "our mother country and our people." Don't you think that you would argue that support of the king was necessary to insure the continued protection of the colony by Britain? Remember that military security was one of the most important reasons why Georgia was established as a colony. And what about economic relations, trade and the sale of agricultural products? What other arguments can you think of for loyalty to the king in 1774? How do you think the loyalists felt about those who were in opposition to the king?

What was the case for loyalty to the king?

Now put yourself in the place of an individual who opposed the king. What case would you make for that opposition? Certainly, you would argue that the king had oppressed the colonies and that the oppression should be resisted. And don't you think you would have put special emphasis on the hated taxes the king imposed? What about the benefits of freedom? Could you have argued that freedom is necessary to both security and economic development? What other arguments can you think of for opposition to the king? How do you think those in opposition felt toward the loyalists?

What was the case for the Revolution?

However these questions are answered, it is important to remember that practically nobody at this time, in Georgia or any of the other colonies, seriously suggested separating from England. Even those in opposition simply wanted the king to stop his tyranny and to correct their grievances. The idea of separation was to come later.

In July, this advertisement appeared in the *Georgia Gazette:*

> The critical situation to which the British colonies in America are likely to be reduced, from the arbitrary and alarming imposition of the late acts of the British Parliament respecting the town of Boston, as well as the acts that at present exist, tending to the raising of a perpetual revenue without the

consent of the people or their representatives, is considered an object extremely important at this juncture, and particularly calculated to deprive the American subjects of their constitutional rights and liberties, as a part of the British empire. It is therefore requested that all persons within the limits of this Province do attend at Savannah, on Wednesday the 27th of July, in order that the said matters may be taken into consideration, and such other constitutional measures pursued as may appear most eligible.

It was signed by four very distinguished Georgians: Noble Wymberly Jones, Archibald Bulloch, George Walton, and John Houstoun.

The meeting these four had called was held at Tondee's Tavern on July 27, with another meeting on Aug. 10. Governor Wright forbade the meeting but it was held anyhow. John Glen was elected chairman of a 31-member committee to draw up some resolutions of protest against the king. They named another committee to gather up rice to send to the starving people in Boston.

What did the meeting at Tondee's Tavern do?

The governor and the loyalists were alarmed by what had happened at Tondee's Tavern. Wright wrote, "The world will judge whether that meeting, held by a few persons in a tavern with the doors shut, can in truth and decency, be called a `general meeting of the inhabitants of Georgia.'" He and the Tories still had enough influence to keep Georgia from sending official delegates to the First Continental Congress which met in Philadelphia in September. The other 12 colonies sent 56 delegates. The Congress met for a month and adjourned, agreeing to reconvene in May 1775. They little dreamed what would happen before they met again.

Wright, who said that the conditions in the other 12 colonies made him shudder, warned the Georgia Assembly, "Do not listen to voices and opinions of men of overheated ideas. Do not catch at shadows." On Oct. 14, 1774, he was reporting to

England that "the poison of rebellion has affected the whole province. There is hardly a shadow of government remaining."

Georgia Delegates Refuse To Go to Philadelphia

What actions did the First Provincial Congress take?

On Jan. 18, 1775, Georgia held its first Provincial Congress. It elected three delegates to go to Philadelphia. They were Noble Wymberly Jones, Archibald Bulloch, and John Houstoun, but they refused to go! They pointed out that only five of Georgia's 12 parishes had sent representatives to the Provincial Congress that elected them. This meant that they could not represent all of Georgia even if they did go to Philadelphia.

Who were Georgia's delegates and what position did they take?

All three of them were re-elected later to the larger delegation from Georgia, but not one would be there to sign the Declaration of Independence.

Moreover, the First Provincial Congress did not adopt the resolutions that other colonies had adopted. So Georgia remained outside the organization of colonies and was increasingly unpopular with them, especially with South Carolina.

The Impatient Puritans Send Their Doctor

What was the position of the Puritans?

The Puritans at Midway were especially impatient since their kinsmen in Boston were undergoing hardships because the British closed the port. South Carolina, wanting to have nothing to do with anybody from Georgia, had refused to allow the Puritans to join with them in sending delegates to the Second Continental Congress. The Puritans, believing that they could wait no longer, decided to send their own delegates. On March 21, 1775, the people of St. Johns Parish sent their physician, Dr. Lyman Hall. He started on his long journey north with 60 barrels of rice and 50 pounds of sterling for the Boston people. Hall arrived in Philadelphia on May 13,

Dr. Lyman Hall

1775, three days after the Second Continental Congress had opened in Carpenters' Hall. He sat in on the deliberations but he did not attempt to vote.

THE REVOLUTION BECOMES A SHOOTING WAR

On April 19, 1775, while Dr. Hall was still far from Philadelphia, the anger and frustration felt in Boston broke into a shooting war at a place called Lexington, about 16 miles outside of Boston. This was 14 months after the Boston Tea Party. For more than a year, emotions had been seething. The Boston leaders of the movement against the king had stirred New England and the whole of colonial America.

In Georgia, on May 10, patriots broke into Governor Wright's ammunition stores east of Savannah. They took 600 pounds of the king's ammunition and sent part of it to Boston. The stores were 12 feet underground and made of brick. Wright had thought them so safe that he had not even put guards there.

Georgians Organize a Council of Safety

What was the purpose of the council of Safety?

On June 22, 1775, two months after the war had started at Lexington, Georgians organized a **Council of Safety**. Similar councils were also being organized in the other colonies. These councils were to be the focus of government when legislative bodies were not in session during the coming years. Georgia's Council was organized at Tondee's Tavern. The *Georgia Gazette* reported:

> On Monday last (June 5, 1775) a considerable number of the Inhabitants met, and having erected a Liberty Pole, afterward dined at Tondee's Tavern in the Long Room. They spent the

day with the utmost harmony, and concluded the evening with great decorum.

When the Council of Safety was organized, it was given instructions to keep in touch with the other colonies and to meet at the tavern every Monday. It also issued a call for the Second Provincial Congress of Georgia to meet on July 4, 1775. When it met at Tondee's Tavern the 12 Georgia parishes had sent a total of over a hundred delegates.

Archibald Bulloch was elected president. He was also named as one of the five Georgia representatives to go to Philadelphia to the Second Continental Congress. Lyman Hall was already there but he represented only the one parish of St. Johns. Hall was named one of Georgia's five to represent the whole colony. John Houstoun and Noble Wymberly Jones were also elected delegates.

The fifth delegate was a minister, Rev. Joachim Zubly, the scholarly pastor of the Calvinist Independent Presbyterian Church in Savannah. He was a 51-year-old Swiss who spoke six languages and had come to Georgia from South Carolina in 1760. It turned out that he was not for independence at all. When the other delegates found out his true sentiments, they expelled him from the delegation. John Houstoun returned to Georgia at that time. Jones had to stay in Georgia because his aged father, who had come over with Oglethorpe in 1733, was ill and dying. Bulloch was too busy with his duties as president of Georgia to be in Philadelphia. So Button Gwinnett and George Walton were appointed to fill the vacancies.

Governor Wright Is Arrested

The patriots were now in control of Georgia but the Liberty Boys had no intention of harming the governor. Georgia had prospered under him and he was a popular and influential

figure. They wanted him to relinquish the government, however, and on Jan. 18, 1776, the Council of Safety adopted a resolution: "Resolved, that the person of his Excellency, Sir James Wright, Baronet . . . be forthwith arrested."

As Wright sat in his home with members of his Council that day, 24-year-old Maj. Joseph Habersham walked in. He laid his hand on the governor's shoulder and said, "Sir James, you are my prisoner." The Council members fled.

Wright was allowed to remain in his own home, but on Feb. 11, 1776, he escaped. The British ship *Scarborough* was in Savannah harbor, and the captain received him on board at three a.m. on Feb. 12, 1776. He went to Nova Scotia and was away from Georgia for three and a half years.

Georgians Elect Bulloch President

After Governor Wright was arrested, Georgians took over the government and elected Archibald Bulloch as its head. Bulloch was a very democratic man. When Gen. Lachlan McIntosh wanted to place guards at his door, he declined. He thought it would look as if he were trying to display his position.

What actions did Georgia take to prepare for the war?

The colonies were now joining together to strengthen their defenses and to support the Continental Congress. The Liberty Boys had already organized a battalion commanded by General McIntosh. Georgia's Provincial Congress had named McIntosh Continental Commander in Georgia with the rank of brigadier general. This angered Button Gwinnett who had wanted the post. The appointment of McIntosh was to cause deadly trouble later.

Early in January 1776, McIntosh headed a delegation sent by Georgia to Charleston to confer with the American commander in charge of the south, Gen. Charles Lee. Lee also came to Savannah to review the troops and to look at

Georgia's defense plans and at the forts on the coast.

General Lee thought the Georgians were too optimistic about their ability to defend their part of America. This bitter and cynical man wrote:

> These Georgians would tackle anything. They propose to defend their frontier with Horse Rangers, and it turns out that they do not have there a single horse. Later, they planned to defend it by boats—and they had no boats! I would not be surprised to hear them propose to defend the coastal country with mermaids mounted on alligators!

Georgia and the Declaration of Independence

Three of the men chosen to represent Georgia at the Continental Congress in Philadelphia were there on July 4, 1776, when the Declaration of Independence was adopted. They were Dr. Lyman Hall, Button Gwinnett, and George Walton. Later each of them became a head of government in Georgia and was to have a county named for him. Two signers, Hall and Walton, are buried under the Signer's Monument in Augusta. It was built in 1848 and designed like the Washington Monument in Washington, D.C. Gwinnett's body was lost to history for a long time. It is now in Savannah's Colonial Cemetery.

Who from Georgia were present when the Declaration of Independence was signed?

News of the Declaration reached Georgia in early August and a copy of it arrived in Georgia on Aug. 8, 1776. The Declaration was read several times in Savannah: to the Assembly members in the Council House; to the public gathered around the Liberty Pole near Tondee's Tavern and to another crowd in the Trustees' Garden.

How did Georgians react to the Declaration?

The crowds were very excited. They held a mock funeral service in Savannah and buried an effigy of King George III. They rang bells: 13 cannons boomed. At Tondee's Tavern

they had a feast and drank toasts to the success of their new country.

But not all Georgians were in favor of independence and in the next few months, about 2,000 moved away. Some went to Florida, some went to Nova Scotia, some to Jamaica, and some, like the Tattnalls, back to England. A son, Josiah Tattnall, returned and was later elected governor. He signed "with lively expressions of gratitude" a legislative bill restoring to him his family's confiscated property.

GEORGIA GETS ITS FIRST CONSTITUTION

How did Georgia adopt its first constitution?

In 1776, the second year of the American Revolution, President Archibald Bulloch set up a committee to draft a constitution for Georgia. The committee worked hard all through the winter of 1776-1777. By February 1777, a constitution of 63 articles was ready and the legislature adopted it. One of the things it provided was that schools should be erected in each county, "supported at the general expense of the State." The official church was disestablished. Georgians, who had been taxed to support it and fined if they did not go to church on Sunday, were free to worship as they pleased.

What provisions did the first constitution contain?

The constitution provided for eight counties instead of the 12 Church of England parishes that had existed. Liberty County, one of the few not named for a place or a person, honored the Midway Puritans who had been so insistent in the cause of liberty. The others were named for Britishers who had championed the cause of the colonies.

The constitution provided for two members from each county to form an advisory council for the governor, who was to be the state's chief executive. Superior courts and *courts of conscience* were set up. The governor was to be elected by the legislature and to serve for only one year. He would also be required to swear that he would not try to "hold over" in the office. Patriots were fighting a war to get rid of tyrannical British governors and they did not want new governors to hold office for long periods. This rule was to cause trouble when the British suddenly swooped down on Savannah and the government had to flee.

The constitution was adopted on Feb. 5, 1777. President Archibald Bulloch set May 7, 1777, as the date for the meeting of the first legislature. Its biggest task would be to elect Georgia's first constitutional governor. This would undoubtedly have been Bulloch himself, but early in March he died. He was buried in Savannah's Colonial Park Cemetery. A strange mark is on his tomb: a figure carved in a circle.

Gwinnett Fails To Become First Governor

Button Gwinnett

Even though Button Gwinnett had been somewhat late siding with the patriots, he had achieved considerable prominence in the new state. He had worked on the first state constitution and had been assistant to President Archibald Bulloch.

When Bulloch died, Gwinnett was named acting president. The commission issued to him on March 4, 1777, began with the quaint wording formerly used by King George:

> To Our Trusty and Well-Beloved Button Gwinnett . . . We elect you in the name of the good people of Georgia, reposing special trust and confidence in the Prudence, Courage, Patriotism and integrity of you, the said Button Gwinnett.

Why was Gwinnett not named Georgia's first governor?

But Gwinnett was not the well-beloved of all. He had incurred the enmity of the powerful Scotch Highlander clan of McIntosh. There were two reasons for this. First, Gen. Lachlan McIntosh had been appointed by the Continental Congress in

Philadelphia as commander of the military forces in Georgia and worked hard at his job. But when Gwinnett became acting president of Georgia and found himself automatically commander-in-chief of the state's soldiers, he planned an expedition to Florida without even consulting McIntosh. The expedition was a failure. Then McIntosh led a group of his own. Georgia's Council of Safety summoned both Gwinnett and McIntosh to explain. They hurled charges at each other. In the exchange, McIntosh called Gwinnett a "rotten-hearted, lying scoundrel."

The second reason the McIntoshes disliked Gwinnett was that he had arrested and had put into irons George McIntosh, their youngest brother. Gwinnett had received a letter from John Hancock, president of the Continental Congress, informing him that George McIntosh was suspected of trading with the British in Florida. Even though George McIntosh had been a member of the Council of Safety, Gwinnett refused to allow him out on bail. He finally got out, went to the Continental Congress to answer the charges, and was cleared.

When the election for governor was held on May 8, 1777, the day after the first state legislature under the new Constitution convened, Gwinnett was defeated by John Adam Treutlen, a staunch old Salzburger who was to serve six months. Gwinnett was bitterly disappointed. Lachlan McIntosh was delighted and said so.

Gwinnett and McIntosh Fight a Deadly Duel

Things had come to a crisis between the two men. The humiliated Gwinnett challenged McIntosh to a duel at dawn on May 15. "Dawn is earlier than I usually rise," said the general, "but I will be there."

They met in the meadow of the house in which Royal Governor Wright had lived and within the present city limits of Savannah. Both men were shot, Gwinnett the more seriously. He had a bone shattered above his knee. As he fell, he called out, "My hip is broken." McIntosh, who was shot in the fleshy part of his leg, replied, "Do you want another shot?" Gwinnett said, "Yes, if somebody will help me up." But their seconds stopped the duel. The men shook hands and went home. McIntosh recovered, but Gwinnett had gangrene in his wound, and he died four days later.

What was the result of the Gwinnett-McIntosh duel?

There came a time when nobody remembered where Gwinnett was buried. In 1964, bones thought to be his were found and placed in a new tomb in Savannah's Colonial Park Cemetery. He has no living descendants but Gwinnett County is named for him.

Feeling ran high against McIntosh. More than 500 Georgians signed a petition asking that he be transferred out of Georgia. He was sent to Valley Forge just in time to spend the bitter winter there with Washington. When the fighting moved to Georgia he asked to be sent back. He returned and fought valiantly. After the war, he lived out his remaining years in Savannah. He, too, is buried in Colonial Park Cemetery.

The First Governor Disappears

John Adam Treutlen

John Adam Treutlen, the man who defeated Gwinnett for governor, was a Salzburger born in Austria. When the Revolution came, the Salzburgers were divided about what they should do. Some thought they should remain with the British, since the Trustees had allowed them to join the British colony when they needed a refuge. Others believed that since they were victims of British tyranny like the others, they should join in the protest. Treutlen was on the side of the patriots.

He was a member of the Council of Safety and later of Georgia's Provincial Congress. Then, after Archibald Bulloch

What did Truetlen accomplish as governor?

died and Gwinnett's enemies were strong enough to keep him from the governorship, Treutlen became governor. His term was very short, since he was elected on May 8, 1777, and the constitution provided that a new governor should begin his term each January.

Treutlen resisted the pressure of South Carolina to absorb Georgia. He strengthened the state's defenses for the war with England, mortgaging his home to help pay for them. This made the British angry and they burned his house.

When Treutlen's brief term as governor was finished, he took his family to Orangeburg, S.C. Mystery surrounds his last days and accounts differ. One account is a letter dated March 18, 1782, from Dr. Jenkin Davis to H. M. Muhlenburg, head of the U.S. Salzburgers. Davis' letter said that five Tories came to Treutlen's house, burned his home and took him into the woods and cut him to pieces with swords. Whatever happened, Treutlen's experience teaches us that America's independence was won at great cost to those who participated in the Revolution.

For Extended Thinking

1. What reasons led Georgia to be slower in joining the Revolution than other colonies?
2. Why did Georgia's delegates refuse to go to the Continental Congress in 1775?
3. How did Georgians organize for the Revolutionary War?
4. What was the basis for the differences between Button Gwinnett and Lachlan McIntosh?
5. What important things did Georgia's first constitution establish?

Names, Terms and Concepts

Tories
Tondee's Tavern
Archibald Bulloch
Whigs
boycott
Button Gwinnett
Sons of Liberty
Provincial Congress
Lachlan McIntosh
Council of Safety
John Adam Treutlen
Stamp Act

To Help You Study

1. When and where did the American Revolution start?
2. What was the population of the 13 colonies?
3. Why was Georgia slow in joining the revolution?
4. What was the Stamp Act? How did Georgians react to it?
5. Who were the Liberty Boys? What was their slogan?
6. Tell about the factions for and against England in Georgia.
7. What did the Puritans do at Midway?
8. How did Georgia organize after taking over the government from Governor Wright?
9. What did Georgians think of Governor Wright?
10. What were the main provisions of Georgia's first constitution?
11. Describe the feud between Gwinnett and McIntosh.
12. What happened to Georgia's first governor?

CHAPTER 6

GEORGIA BECOMES A BATTLEGROUND

THE REVOLUTIONARY WAR AND ITS RESULTS

The first three and one-half years of the Revolutionary War were fought in the north. Georgians hardly knew, except by news reports and word of mouth, that a war was going on. But the strategy of England changed, with momentous consequences for Georgia.

What strategy change occurred?

Losing to George Washington in the north, strategists in England decided to move the war south. There were a number of reasons for this. Among the most important was the belief in England that the king had many friends and supporters in the south. With the support of these loyalists, England could win in the south. Then, having won in the south, British troops could fight their way back up the Atlantic coast and retake the territory that had been taken from them.

Why did Britain's strategy change?

However, there were additional factors on the international scene to be considered. France, Spain, and Holland were all roused against Britain. This meant that King George had to keep some soldiers in Europe. He could not hire enough Hessians to help British soldiers fight in America. The king was still poring over maps and trying to tell his generals how to run the war in America from his palace 3,000 miles away! To make matters worse, Gentleman Johnny Burgoyne, a British general who also wrote plays, surrendered to Americans at

Saratoga on Oct. 17, 1777. This had impressed the French, who were still angry at having lost their American territory to England in the French and Indian War. As a result, the French agreed to help America, signing a treaty of aid on Feb. 6, 1778.

King George III and his ministers wanted to regain control of the war before this French aid reached the colonies. The king thus made the decision to move the war south. His ministers figured that it would take about 2,000 British soldiers to capture Savannah and about 5,000 to take Charleston, S.C. On March 8, 1778, the king appointed Sir Henry Clinton to put his plan into effect.

ENGLAND'S FIRST PLAN TO CAPTURE GEORGIA

The new British commander's strategy to capture the south did not at first succeed. His idea was to move on Savannah first from Florida and then from New York. The attack from Florida was to be a two-pronged one, by land and by sea. The land forces entered Georgia from Florida on Nov. 10, 1778, marching toward Midway and Sunbury. There they were to join forces with a sea force under the command of Lt. Col. L. V. Fuser. But strong winds delayed this sea expedition and it did not keep the appointment. So, after burning Midway Church, the British marched on back toward Florida, by way of Frederica on St. Simons Island.

What was Clinton's plan to capture Georgia?

After they left, Fuser arrived by sea with 500 men. He demanded the surrender of Ft. Morris, which guarded Sunbury. Col. John McIntosh was in command. He had only 200 soldiers there but he sent back a defiant retort: "Come and take it!" Fuser, having missed connections with the land forces, decided not to fight for the fort, and he left. Later, the Georgia legislature presented McIntosh with a sword inscribed with his brave words, "Come and take it!"

Thus the first effort of the British to move the war south failed. But a bigger British force was getting ready to sail from New York, under command of Gen. Archibald Campbell.

The Secret Path and the Fall of Savannah

Gen. Robert Howe, an American from North Carolina, was in command of the American forces at Savannah. At sunset on Dec. 23, 1778, sails came into sight, and the British fleet was seen approaching the shore. It had taken them 17 days to come from New York on the wintry seas.

Gen. Howe had only 672 men, most of them new and untrained. On the British ships were 3,500 men. He called his officers together to decide what to do. They voted to try to hold the city. George Walton and Samuel Elbert warned Howe to guard the jungle-like swamps, but Howe was scornful. "Only a tiger could get through those jungles," he said, and he prepared to fight. Later, at Howe's court-martial, Walton said he knew the place well because he had walked along the river there with young ladies, picking jessamine.

What warning did Howe ignore?

In the meantime, the British commander was coping with the problem of getting through the swamp. "Surely there must be somebody around here who knows how to get through that swamp," said Campbell. Somebody had heard of a black man named Quash Dolly, an expert woodsman who lived on the Giradeau plantation. Dolly, who probably did not even know there was a war on, led the redcoats through the swamp, enabling the British to overpower the small American force on Dec. 29, 1778. About 300 Americans were killed. The British lost only 15. The battle was over so quickly that the town itself was not greatly damaged.

Washington named Gen. Benjamin Lincoln to replace Howe as southern commander. Howe was later court-martialed. He was cleared but he was never again given a responsible command. Howe was always sensitive about this. He once shot off the ear of Gen. Chris Gadsden in a duel when Gadsden criticized him for losing the city.

Georgia's Government Moves

Gov. John Houstoun, who had succeeded Treutlen, was just going out of office when the British captured Savannah. He could not hold over as governor because Georgia's constitution forbade it, so he held his last Council meeting on Dec. 26, 1778. He took Georgia's papers to the home of his father-in-law, Jonathan Bryan. Then he went to Retreat, the home of his brother George on the Vernon River. He escaped the British by climbing a tree and hiding.

What did Georgia's government do after the fall of Savannah?

The British held Savannah for three and a half years, from Dec. 29, 1778, to July 11, 1782. In July 1779, the civil government, temporarily headed by Lt. Col. Mark Prevost, was again turned over to Royal Gov. James Wright. When Wright returned he hanged many patriots and confiscated the property of others.

The British Stable Horses in Ebenezer's Church

With Savannah secured, Gen. Archibald Campbell was free to push into northern Georgia and capture the rest of the state if he could. His first stop was at Ebenezer, the spot where the Salzburgers had settled, which he took on Jan. 2, 1779. First the British used the fine old Jerusalem Church, built in 1767, with Martin Luther's swan on the steeple, as a hospital. Later they used it as a stable for their horses. They moved into the homes of the people and were often insulting and offensive to them. They brought to Ebenezer the prisoners they took in battles in upper Georgia. Sometimes they were very cruel to these prisoners.

How did the British soldiers conduct themselves?

Sgt. William Jasper, already famous for saving the flag at a battle in South Carolina, rescued a group of these prisoners.

He and his friend, Sgt. Newton, surprised British guards who had stopped at a spring above Savannah for a drink of water, freed the prisoners and took the guards away. The spring, nine miles from Savannah on U.S. Highway 17, is named Jasper Springs.

Sunbury Falls to the British

Sunbury and Ft. Morris were captured by the British on Jan. 9, 1779. Gen. Augustine Prevost marched his troops into the village, and the British guns almost destroyed the fort before the outnumbered little band of patriots surrendered it. The British renamed it Ft. George. This site stands there by the water today with its deep ditches under the old trees.

What happened to Sunbury?

Sunbury, which had been a bustling little port, never recovered from this attack. It began then to become the ghost town that it is today; a few buildings in the sun, an old cemetery and markers that relate its history. The last big ship to dock at the port of Sunbury came in 1815.

Augusta is Handed Over to the Enemy

By early February, Gen. Archibald Campbell had moved his troops into Augusta. He had taken Ebenezer and put down the brave resistance of patriot troops in Burke County. With this accomplished, he put 2,000 troops in Augusta, some by land and some by the Savannah River.

The American commander in charge of Augusta, Col. Andrew Williamson, believing that the British controlled Georgia and would soon win the war, practically handed over Augusta to Campbell. He later joined the British army.

What happened when the British controlled Georgia?

In control of most of Georgia, Campbell began sending out soldiers to burn homes, destroy crops, and kill livestock. He spared those who took the oath of allegiance to the king. More than a thousand Georgians signed the oath. There was much distress in upper Georgia. The government had moved to Heard's Fort. Men in Wilkes County were carrying on such guerrilla warfare as they could, but despair gripped many.

Campbell heard that Washington had sent Gen. Benjamin Lincoln, the big, fat hero of Bunker Hill, and that Lincoln had set up headquarters at Smoking Camp near Purrysburg and was drilling troops.

THE ATTEMPT TO TURN THINGS AROUND

Gen. Lincoln Takes Command in the South

Gen. Lincoln kept two servants to get him into his uniform. It had a colorful sash and included the sword that Congress had given him for his spectacular victories at Saratoga and his service at Bunker Hill. At first the soldiers of the Georgia militia hesitated to fight under the heavy, lumbering general. But they came to see his remarkable ability and his fine personal traits. His chief aide was Gen. Lachlan McIntosh, who had requested to be sent back to his native Georgia now that it was in danger.

The Patriots Win at Kettle Creek

On War Hill, near Kettle Creek, about eight miles from Washington, Ga., the Americans won a battle on Feb. 14, 1779. British Col. Thomas Boyd started from South Carolina with about 800 British soldiers to meet Dan McGirth at Little River. McGirth did not come. Boyd's men had been marching for three days and were tired and hungry. They came to Kettle Creek, six miles from Little River, and stopped to rest and to eat. They turned their horses loose to forage, and they caught a farmer's cow to roast. With some parched corn to go with the browned beef, they had quite a feast.

At daylight, a patriot force under two generals, Elijah Clarke and Andrew Pickens, launched a surprise attack. Clarke's horse was shot from under him, but the British commander, Boyd, was fatally wounded.

"What can we do to make your last hours more comfortable?" asked Pickens.

"Leave two soldiers here to give me water through the night, and send my watch and other things to my wife in England, please," he answered. This Pickens did. When Mrs. Boyd died she left the watch to the Pickens family.

What was the result of the victory at Kettle Creek?

Americans rejoiced at their Kettle Creek victory. It encouraged them since the battle broke the grip the British had on Georgia. A gray stone shaft stands now on the hill above the creek commemorating the battle.

The Siege of Savannah

In the autumn of 1779 Gen. Augustine Prevost, known as Old Bullet Head, was in command at Savannah. The American Gen. Benjamin Lincoln had laid plans for the recapture of Savannah with the help of Count Charles Henri D'Estaing. D'Estaing was the dashing French naval commander who was to bring his ships from the West Indies to meet Lincoln at Savannah. Lincoln was now plodding on his way with two aides, Gen. Lachlan McIntosh and Polish Count Casimir Pulaski, commanding two sections of his soldiers.

What was D'Estaing's role in the siege of Savannah?

D'Estaing reached Savannah before Lincoln, landing at Beaulieu, the old home of William Stephens, on Sept. 11, 1779. He had 36 ships and 4,500 men. Then the Frenchman did a very foolish thing. Instead of waiting for Lincoln, he demanded in the name of the French king that Prevost surrender the city.

Actually Savannah was not well defended. One British officer said later, "They could have taken this pile of sand in ten minutes." So the British commander made a desperate play for time. He replied, "Sir: I am honored with Your Excellency's letter. The business we have in hand being of great importance, a just time is absolutely necessary to deliberate. I am therefore proposing a cessation of hostilities for 24 hours. You are to draw your columns back out of sight during that time."

The Frenchman actually agreed to a truce "till the signal for retreat tomorrow night, Sept. 17, 1779." At once the British called for help from all the plantations near Savannah and worked feverishly all night strengthening the defenses of the city. Moreover, they sent an urgent message to Col. John Maitland in Carolina for help. Through fog, he slipped in with his ships right under D'Estaing's nose, and reinforced Prevost's forces with 800 men. Finally, Prevost had 2,500 men and a stronger defense. He wrote D'Estaing, "The King, my master, pays these men to fight, and they must fight. I decline your terms."

What was the effect of the truce?

In the meantime, Gen. Lincoln had arrived Sept. 16. He was astonished to find what the French commander had done. The rains poured, tempers were short, and three weeks later Savannah was still holding out.

D'Estaing was growing impatient. The hurricane season was at hand and his men were sick. They did not like American food, especially rice, and meat was becoming scarce. They also suffered from the climate. They said the days were too hot and the nights too cold.

Finally D'Estaing insisted on an all-out attack. Lincoln agreed. It was set for Oct. 9, 1779. D'Estaing, who was brave, led his troops, with the Americans under their commanders, in a bloody, savage, all-day attack. The British lost 264, the French 600. The Americans, who had 2,500, lost 600. In spite of these losses, the siege of Savannah failed.

Jasper Becomes a Hero

Sgt. William Jasper, who had already become a hero at the battle of Ft. Moultrie, was killed that day. Sgt. Jasper's last words were, "I have got my furlough."

On the Jasper monument on Bull Street in Savannah, placed there on Feb. 2, 1988, is this inscription:

> To the memory of Sgt. W. Jasper, who, though mortally wounded, rescued the colors of his regiment, in the assault on the British lines about the city, Oct. 9, 1779. A century has not dimmed the glory of the Irish-American soldier whose last tribute to civil liberty was his life. Erected by the Jasper Monument Association.

Jasper County in Georgia, the town of Jasper in Pickens County, and Jasper Springs two miles above Savannah, where he rescued the six prisoners, keep his name alive in Georgia.

Savannah's monument to Sergeant Jasper.

Count Pulaski is Killed at Savannah

Among the officers who died in the siege of Savannah was the young Polish commander, Count Casimir Pulaski.

He had come to America to fight for freedom at the suggestion of Benjamin Franklin, whom he had met in Paris in 1776. Washington made him a brigadier general. Once Pulaski resigned from the Continental Army because he disagreed with Gen. Anthony Wayne; but they both came later to fight in Georgia.

At Savannah, Pulaski charged into battle on his spirited black horse. One of his men later described the fight:

What happened to Count Pulaski?

> For a half hour after the battle started, the guns roared and the blood flowed. Seeing an opening in the enemy line, Pulaski told General Lincoln that he would dash in with his men, confuse the enemy and cheer up the people of Savannah. Lincoln approved. We dashed in. At first, all went well. Then we were caught in a cross fire. I looked around. Oh, sad moment ever to be remembered! Pulaski lay prostrate on the ground. I leaped toward him, thinking that possibly his wound was not dangerous, but a shot had pierced his thigh and blood was flowing from a wound in his breast. Falling on my knees, I tried to raise him. I heard him say faintly, "Jesus! Mary! Joseph!" Further I knew not; for at that moment a shot grazing my scalp blinded me with blood and I fell to the ground insensible.

In the retreat, Pulaski was left where he fell. A brave Georgia officer, Capt. Thomas Glascock, for whom Glascock County is named, went back through gunfire and rescued his wounded leader. Pulaski was not dead, but a few days later he died of gangrene. He was 31.

Georgia named Pulaski County for the count. A monument to his memory was erected in Savannah and Ft. Pulaski at Savannah was named for him. It took brick masons 20 years to build its massive walls, in which there are 25 million bricks. The fort was to play an important part in the Civil War in the next century. Robert E. Lee, as a young army engineer, assisted in the construction of Ft. Pulaski.

After the Siege of Savannah

The Americans were surprised at the outcome of the battle which they had thought would be an easy victory. Count D'Estaing, humiliated at his defeat, and wounded, sailed away. The disastrous failure of the siege of Savannah was largely his fault. In spite of that fact, Gen. Lincoln generously wrote an appreciative letter to Congress about the brave, quarrelsome Frenchman and Georgia gave him 20,000 acres of land. He was grateful. He wrote, "The mark of its satisfaction, which Georgia gave me after I was wounded, was the most healing balm that could have been applied to my pain."

Gen. Lincoln and his troops retreated to Ebenezer. They later moved to Charleston, S.C., where smallpox broke out and weakened the armies. Outnumbered there, Lincoln surrendered to Cornwallis on May 12, 1780. The British moved back into Augusta with Col. Thomas Browne in command. Gen. Henry Clinton, the British commander, was jubilant over the success of his plan to capture and hold Savannah and Charleston. He left Cornwallis to mop up in the south.

How did Georgia come under the iron grip of the British?

Georgia was in the iron grip of the British. Gov. Wright was hanging patriots in Savannah and confiscating their property. People on the frontier were suffering incredible hardships. One was the Tyner family. While Richard Tyner was away fighting for the patriots, the Indians killed and scalped his wife, killed their baby, and carried off their daughters Mary and Tamar to live in Indian country at Coweta Town. Later, the girls escaped.

What conditions did Georgians face?

Maj. Micajah Williamson had left his family at home to go fight. The Tories hanged his 12-year old son in his wife's presence. Mrs. Williamson took her older children and escaped to South Carolina.

Col. John Dooly, who had come from the Carolinas and settled in Wilkes, was dragged out of bed and killed, with his wife and children looking on.

But there was a small, determined guerilla resistance. Across the border was Gen. Francis Marion, called the Swamp Fox, fighting with his little band, living off meager fare. In part of Wilkes County Elijah Clarke and his son John were fighting. They were aided by Nancy Hart, a rough old heroine who was six feet tall, with red hair, blue eyes, and a fiery temper. She spied on the British and reported their movements to the patriots, doing much to help the cause.

Who were the guerillas?

A replica of Nancy Hart's cabin.

Gen. Clarke never learned to read or write, yet the rough old warrior almost single-handedly saved this section of Georgia from the British. Sometimes he had 300 soldiers; sometimes he was down to 20. After the British had driven Mrs. Clarke and her children out in the snow and burned his home, Clarke thought it was time to take his own family and the families of his neighbors to a safe place while the war was being fought in Georgia. He managed the feat of taking 400 women and children over the mountains, out of Georgia, to the safety of Watauga Valley, N. C.

Gen. Clarke fought up and down Georgia. What he really wanted to do was to take Augusta back from the terrible Tory turncoat, Thomas Browne. By September 1780, he had rounded up about 300 fighting men. They began the siege, driving Browne and 40 men into a building then called Seymour's Trading Post. Clarke had no cannon, so he cut off Browne's supplies. Thus Browne's men inside had no food and no water, and some of them were badly wounded. The Americans outside could hear their pitiful cries for water, but Browne would not surrender. He himself was wounded in both thighs, but he sat in a chair and kept shooting out the window. He was as brave as he was cruel.

How did Clarke attempt to recapture Augusta?

Clarke and his soldiers besieged the house for four days. On the fifth day, Browne got reinforcements and Clarke finally had to give up the siege. He took most of his men with him, but 30 were so badly wounded that he was forced to leave them behind. He thought they would be treated as prisoners of war, but he was wrong. Historical accounts differ. It generally is believed that Browne had 13 of them dragged inside the house, and hanged them, one for each of the 13 colonies, from the stairway.

Clarke, defeated but not discouraged, kept his men fighting guerrilla fashion, swooping down on the British, doing what damage they could, and vanishing.

Robert Sallette and the Pumpkin Head

A mysterious man of the revolution was Robert Sallette of Liberty County. He became known as a terror to the Tories. One rich Tory farmer offered a hundred guineas for the head of Robert Sallette. One day a man appeared with a sack. He said to the farmer, "I hear that you have offered a reward for the head of Robert Sallette. I have it here." The farmer looked at the sack, then he counted out the money. The young man took the money, and then removed his hat and pointed to his own head.

"Here is the head of Robert Sallette," said the man. The farmer was so frightened to be face to face with the notorious fighter that he could not move. Sallette, with the money, ran, got on his horse and left. In the sack was a pumpkin.

Gen. Nathaniel Greene

THE TIDE BEGINS TO TURN— WASHINGTON SENDS GREENE SOUTH

What was Nathaniel Greene's idea about how to fight?

After Charleston fell to the British in May 1780, and after some further reverses, Washington sent his ablest general, Nathaniel Greene, to command the troops in the south. Greene was from Rhode Island, a blacksmith and an iron forger with no military experience whatsoever. He was, however, a natural military genius.

When he came south, Greene found troops poorly clothed, fed, and trained. "We fight," Greene said, "get beat, then get up and fight again." His courage was contagious. He knew that even if he did not win the battles, he could keep enough British soldiers in the south so that they could not go to fight Washington in Virginia.

Gen. Lighthorse Harry Lee

Once Greene marched his men 900 miles in pursuit of Cornwallis. The British commander was so harassed that he burned his heavy baggage so he could travel lighter and faster to get away from Greene and his soldiers.

Gradually, the picture brightened. In May 1781, Greene ordered Gen. Henry (Lighthorse Harry) Lee, father of Robert E. Lee, to help Clarke and others attack Augusta and try to take it back from the British.

What was Green's plan to retake Augusta?

First the Americans took a fort at Silver Bluff. After that, they began their siege of Augusta where Browne was still in command. An officer named Hezekiah Mayham, who had been fighting with Lee in the Carolina battles, remembered a curious device used by ancient warriors: a wooden tower raised so high that guns placed on it could fire down into a fort which could not be stormed any other way. This tower, which came to be known as Mayham's Tower, had been used in one of the battles in South Carolina. The Americans built another one on the flat land around the Augusta fort. Browne tried desperately to destroy it but could not. With the advantage of the tower, the Americans won. Browne delayed surrender a few hours, until June 5, because he did not want to surrender on the king's birthday.

Gen. James Jackson, then 25 years old, was left in charge of Augusta after the surrender, along with Gov. Nathan Brownson, who had been elected in June, 1781. Augusta was short of food and other supplies, and some people were starving. But the good news was that on the northern front George Washington was winning.

What was Wayne's plan to retake Georgia?

Mad Anthony Wayne Comes to Finish the War

In January 1782, Washington sent Gen. Anthony Wayne of Pennsylvania to Georgia. He set up headquarters at Ebenezer. Even though Cornwallis had surrendered at Yorktown Oct. 19, 1781, there were still some British soldiers fighting in Georgia. Wayne's idea was to push all the remaining British back into Savannah and then capture the city. The British there were getting desperate. Gov. James Wright had written the British commander, "The rebels hold Georgia from Augusta to Ebenezer. Here in Savannah we have no beef or pork and no money to buy any. Do not let any women and children be sent here."

The last battle of the Revolution fought in Georgia was at Ogeechee Ferry. The British and Tories were led by the notorious Col. Thomas Browne. Browne had been allowed to rejoin the British after he had surrendered Augusta, despite the terrible cruelties he inflicted. Wayne surprised them in the night, took their horses and ammunition, and captured 30 prisoners. Then he pushed on toward Savannah.

Sir Henry Clinton wrote, "All has gone except Savannah." In the spring, Gov. James Wright was notified to get ready once more to leave Savannah.

"All is lost!" mourned King George III in England; "at last the fatal day has come." Lord North said, "Oh dear God, it is all over." The defeat of England brought the downfall of North's ministry. He resigned in March.

On July 10, 1782, Gen. Wayne wrote an official order:

> As the enemy may be expected daily to evacuate the town, the troops will take care to be provided with a clean shift of linen and to make themselves as respectable as possible for the occasion. Lt. Gen. James Jackson, in consideration of his severe and fatiguing service in the advance, is to receive the keys to Savannah and is allowed to enter the western gate.

Gen. Jackson was just 26 years old.

How was the transition from British rule to civilian rule accomplished?

Wayne and Wright agreed on July 11, 1782, for the surrender of the British in Savannah. They had held the city since Dec. 29, 1778—three years, six months, and 13 days.

THE WAR ENDS

After Savannah had been surrendered, and the state government was back there from Ebenezer, Gov. John Martin gave the Tories time to get their affairs in order and leave. Some took the oath of allegiance and remained, but 7,000 left, starting on the day of surrender, July 11, 1782. They took about 5,000 slaves with them. Some went to Nova Scotia, some to the West Indies, and some to England. Georgia confiscated the property of many of them.

Gov. Martin called the legislature into session on the first Monday in August, 1782. On Jan. 7,1783, Dr. Lyman Hall was elected governor.

Georgians started rebuilding their lives in a state ravaged by war. Money and food were scarce. The government could at first be of little help to them. It had to get started again, too. The governor and his advisers had to decide which British property would be confiscated and sold. Some property was given to generals and soldiers who had fought for Georgia. Some was sold to provide necessities for the government and to start schools.

The Treaty of Paris, which ended the war, was signed on Sept. 3, 1783. Benjamin Franklin, John Adams and John Jay went to Paris to settle these terms. The United States got all the land below Canada, and east of the Mississippi, except for Florida, which went again to Spain.

How did Georgia show its gratitude to those who fought?

Georgia Rewards Generals and Soldiers

The new state of Georgia was so grateful to the generals who had helped rid them of the British that they rewarded many of them. It also rewarded many of the men who had fought under them. Much of the land given was either confiscated Tory property or was bought with money appropriated by the legislature. Gen. Nathaniel Greene, the only general who had fought under Washington for the entire eight years of the Revolution, was given Mulberry Grove plantation and the Greene family came there to live in 1785. The 2,170-acre plantation had belonged to John Graham, the assistant to the third royal governor, Sir James Wright.

Savannah's monument to Gen. Nathaniel Greene.

Greene's wife Kitty was regarded as one of the most charming women of her time. When she went to Valley Forge to be with her husband, then Washington's quartermaster-general, she was Washington's favorite dancing partner. Once they had danced four hours without sitting down! When Washington came to Georgia in 1791, he stopped at Mulberry Grove to pay his respects to the widow of his old friend.

Greene enjoyed his Georgia home. He had only a year of life remaining and he lived it there. In October 1785, he wrote to a friend:

> We found the house, situation and outbuildings more convenient and pleasing than we expected. The prospect is de-

lightful, and the house magnificent! We have a coach house, a poultry house, a large out-kitchen, stables, a pigeon house that will contain a thousand pigeons, a fine smokehouse, and a garden that is now in ruins but still with a variety of shrubs and flowers.

Gen. and Mrs. Greene went to Savannah from Mulberry Grove in June 1786. On the way home, he stopped at a neighbor's house and strolled out with him to look at his fields. The sun was hot and Greene suffered sunstroke. They took him back to Mulberry Grove where he died at 6 a.m. on June 16, 1786. He was 44. Georgia named Greenesboro and a county for Gen. Greene.

New Ideas Out of the Revolution

What were the key lessons of the Revolution?

The colonists had discovered that together they had strength that none of the 13 had alone. Together they had defeated the power of England, which had itself defeated France and Spain.

The colonists also learned that a representative government suited them better than a monarchy. But they also learned that there must be some kind of central government, with law and order, even in a democracy. After the war, there were 13 separate states, only loosely held together by the Articles of Confederation. Their paper money had little value. The Articles provided no way to make the states pay their share of the war or for administering a central government. There were few roads or means of communication. To top it all off, some states were quarreling among themselves. For instance, Maryland would not let Virginians fish in the Potomac River, and Virginia would not let Maryland's ships through the Chesapeake Bay.

Then Alexander Hamilton of New York suggested that the Continental Congress call a meeting to work out the problems that were troubling them and to strengthen the Articles of

Confederation. It was a powerful idea, and it resulted in the Constitution of the United States of America, one of the most remarkable and enduring documents in the world. American representative democracy was getting its start.

A THOUGHT EXPERIMENT

The Legacy of the Revolution for Modern Georgians

What was the legacy of the war for many Americans?

The American War of Independence ended with the signing of the Treaty of Paris on Sept. 3, 1783. The United States is now well into its third century of independence.

Throughout this chapter, and in the previous one, we tried to give you some insight into what the war meant to those who lived at the time. There was great hardship and suffering. You should remember that the suffering and hardship associated with the war was not restricted to those men who actually fought in its battles. Families suffered too—wives, mothers, and children endured great hardship. Some were killed; others faced the torture of watching their husbands and fathers killed. One mother was forced to watch her young son die by hanging. The legacy of the war for them was one of hardship, suffering and sacrifice. But the final result was a legacy of freedom—a freedom, as we have tried to show, that brought exhilaration and great joy to the people of that time.

What about the legacy of the war for modern Georgians? The thought experiment for this chapter is for you to think carefully and analytically about the war's legacy for you. What does the freedom won for Americans by the Revolution mean to you? Think of all the things that you are free to do that are not possible in a society that is not free. Be specific in your thinking.

Now, think of the opportunities that are yours. What opportunities for the good life in the future do you have that are made possible by our freedom? Be specific in your thinking. For example, can you choose what career you will pursue? Can you choose how you will spend your leisure time? What about what you will do in your everyday life?

At the news that the Declaration of Independence had been signed, Georgians of that day celebrated with great exhilaration. In your thought experiment, ask yourself how you react to the great symbols of our freedom. Do the words, "We hold these truths to be self evident . . ." stir emotions in you? Does the concept of unalienable rights lead you to a sense of commitment to preserve the freedom that we enjoy?

What is the legacy of the American War for Independence for you, a modern Georgian?

For Extended Thinking

1. What were the major factors that caused Britain to change its Revolutionary War strategy?
2. Describe what happened to Georgia when it fell under British control.
3. What was the strategy of both sides in the siege of Savannah?
4. How did the Americans recapture Augusta?
5. What happened to Georgia at the end of the Revolutionary War?

Names, Terms and Concepts

Robert Howe
Kettle Creek
Pumpkin Head
Quash Dolly
Old Bullet Head
Mayham's Tower
William Jasper
Casimir Pulaski
Mad Anthony Wayne
Benjamin Lincoln

To Help You Study

1. What was England's plan to capture Georgia?
2. How did the British use Quash Dolly? Who was he? Did he do right or wrong?
3. What happened to Gen. Howe?
4. What battles occurred aroundAugusta?
5. Who was Count Pulaski and what happened to him?
6. What do you think of the way Britain treated some Georgians?
7. Describe Thomas Browne.
8. Why was Mad Anthony Wayne sent to Georgia? What did he do?
9. What treaty ended the Revolutionary War? Where and when was it signed?
10. What did Georgia do for some of the Revolutionary War generals and soldiers?
11. What were some of the things the colonists learned after they won the war?
12. Who was Kitty Greene's dancing partner for four hours without stopping?

CHAPTER 7

A NEW STATE IN A NEW NATION

Georgians, emerging from the dark and bloody days of the Revolution, had a kindred feeling with the other 12 states that had been colonies. Having suffered together through the war, the new states shared a feeling of triumph. Their new freedom brought many opportunities to build the kind of society they had fought for in the Revolution. And with the opportunities, the new state faced some big problems. Among the most immediate of the needs facing the new state was the formation of a government that could effectively serve the state. Equally important was the opportunity to build institutions, like schools and churches, that make any society great. And for the young state to establish itself, it had to stabilize and develop its economy.

What needs did the new state have?

Georgia was growing rapidly during this period. New settlers were coming in, more than making up for the population loss that occurred when the Tories took their slaves and left the state. All soldiers who had fought in Georgia were given free land, whether they were Georgians or not. By 1790, the official census showed 82,548 people living in Georgia.

With the opening up of new lands, Savannah was no longer the center of the state. With the Government having to meet in Augusta during the Revolution to escape the British, the legislature began to debate the appropriateness of a new capital "within 20 miles of Galphin's old town." They decided to name the new capitol **Louisville**, for France's king, Louis XVI.

The Great Seal of the new state, 1777 to 1798.

THE GOVERNMENTS ARE BUILT

The National and Georgia Constitutions

What were the problems with the Articles of Confederation?

The first effort to establish a government at the national level was the **Articles of Confederation**. This document was ratified by the 12 states in 1781. But trouble with the new government developed very quickly. Many in the states were worried about the ability of the government under the Articles to defend the country. This was especially a concern since the national government was dependent on the states for troops. It was also dependent on the states for money. Being unable to tax, it had to **requisition** the states for money. Some states did fairly well in sending money; others were negligent in doing so. Commercial difficulties began to develop between the states, particularly between Virginia and Maryland. Many people at the time thought that these commercial problems would spread to all states. As a result of these problems, the new nation, having concluded that the Articles of Confederation would not work, called for a convention to meet in Philadelphia to work out the problems.

What was the role of Georgians in the Constitution of 1787?

When the call for the Philadelphia convention was made, Georgia's legislature was still meeting in Augusta since the new capitol in Louisville was not ready. In February 1787, it named delegates to go to Philadelphia to work with those from other states in writing the constitution. In all, 55 delegates were sent from 12 states. Rhode Island did not send delegates to the convention. Of the 55 delegates, 39 actually signed the constitution when it was completed. William Few and Abraham Baldwin from Georgia were among the signers. William Pierce brought a copy of the constitution to Georgia when he returned south on October 10 and it was printed in the *Georgia Gazette*. This gave Georgians their first opportunity to read the new Constitution.

William Few

Some states were slow in ratifying the new national constitution. Georgia did so unanimously on January 2, 1788, the fourth state to ratify. On ratification of 9 of the 13 states, the constitution went into effect. This meant that Georgia's state constitution had to be brought into line with the national constitution.

The way the state changed its constitution to accomplish that objective tells us a great deal about what people believed at that time. A convention was to be held to draw up a new state constitution. Each of the eight counties were to name three representatives to that convention. Then each county would name three more and these 24 would review the draft prepared by the first group. A third group of 24 was designated to meet later to ratify the new constitution.

How did Georgia change its constitution?

Georgians, who had cast off the rule of the king, were determined to have a representative government that assured that no person or single group would be in control. A significant feature of the new Georgia constitution was the weak power that it gave to the governor. With the bitter experience of tyranny still fresh in their minds, those who wrote Georgia's new constitution would not entrust too much power in one man. Additionally, the governor was elected by the legislature. The Georgia House of Representatives chose names and the Senate selected one individual from the list to be governor. The new constitution, ready in 1789, did extend the term of office of the governor to two years.

What did it provide for a weak governor?

But this constitution was not the end of Georgia's efforts at state-building. In 1795, another convention met in Augusta to consider whether a new constitution was needed. This was probably due to the influence of Thomas Jefferson, who had advised the states to have meetings about every five years to look at their constitutions. While nothing came of this meeting in Augusta, Georgia has seemed to follow Jefferson's advice. The state had nine constitutions in the period 1776-1976. Three of those constitutions were adopted in the 18th century.

The next constitution, adopted in 1798, did provide for

significant changes. It removed the fine for not voting that had been levied under the 1789 constitution. However, before a person could vote, the constitution provided that he must have paid all his taxes. The 1798 constitution abolished the ban against ministers becoming legislators. And it was this constitution that provided for the seal of Georgia with words from Plato's *Republic*, "Wisdom, Justice, and Moderation." In this document, as in future constitutions, the governor gradually gained more power.

What were the changes in the 1798 constitution?

The 1798 constitutional convention did its work so well that this constitution lasted until 1861 when Georgia pulled out of the Union and joined the Confederacy. This secession meant that Georgia needed another constitution to suit the peculiar circumstances of that period. After the war, Georgia had two constitutions in rapid order. One was in 1865, immediately after the war, and the second was 1868, marking the end of Reconstruction. Fairly soon, in 1877, another constitution was adopted. By 1945, the 1877 constitution had 301 amendments, making it one of the longest state constitutions in the nation. Ironically, the 1945 constitution was adopted as an amendment to the 1877 constitution. The same practice was followed in 1976.

EDUCATION AND RELIGION IN THE NEW STATE

What was Georgia's early experience with schools?

There had been a strong commitment to education and to the cultural and religious growth of the people from the earliest days of the colony. The first colonists brought books with them, the church sent teachers and other teachers came on their own. Whitefield had set up his orphanage and school and had dreamed of a college. By 1752, the Trustees had set up a small budget for schools—actually a part of the appropriation by the British Parliament. Teachers in the colonial

An old field school.

period were certified by the royal government. The first public school in Savannah was taught by Charles Delamonte with the help of John Wesley. At Ebenezer, the Salzburgers had employed Christopher Ortman as the first teacher in Georgia and then fired him because he displeased the preacher.

As a new state, Georgia began to build on this tradition of educational, cultural and religious advancement. The academies began to develop about this time. First was the Richmond Academy in Augusta, opened in 1785. In the same decade, academies were started in Chatham, Glynn, Waynesboro, Sunbury and Louisville. In 1783, the state legislature set aside a thousand acres of land in each county for a school. Private schools began operating too. James Cosgrove had one in Chatham County with girls as well as boys for pupils, possibly making it among the first co-ed schools in the country. Mrs. Cosgrove may have been Georgia's first woman teacher.

Schoolteachers often wandered from one community to another, teaching a short term and moving on to another place. They often boarded with families of pupils. The board was a part of their pay. The remainder of their pay usually came from a small tuition fee charged to students.

What kind of teachers did early Georgia have?

Most of these early teachers were good teachers, but some were disreputable. One Irish schoolmaster, described by Richard Malcolm Johnston in *Early Education in Middle Georgia*, told his pupils:

> Boys, I suppose ye know that the races is to be in town tomorrow. Now I advise that ye don't go into town at all, and so keep yourselves out of temptation; but if yer parents let you go, don't go near the racetracks. That's no place for boys. But if ye just will go to the races, don't bet! Betting is a bad thing for grown people, to say nothing of boys. But if ye just will go to town, and if ye will go to the races, and if ye will bet, be sure to put money on Abercrombie's mare.

And there were outstanding teachers. One of the most exceptional schoolmasters may have also been one of the ugliest. William McWhir, schoolmaster at Sunbury for 30 years, told this story on himself: "Once when I was still living in my native Ireland, I was walking down the road when an old lady stopped me, stared, and said, `You are the ugliest man I ever saw. Your face looks as if the devil had been threshing peas on it.' " But McWhir's school attained such a fine reputation that he had to turn students away. George Washington's nephews were among his pupils. While smallpox had scarred his face, he had lost one eye and he was prematurely gray, McWhir was such a remarkable character that people considered him one of the most attractive personalities in Georgia.

This is a good place for you to engage in another thought experiment. Imagine yourself a student in Mr. William McWhir's school. What would it be like? Would there have been a lot more rules and more strict discipline? Would you have had fewer activities like athletics and social clubs than you have now? What would school life have been like then? And do you think you would have studied the same things? Do you think you would have enjoyed courses like rhetoric, elocution and Latin? Does education need to change with the times and if so, how?

Georgia Charters the Nation's First State University

How was the University of Georgia formed?

During the term of Gov. John Houstoun the state had set aside 40,000 acres to be sold to raise money to charter the University of Georgia. John Milledge, Georgia's eighth governor, gave a 633-acre tract for the actual college site—on the edge of the Indian territory on the Oconee River. The Indians watched in wonder from the forest as the college went up. The city of Athens began to grow around it.

Harvard had been founded in 1636, the College of William and Mary in 1693, and Yale in 1703, but Georgia's was the first state university in the nation to be chartered. The legislature, still meeting in Savannah, granted the charter in 1785. Lyman Hall, Abraham Baldwin, and Nathan Brownson, all Yale graduates, had a big part in planning the university. They saw it as the capstone of a complete educational system for the state.

Josiah Meigs

The university did not actually get into operation until after 1800. The first graduating class had ten members. The sheriff led the first graduation procession, a custom now traditional with the college. Baldwin acted as president until 1800 when he persuaded his friend, Dr. Josiah Meigs, also a Yale man, to take the presidency.

Georgia's First Churches— and a Preacher Arrested on his Knees

What was the official church in Georgia?

Until after the Revolution, the official church of Georgia was the Church of England. Georgians were taxed to support it and were expected to attend it. But when the Scotch Highlanders came they brought with them their Presbyterian faith, for which John Knox had crusaded in Scotland. The first Presbyterian minister, John Springer of Delaware, was ordained in Georgia on Jan. 21, 1790, under a tree that still stands in Washington, Ga. Even though the tree is a poplar it is known as the Presbyterian Oak.

The Independent Presbyterian Church in Savannah stands on the site where a Presbyterian congregation was organized in 1755, about 20 years after the Scotch Highlanders had come to Georgia. The present building was erected in 1890, a copy of the one which burned in 1815. This particular church has never been affiliated with the Scotch Presbyterian church's organization in America.

How were the early church groups formed?

The first Methodist conference, with ten members, was held in Georgia in April 1788. Bishop Francis Asbury and Rev. Hope Hull, who on horseback rode the preaching circuits in Georgia, really established this organization. Bishop Asbury had come to the United States in 1771. He rode over 300,000 miles on horseback, often studying his Latin and Greek while riding. But the trail in Georgia had been blazed for Asbury and Hull by two preachers named John Major and Thomas Humphries, who began to hold cabin prayer meetings on the frontier about 1784. The first Methodist church was Grant's Meeting House in Wilkes.

The Baptists were the first to protest being taxed to support the Church of England. The first Baptist church in Georgia was at Kiokee, 20 miles above Augusta. It was started in 1772 by 65-year-old Daniel Marshall. At that time, the Church of England was still the official church in Georgia and it was against the law to preach any other doctrine. In 1779, Marshall was arrested while on his knees praying. The warrant was served on him by a court officer named James Cartledge. Marshall's wife gave Cartledge such a tongue-lashing that he agreed to wait until Marshall was through with his prayer and sermon. Listening, he was converted to the Baptist faith. Even so, he arrested Marshall and took him to Augusta, where he was tried and cleared. Afterwards Marshall baptized Cartledge into the Baptist faith. He became a deacon in the church, and finally a Baptist preacher.

The Baptists were incorporated on Dec. 23, 1789. By then Georgians were not required to go to church. However, if they disturbed others who did go, they could be fined five pounds, sentenced to ten days in prison, or get 39 lashes on a bare back!

The first Catholics to set up a church came to Wilkes from Maryland at the end of the 18th century. The Spanish Catholics had really been the first religious group in Georgia, when they set up missions along the Georgia coast to convert the Indians in the 16th and 17th centuries.

Many other denominations have come, but these were the first.

WHITNEY'S GIN SPURS THE DEVELOPMENT OF THE AGRICULTURAL ECONOMY

The most far-reaching event that happened in these postwar years was the invention in Georgia of the cotton gin. Its inventor was a New England school teacher named Eli Whitney.

Whitney, who had an inventive mind, had set up a nail manufacturing business when he was only 14. It did so well that he had to hire an adult to help him. He was late starting to college and was 26 when he graduated from Yale. He was interested in a job as a tutor on a plantation in South Carolina.

What role did Kitty Greene have in the invention of the cotton gin?

On the boat coming down, he met Kitty Greene, the widow of Nathaniel Greene, and her children. She invited Whitney to visit them at Mulberry Grove. A Yale alumnus, Phineas Miller, whom Kitty later married, was already there as farm boss and tutor to her children. He later became Whitney's business partner.

There at Mulberry Grove Whitney heard Georgia planters talk about how difficult and expensive it was to separate cotton from its seeds. Mrs. Greene, whose watch and embroidery hoops Whitney had repaired, said, "Talk to Mr. Whitney about it. He can solve any problem."

He solved their problem by inventing the cotton gin. An old story says that Mrs. Greene herself put the finishing touch on the invention by handing him her hair brush when he could not find a way to pull the cotton lint through. The cotton engine, soon shortened to "gin," quickly did work that had taken a whole family an entire day to do.

What effect did the gin have on Georgia's economy?

Whitney's cotton gin had a powerful effect on the country. Up to this time, with hand labor involved, the raising and marketing of cotton had been so expensive that there was little money in it. With the gin, farmers began to plant more cotton. They also needed more slaves to work in the hot cotton fields. This helped entrench the institution of slavery in the South and gave it new importance.

How did the gin affect national politics?

There was also a larger angle to the matter. Men began to move west in search of more land for cotton. They took their slaves. When a western territory became a state, it got representation in Congress. The North had a growing group fiercely interested in the abolition of slavery. This group feared that slaveholders would get power enough to control the nation, shaping it to the interest of those who owned slaves. The hot question of the moment became, "Should a new state come in as a free state or a slave state?" It was the matter of slavery that brought the states' rights issue to a head. Eli Whitney's cotton gin was more important than anybody dreamed.

A Near Miss for Another Georgian on an Important Invention

About this same time, another Georgian developed and patented the steamboat but missed the opportunity to gain from the invention. William Longstreet worked on the steamboat for 10 years, suffering poverty and derision in the process. Longstreet wrote Georgia's Gov. Edward Telfair, "I make no doubt that you have heard of my steamboat, and as often heard it laughed at." But he finally succeeded in making it run and actually made a short trip up the Savannah River. He obtained a patent for it from the state. This was the only patent ever granted by the State of Georgia before the national government took over the granting of patents. It was issued on Feb. 1, 1788, almost 20 years before Robert Fulton launched his *Clermont*. When Longstreet heard that Fulton had patented and demonstrated a successful steamboat in New York, he gave up his dream since he had no money to pursue it further. He is buried in St. Paul's Churchyard in Augusta.

What is the only patent granted by Georgia?

OPPORTUNITIES ARE ACCOMPANIED BY PROBLEMS

Even as Georgia was realizing opportunities to develop as a new state, several very important problems occurred. A number of the problems centered on land. These included disputes with Indians over ownership and some graft and corruption relative to public lands.

Indian Troubles Loom

Some of the Indians, especially the Creeks, had been on the British side during the Revolution. This, added to the clashes that naturally occurred on the frontier between Indians and settlers, created a problem for Georgia in these years.

What problems occurred between Georgia and the Indian tribes?

Chief Tecumseh had tried hard to persuade Indians in the southeast to join in an Indian confederacy against the encroachments of the white man. He had little success. But the Creeks did listen to one leader, a chief who hated Georgia. His name was Alexander McGillivray. He believed he had two reasons to hate Georgia. First, he thought that the white men were taking too much of the lands of his people. Second, the State of Georgia had confiscated the property of his father, Lachlan McGillivray of Savannah, who had been on the side of the Tories during the Revolution.

Lachlan McGillivray went among the Creeks in Georgia and Alabama with his wares. He married Sehoy Marchand, daughter of a French officer and an Indian woman, who was a member of the Tribe of the Winds. He settled in Savannah, acquired a great deal of property, and sent his 10-year-old son, Alexander, to school in Charleston. There he learned the classics and, more importantly, he learned to write well. It probably was his education that influenced his Indian people to make him a chief.

Young McGillivray went back to his mother's people because he found it dull to work in his father's business in Savannah. He was already a young chief of the Creeks when he was only 23. His Indian name was Hobo-Hili-Miko, which means "the good child king." He had a plantation, many herds of livestock, and dozens of slaves.

McGillivray influenced the Indians, in Georgia especially, to repudiate the treaties they had signed ceding their lands to the white men. He wrote Andrew Pickens, a general and later governor, "We want our hunting grounds preserved from encroachment. They have been ours since the beginning of time. I trust that with the assistance of our friends, we shall be able to maintain them against any attempt to take them from us."

McGillivray agreed to bring his Creeks to meet the white leaders at Rock Landing, just below the present Milledgeville on the Oconee River. President Washington thought this meeting was so important that he sent back to Georgia former Gen. Benjamin Lincoln, who was Secretary of War. Lincoln and his fellow commissioners met with McGillivray and his 2,000 Creeks at Rock Landing on Sept. 20, 1789.

Gen. Lincoln told the Creeks, "We are now governed by a President, who is like the old King over the waters. He commands all the warriors of the 13 great fires. He has regard for the welfare of all Indians, and when peace is established between us, he will be your father and you will be his children so that none can do you harm."

What happened at Rock Landing?

The commissioners woke up one morning to discover that the whole Indian camp at Rock Landing had vanished in the night. McGillivray sent a messenger with a note saying, "Your terms are not satisfactory and we have left to find forage for our horses."

Georgia had been plagued with a whole series of little wars known as the **Oconee Wars**. Gen. Elijah Clarke led soldiers against these Indians and asked the federal government for troops to deal with them. President Washington first thought of waging war against the Creeks, but decided that it would be cruel and costly. He decided to try talking personally with McGillivray. He sent Col. Marius Willett to invite the Creek chief to New York. McGillivray agreed to go back with him to New York to see the President. With their party, they left Stone Mountain on June 9, 1790.

Why was McGillivray invited to New York?

The Creek chief was royally welcomed in New York. The most fashionable hostesses entertained him, including Abigail Adams, whose husband was vice president and would become the second president. Mrs. Adams wrote of the Indians, "We entertained them kindly and they behaved with much civility. McGillivray could talk politics, philosophy, art and literature—and in several languages."

McGillivray and Washington came to an understanding. The Creek did not tell the president that he was already on the

Spanish payroll. This meant that he was committed to help Spain acquire lands between the Chattahoochee and the Mississippi. In exchange Spain would help Creeks keep their lands in Georgia. On Aug. 6 McGillivray signed a treaty agreeing to restore the Oconee lands that had been fought over. The treaty reserved for the Creeks the Tallassee country between the Altamaha and the St. Mary's, which the Creeks had already ceded to Georgia.

What was the reaction to the treaty?

McGillivray was astonished to find that he had angered everybody with his treaty. The Indians did not want to give up their Oconee lands. The Georgians were angry because the treaty took back the Tallassee country for the Indians. They also resented the federal government bypassing the state government in dealing with the Indians—the first states' rights issue in Georgia. Spain was angry because the Creek chief was planning to work with the United States when he was already on their payroll.

The angry Creeks turned against their chief. Saddened, he left the tribe. When he died in 1793, the Creeks felt an upsurge of their old affection for him and mourned him throughout the land.

Elijah Clarke and the Troublesome Trans-Oconee Republic

A Frenchman named Edmond Charles Genet—"Citizen Genet," the French minister—had come to America in 1793 to stir up sympathy for the French Revolution. Among the things he wanted to do was drive the Spanish out of Louisiana and set up a French republic there.

Why did Clarke raise an army?

Genet met Gen. Elijah Clarke and authorized him to raise an army. Many of the general's old Revolutionary soldiers came flocking to fight with him again. But George Washington disapproved of Genet's scheme. When the plan failed, Clarke was left with his soldiers and no money to support them. He thought of the lands beyond the Oconee. In 1794, he marched his army across the river, gave each man 640 acres and promised each 500 more. He designed the **Trans-Oconee Republic**, 10 miles wide and stretching 120 miles along the Oconee. Clarke said Georgia owned this land because the Indians had ceded it to the state in the treaty of 1773 at Augusta.

George Washington advised Gov. Mathews to stop Clarke's actions. Washington said that the settlement might bring on a war. Washington decided that the land belonged to all Georgians if it belonged to any and that Clarke could not give it away himself. Gov. Mathews sent the Georgia militia under Jared Irwin, who later became governor, to destroy the new settlements. They burned the forts, all three of them on the same day.

Clarke, then past 60, went home to his wife Hannah, in Wilkes County. He died on Dec. 15, 1799, one day after George Washington died.

The Yazoo Scandal

The first political scandal in Georgia's history occurred between the end of the Revolution and 1800. It was known as the **Yazoo Fraud**. The name came from the western river to which the claim extended.

Land speculators had been trying for years to buy Georgia's western territory, the land that is Alabama and Mississippi today. George Washington had warned the Georgia legislature about this, pointing out that the titles had never been really cleared and that Spain claimed some of the Yazoo territory.

What were land developers after?

But the land schemers kept trying. They attempted to bribe some legislators. Other legislators were convinced by the argument that it would be a good thing for the state to sell these unused western lands to get money to pay debts still due the Revolutionary soldiers. The speculators offered some influential men thousands of acres of the land free. Finally, the 1795 legislature, the last one to meet in Augusta, voted to sell the land at a ridiculously low price. Opponents of the sale, appalled, hoped that Gov. George Mathews, the Irish governor from Goose Pond, would not sign the bill.

Mathews had fought in Georgia in the Revolution, had liked the state, and later acquired a farm on Goose Pond in Wilkes County. He was a somewhat eccentric man who was married three times. He divorced one wife, when divorces could only be granted by an act of the legislature, because he was angry that she went to visit her relatives against his wishes. When she sent for him to get her, he refused. "I did not take her, and I will not go to bring her back," he said. Mathews spelled coffee "kaughy," dictated his speeches and sent them to an Irish schoolmaster to be "grammared up."

Mathews had vetoed a bill similar to the Yazoo bill in 1794. He was an honest and able man. But this time the pressure on him, from very influential people, was too great. He signed the Yazoo bill on Jan. 7, 1795. Two of his sons bought western lands.

Jackson Fights the Yazoo with Pen and Pistol

What was Jackson's response?

Fiery little James Jackson, with the king-sized sense of honor, was in Washington when he heard that the Yazoo bill had become law. He was furious. The Yazoo men offered him a half million acres just for the use of his name. He scorned them.

Jackson had been given a house, The Cedars, in Savannah, by the state because of his valor in the war. He married Mary Charlotte Young, with whom he was so happy that he did not like to leave home, even on matters of business. Once he wistfully wrote her from Washington, "I got no letter today.

Two boats have arrived, and still no mail for me. What am I to think, darling?"

This hot-tempered, honorable little man resigned from the senate and came charging home, indignant, to right the wrong of the Yazoo Fraud. He went up and down the state telling the people that the Yazoo lands belonged to them. "I and my comrades fought for them in the Revolution. They belong to you and your children. The legislature has no right to vote them away. This dreadful wrong must be righted." The 1796 legislature, meeting in Louisville, voted to rescind the Yazoo law. Jared Irwin was governor. He signed this bill Feb. 15, 1796, and the legislators and state officers filed out of the new capitol and burned the infamous papers the same day.

What was the result of Jackson's actions?

When Jackson became governor, he led in the adoption of a new constitution. Among other things, it decreed that any bill must mention in the title every matter that is contained in the body. He believed that one of the reasons for the passage of the Yazoo bill was that its title was simple, and the damage was down in the fine print which some legislators did not read carefully. Modern bills still have long titles.

The Yazoo matter was really not ended until long after Jackson's death in 1806. The U.S. Supreme Court, with John Marshall as Chief Justice, handed down a decision in 1810 which denied Georgia's right to repeal the Yazoo Act. The Court said the repeal affected the validity of a contract which the U.S. Constitution guaranteed. The case was Fletcher vs. Peck. George Walton, then a Georgia judge, had said the same thing. By this time the lands had passed into the hands of some people who were innocent of wrongdoing. The United States, to which Georgia sold its western lands in 1802, had to pay about $4 million to the owners of Yazoo lands.

What settled the Yazoo affair?

J. Harris Chappell, first president of the Women's College of Georgia, wrote in his history that "The Yazoo was the strangest instance of wholesale corruption of public officials in American history."

AS THE CENTURY COMES TO AN END

Among the most colorful events in Georgia as the century came to an end was a visit by George Washington to the state at 11 a.m. on March 12, 1791. This was two years after his inauguration as the first president of the United States. Washington left Philadelphia, then the capital, in a carriage drawn by four horses, for a ceremonial trip to the south. Georgia's Gen. James Jackson was with him. Washington's diary notes: "May 12, 1791. By 5 o'clock we set out for Purrysburg, driving 22 miles to breakfast. I was met by a committee from Savannah, Mr. Jones, Colonel Habersham, Mr. John Houstoun, and Mr. Clay, to take me in a boat down the Savannah River. On the way down, I called on the widow of the deceased General Greene, at a place called Mulberry Grove. I asked her how she did." He also stopped to see her on his way back to Augusta.

What did Washington do in Georgia?

In Savannah, he was saluted with guns and lavishly entertained. He visited Gen. Lachlan McIntosh, who had been with him at Valley Forge. With McIntosh and Anthony Wayne he inspected the forts. Then on Sunday, May 15, he started by carriage to Augusta. He attended a brilliant ball given by Gov. and Mrs. Telfair in his honor, and wrote in his diary about the

George Washington was a guest of Georgia in 1791.

The Washington Oak at St. Marys was planted the day George Washington died.

well-dressed ladies he had met in Georgia. He also visited Richmond Academy and heard the pupils debate. After his return to Mount Vernon he sent each of the students a book. One, inscribed "a premium due to merits," was treasured for years by Judge Adam Smith Clayton of Athens.

Washington, who hated to shake hands even with his close friends, bowed to each person. He wore elegant clothes, often with velvet, lace and silver buckles. He wore his sword in a white leather scabbard. He had a commanding presence. He was over six feet tall, weighed about 220 pounds, and had blue eyes. His powdered red hair was caught up in a silk bag behind.

By the end of the century, the end of life had come to several men who had been a part of Georgia's history. Oglethorpe, founder of the little colony in 1733, had died in England at the age of 89. George Washington, who had made the colorful visit in 1791, died on Dec. 14, 1799. John Wesley, the powerful preacher who was so sadly unhappy in Georgia, had died. So had Benjamin Franklin.

At the turn of the 19th century, John Adams was president. Men were seeking new lands in the west. Where settlers went, states developed. The question of whether the states would be slave or free had to be decided. The decision would involve a terrible and bloody war. But before then, 60 colorful and important years intervened.

For Extended Thinking

1. What would have been your view of the problems and prospects for Georgia just after independence?
2. What were Georgia's early efforts to provide education for its people?
3. Who were some of the earlyreligious leaders in Georgia?
4. Why was the invention of the cotton gin so important?
5. Why did Georgia have continuing problems with the Indians?
6. What was Georgia's first big political scandal and why did it happen?

Names, Terms and Concepts

Articles of Confederation
Grant's Meeting House
Oconee Wars
William Few
Eli Whitney
Trans-Oconee Republic
Abraham Baldwin
WilliamLongstreet
Yazoo land fraud
Richmond Academy
Alexander McGillivray
Fletcher vs. Peck
William McWhir
Rock Landing

To Help You Study

1. Why was Georgia's capitol movedfrom Savannah to Louisville?
2. What was the most important reason that Georgia had three constitutions prior to 1800?
3. Why did these constitutions give so little power to the governor?
4. What is the motto on Georgia's seal and where did it come from?
5. What were the early schools and academies in Georgia?
6. What do you know about William McWhir? Do you think he had a sense of humor?
7. How was the University of Georgia founded? Who were the leaders in that effort?
8. What do you know about Daniel Marshall? What did his wife do? What happened to James Cartledge?
9. Why is Alexander McGillivray important to Georgia? Why did some consider him to be a double-crosser?
10. What effect did the cotton gin have on Georgia agriculture?
11. Why was the Trans-Oconee Republic formed?
12. What did the U.S. Supreme Court rule about the Yazoo land fraud?

CHAPTER 8

THE 19TH CENTURY TO THE CIVIL WAR

According to the 1800 census, there were 162,686 people in Georgia. The first official census, taken in 1790, listed only 82,548. Fiery little James Jackson was governor of Georgia. The plantation system was developing. Men who had money acquired huge tracts of land, especially in the coast country. Up-country were small farmers and frontier settlers who had acquired small tracts of cheap or free land after the Revolution. They were often uneducated but fiercely independent. Later these two groups, the great planters and the frontier farmers, were to shape the pattern of Georgia politics into two bitterly feuding factions.

AT THE BEGINNING OF THE NEW CENTURY

Georgia Sells Western Lands to the United States

Among the problems confronting Georgia as the new century began, none had caused more trouble than the lands the state claimed between the Chattahoochee and the Misissippi rivers. This is the area that is now Alabama and Mississippi, the lands sold in the infamous Yazoo Fraud.

Tired of the whole affair, the legislature in 1802 voted to sell the western lands to the United States government. The price for the land was $1.25 million and the federal government's promise to remove the Indians from its remaining territory.

This promise was to cause real trouble later; 20 years afterward it had not been kept.

Why should Georgia sell the land west of the Chattahoochee?

Why should the land not be sold?

This sale of Georgia's western lands is an excellent basis for another thought experiment. Imagine yourself a member of the state legislature at the time. The crucial policy issue of whether or not to sell territory in the west is being debated. Start by thinking carefully and analytically on the pro side of the argument. What points would you advance in the debate to support the position that the western lands should be sold? For example, would you argue that the state needed money, that those lands would be difficult to occupy because of hostile Indians, or that the territory (after all, it consisted of what is now Alabama and Mississippi) is not worth very much? Build your case for the sale so that you would convince as many of your co-legislators as you can. Then, think carefully and analytically about the case against the sale. What arguments would you advance for not selling the land? For example, would you argue that the land is too valuable, that Georgians had fought and died for that land, or that the land was critical to Georgia's economic development? Build your case against the sale so that you would convince as many of your co-legislators as you can. Now that you have built the case for and against the sale, with which one do you really agree? Obviously, Georgia would be a very different state if Alabama and Mississippi were still part of its territory.

The Capitol is Moved to Milledgeville

Why was the capitol moved?

On May 11, 1803, the Georgia legislature, meeting at the capitol in Louisville, appointed a committee to pick the site for a new capitol. Louisville had become malarial, and was no longer close to the center of the state's population. Gen. John Clark was chairman of the committee. They had evidently already decided to name the new capitol for the governor, John Milledge. On Sept. 27, 1804, Clark wrote him a letter from

"Milledgeville" in which he reported having suffered "a severe bilous attack" but went on to say,

> I cannot ascribe any part of the cause of my sickness to this place. It is as well watered with good springs as any place I ever saw and every other appearances are in favor of its being a healthy situation. With much respect, I am, Your Excellencys Hble Servant, John Clark.

On Dec. 12, 1804, the General Assembly in Louisville officially proclaimed Milledgeville as the new capitol. Three years later the first legislative session was held in Milledgeville. On Oct. 9, 1807, the *Louisville Gazette* noted, "Yesterday 15 wagons left this place for Milledgeville with the Treasury and Public Records of this State. They were escorted by the troop of horses from Washington county, who had arrived there a few days hence for that purpose."

Milledgeville was to remain the capitol for more than 60 years, until after the Civil War. John Clark himself was to be one of the governors who would serve there.

Georgia in the War of 1812

Most Georgians favored the War of 1812. The war started when Britain, at war with Napoleon, began to stop American ships on the high seas. Britain claimed that some of the sailors were British and took them off. One statesman said, "If all states were as ready as Georgia for this, I should not be afraid for it to come." Troops were placed along the coast and on the frontier.

How did the War of 1812 affect Georgia?

There was as much to fear from the Indians, spurred on by the British in Canada and their Indian allies down the Mississippi, as from the British. The Creek war was actually fought about this time. Gen. John Floyd, a famous Indian fighter, was sent to Savannah and was in command there until the war ended.

British ships attacked the Georgia coast, and there were skirmishes within Georgia's territory. America won the war mainly because Britain had to send its best armies against Napoleon. The War of 1812 was the war in which the British burned the White House, and out of which we got the national anthem, *The Star Spangled Banner.*

NEW VENTURES AND ADVANCES

During the first half of the 19th century, the state experienced many new challenges and made important advances. These occurred in both the government and the economy.

Georgia Establishes a Supreme Court

Why did Georgia create a Supreme Court?

Many Georgians at first opposed the creation of a supreme court, perhaps because they associated the very words with the federal Supreme Court in Washington. Georgia was getting adverse decisions in the Indian problems from the U.S. Supreme Court. But the local courts were interpreting the law to suit themselves. Therefore judges led the movement to establish a supreme court, beginning about 1823. However, it was not until 1845 that the court was actually put into effect.

Joseph Henry Lumpkin

The first chief justice was Joseph Henry Lumpkin of Oglethorpe County. He wore his hair long, in the fashion of the day. Lumpkin Law School at the University of Georgia is named for him. The first meeting of the Supreme Court was at Talbotton on Jan. 26, 1846. It reviewed 72 cases the first year, and decided that the lower courts had been wrong in 44 of them.

Today, the Supreme Court meets in the white Georgia marble Judicial building on Capitol Square in Atlanta. Black-robed justices make decisions on cases appealed to them from the lower courts. Above them is a Latin sentence: FIAT JUSTITIA RUAT CAELUM, which means "Let justice be done though the heavens fall."

Public Health is a Concern

In their concern about public health, the Trustees had provided medicine and money to care for those who were ill on the voyages to America. Oglethorpe was careful to have medicines for the Savannah colony and for the soldiers on Frederica Island.

What steps did Georgia take to protect the public health?

Several important health measures were put into operation early in Georgia. One regulated the quarantine of ships to prevent the introduction of disease into the colony. In 1817, laws in Georgia against the sale of impure foods were much like the present-day Pure Food and Drug Act. The state was second in the nation to require births to be registered.

What kinds of diseases affected Georgians?

During the first hundred years of Georgia's history, the average life span of a man was about 28 years. The most common diseases were malaria, bilious fever, and pleurisy. Pellagra later developed, and smallpox was a great menace during the 18th century. Long jail sentences could be imposed on persons who concealed a case of smallpox, since quarantine was the only method to fight the disease for a long time.

In 1804 the Georgia Medical Society was incorporated in Savannah. Dr. Noble Wymberly Jones was elected president. The founding of the Medical Academy in 1828 at Augusta helped to change many false ideas about the cause and cure of disease.

James Dent, a coastal planter, was first to screen his windows. An early belief had been that fog or "miasma" caused malaria. We know now that mosquitoes spread malaria.

The hospital for the mentally ill was opened on Nov. 1, 1842, near Milledgeville. There were 10 patients the first year. By 1846 there were 67. Sherman sent four soldiers to guard this hospital when he marched through Milledgeville on his way to the sea in 1864.

Epidemics plagued Georgia at intervals for years. Malaria was always present. Yellow fever was brought in on a vessel from the West Indies. It became so bad that Georgia built a crematory and quarantine on Blackbeard Island, the ruins of which can be seen today. The culture of wet rice was also an unhealthful occupation, and fevers plagued the coast country. In the uplands, pellagra became a scourge, and hookworm was rampant.

State Banks Start in Georgia

State banks were started in Savannah and Augusta in 1811. Most of the money came from the state treasury, but this was increased by private investors. The two banks were the Planters Bank in Savannah and the Bank of Augusta. There was in the state capital itself a branch of the State Bank of Georgia.

The state banks were not the first banks in Georgia. A branch of the United States Bank had opened in Savannah in 1802. There was much rivalry between the state banks and the federal bank. In addition, the state banks were backed by plantation owners but were not popular with the upcountry small farmer.

What conflicts occurred among Georgia's banks?

Many followers of John Clark in Georgia's upcountry did not trust banks. He wanted the state to handle the money. In 1823, while he was governor, the Central Bank, set up in Milledgeville, was virtually the state treasury. Clark believed state control of its money might in time do away entirely with the state's need to tax.

Georgia Promotes Transportation

Progress was beginning to be made in roads, canals, and rivers for transportation. A road from Tennessee through the Cherokee country was opened in 1805. The War of 1812 had shown how much roads were needed. When the Creeks began their uprising, a road was built from Gwinnett County to the Chattahoochee River, so that soldiers could move easily to keep the Creeks in line. This was known as Peachtree Road. Part of it is now Peachtree Street in Atlanta. Turnpikes and toll stations helped pay for the roads through Georgia. Some roads were kept up by the people who lived near them. Once, all able-bodied men except teachers and doctors were required to give a certain amount of time to working on roads.

How were roads built and maintained?

In 1821, a road from Augusta through Wilkes County to Athens opened up that section. Carriage travel increased. Travelers stopped at inns like Travelers' Rest, or Jarrett Manor, near Toccoa. A trip from Milledgeville to Washington, D. C., in 1837 took seven days and 19 hours!

Georgians Send First Steamship Across Atlantic

During the War of 1812 England, which had much manufacturing, had been unable to get cotton. By 1819 the price of cotton had risen to 25 cents a pound. Creek lands, the fertile area in middle and south Georgia, were being farmed by cotton growers. In other sections rice, tobacco, and timber were marketable crops. Fast ocean transportation was needed to reach European markets. It was thought, too, that ships might attract paying passengers if they could provide faster travel.

Why did Georgians want a steamship?

In 1819 businessmen from Savannah bought a steamship that had been built in New York. They brought it to Georgia, and held excursions on it up and down the Savannah to attract passengers for the coming European voyage. But people were afraid to travel on a steamship. Glowing advertisements in the newspapers attracted no passengers. So when the ship sailed out of the harbor at Savannah on May 22, 1819, it carried only the crew. Its 32 staterooms were empty.

What was its reception in Europe?

The S.S. Savannah, the first steamship to cross the Atlantic.

The vessel was something really new in ships. It had sails for when the wind was blowing. It also had paddle wheels that could be folded up and put on deck. For fuel, it carried 75 tons of coal and 25 cords of wood. Even with that amount, it had to stop in Ireland for more fuel. As it neared the coast, a British ship thought the American ship was on fire and hastened to aid her. The trip had taken 29 days and 11 hours.

In Europe, the ship was a sensation. Sweden offered to buy it, but wanted to pay in hemp and iron. The owners wanted cash. They thought they could sell it to Czar Alexander I. He didn't want the ship but he gave the captain a gold watch. Some Europeans were hostile because they thought the ship's purpose was to rescue Napoleon, who had been imprisoned on the lonely island of St. Helena. Napoleon's brother Jerome had offered a reward for his rescue.

The return trip from Europe to America took six weeks. Two and half years later the ship ran aground in a storm on Fire Island, in sight of New York's harbor. Curiously, no newspaper reported it at the time.

National Maritime Day in the United States, May 22, commemorates the historic day when the *Savannah* started its voyage across the Atlantic. On National Maritime Day in 1958, the keel of another Savannah was laid. This one, too, made history. It was the first atomic-powered merchant ship in the world. It has now been returned to Savannah. It was dedicated by Mrs. Dwight Eisenhower as a memorial to her husband and emphasizes peaceful uses of nuclear power.

The N.S. Savannah, the first nuclear-powered merchant ship.

EARLY AMERICAN RAILROAD TRAIN.

First in Railroads

What were Georgia's early railroads?

Georgia built more railroads in this era than any other southern state. The first to be chartered was the Georgia Railroad in 1832. It was a venture undertaken by Athens citizens, and it went from Augusta to Eatonton. It was later extended to Athens, and finally west to the Chattahoochee.

In 1836 the state chartered the Western and Atlantic Railroad, which was to figure in politics for years to come. The 1837 depression delayed its completion. The road ran from Rossville on the Tennessee line to a point on the Chattahoochee River known as Terminus. This name was later changed to Marthasville, in honor of the daughter of Gov. Wilson Lumpkin. It is now known as Atlanta.

By mid-century Georgia had more than 500 miles of railroad. Some communities objected to the railroad coming through. It made noise, was dirty and frightened horses and children, they said. Some of these towns later disappeared when businesses moved away to be near the railroads. One of these places was Troupville in Lowndes County, named in honor of Gov. George Troup. The new center that grew up a few miles away near a new railroad they called Valdosta, for Troup's plantation, Val d'Osta, in Laurens County.

POLITICS

Bitter Factions and Colorful Leaders

Georgia's politics in the first half of the 19th century did not exactly follow the pattern in the remainder of the nation. Most of the nation's wealthy and conservative men were members of the Federalist Party. This party, with Alexander Hamilton as one of its leading spokesmen, favored a strong national government. In Georgia, the Federalists were believed to have been connected with the Yazoo Fraud. As a result, conservatives like James Jackson, George Troup and William Harris Crawford were on the opposite side. They were anti-Federalists or States' Rights men.

Planters vs. Frontiersmen

What were the major differences between the two groups?

The two groups pitted against each other in Georgia were the wealthy planters, who lived chiefly in the coast country, and the up-country frontier farmers who were Jeffersonian Democrats, or Union men. But the lines were not always clearly drawn and the chief political differences in Georgia came to be due to personal allegiances. Quarrels were fierce and fights were frequent, but not often over issues. Michael Troup and his colleague from north Georgia, William Harris Crawford, were pitted against the able, tempestuous John Clark. For many exciting years, their followers quarreled and fought over politics.

An old tavernkeeper who tried to be neutral found his business falling off. He complained, "Whenever a Crawford man comes in, he asks whether I am a Crawford man. When I tell him I am neither for Crawford or Clark, he curses me for a Clarkite and refuses to buy a drop to drink. When the Clark men come in, they accuse me of being for Crawford. I sell not a drink to either. Faith, it pays to be a politician in Georgia!"

There were many duels. To control them, the legislature passed a law in 1818 to fine duelists up to $500 and make them liable for a prison sentence of up to two years. But some still went across the state line to fight duels. Not even the legislature could stop it.

After 1829, when the two most colorful leaders, George Troup and John Clark, were out of state, Georgia politics fell more in line with national politics. Georgians became either Whigs or Democrats.

The Colorful Leaders

JOHN CLARK

Small farmers in north Georgia, clearing their acres on the edge of the Indian country and living always in danger, were a sturdily independent crowd. They worked hard and played hard. Often they found their cabins burned and their families scalped by Indians. They had few schools and their children did not have much opportunity to be educated.

Describe frontier farmers.

John Clark was just the kind of man that frontiersmen would quickly follow. Rough, uneducated, brave, and able, he had lived with danger much of his life. His father was the Revolutionary Gen. Elijah Clarke. John dropped the e from his name because he thought his political followers would think it pretentious and fancy. The younger Clark, born Feb. 28, 1766, had started fighting at age 13.

What were Clark's views of politics?

Clark spoke roughly and bluntly. He gave orders, but he did not know how to reason with men and he had no tact or diplomacy. He expected his word to be law and he thought that politics was simply a kind of peacetime war. But he made strong and loyal friends and he was as loyal to them as he was merciless to his enemies. As Andrew Jackson did in the nation, so Clark in Georgia brought in "the era of the common man." Under his leadership his followers developed a powerful political group that was later to make him governor and give them control of the Georgia legislature for a time.

Clark served two terms as governor, from 1819 to 1823. When he was not governor, he was throwing his powerful influence behind his candidates. He and Troup seesawed for power for many years in Georgia. After his years as governor were over, Clark was appointed by his old friend, President Andrew Jackson, as governor of Florida. He died there of yellow fever on Oct. 12, 1832. He said he forgave all of his enemies except William Harris Crawford. Even Troup!

GEORGE MICHAEL TROUP

George Michael Troup was born in 1780 in a part of Georgia that is now Alabama. His father soon moved to the coastal country in Georgia. He went to Princeton University, finishing at 19. He was not quite 21 when his neighbors elected him to the Georgia legislature, and he was in politics for many years after that. He became a follower of James Jackson with whose help he went to Congress 10 years, resigning in 1818 to run against John Clark for governor.

What kind of man was Troup?

Troup, every inch the aristocrat, refused to campaign for anything. He would never ask any man to vote for him; he was too proud. He had contempt for "electioneering," which he considered as "evidence of human depravity."

Troup was scrupulously honest, very able, and stubborn. He said, "If I am wrong in anything, I will surrender, but I will never compromise." Some people considered him stiff, proud and haughty, but his personal friends were deeply devoted to him.

After his retirement from politics, he went home to his farm Val d'Osta in Laurens County, which he named for a beautiful valley in the Italian Alps. He heard that his constituents were planning to re-elect him to Congress. He got in his buggy and drove as hard as he could to keep them from it. He arrived too late, and was persuaded to go back to Congress. But he developed serious throat trouble and soon retired again. He died at 73. Troup County was named for him.

WILLIAM CRAWFORD

William Harris Crawford of Oglethorpe County, Georgia, came within a hair's breadth of being president of the United States instead of John Quincy Adams in 1824.

Crawford was born in Virginia in 1772 and came with his family to Appling, Ga., in 1783. He attended Richmond Academy in Augusta, and taught there for a while. He studied law and went to Lexington, a small town near Athens, to practice.

When Abraham Baldwin died in 1807, Crawford was named to succeed him as United States Senator from Georgia. Crawford rose rapidly to prominence in Washington. He became president pro tempore of the Senate, served in the cabinets of two presidents, Madison and Monroe, and was sent to France as America's ambassador to the Court of Napoleon. The little emperor said that the tall, handsome Georgian was the only man to whom he ever felt inclined to bow. President Monroe came to Georgia and visited Crawford at Woodlawn, and said that much of Crawford's thinking went into the famous Monroe Doctrine. Later, however, the two men quarreled so bitterly that they threatened each other one, with a walking cane and the other with a fire poker. Monroe ordered Crawford to leave his office. Politics could be violent in those days!

What were Crawford's accomplishments?

Crawford had seemed a logical candidate for president in 1820. He had stood aside for Monroe. In 1824, he became the most promising of four candidates for the presidency. The others were Henry Clay, Andrew Jackson and John Quincy Adams. But Crawford was stricken with some kind of paralysis. It temporarily crippled him and made him almost deaf

Why was he not elected President?

and blind. His family and friends tried hard to keep his condition a secret, but the word leaked out. The newspapers termed his condition pitiable. Still, his friends hoped. A caucus showed that he was the most popular candidate.

When the showdown came, however, he did not win the election. Jackson got the most votes, both of the people and in the Electoral College. He did not get a majority in the Electoral College so the election went to the House of Representatives. It chose John Quincy Adams, whose father, John, had been the second president. Jackson was furious. He felt that Clay had betrayed him by teaming up with Adams to cheat him out of office. Jackson did become president in 1829.

Adams offered Crawford a place in his cabinet, but the Georgian declined. So the Crawfords came home to Woodlawn where, outside the window of his room, Crawford had planted a cherry tree given to him by Napoleon. He died in 1834 and was buried on the hill behind his home. A magnolia tree shades the lonely grave, and in the spring yellow jonquils make a small patch of sunshine there. The uniform in which Crawford was presented to Napoleon is at the Department of Archives in Atlanta. The towns of Crawford and Crawfordville and the county of Crawford keep his name alive on the Georgia map.

Georgia-born Fremont First Republican Presidential Candidate

The Republican party, which Lincoln was later to bring to fame, was organized just before the Civil War. Its first candidate for president was not Lincoln. It was a Georgia-born explorer named John C. Fremont, who ran in 1856 and lost to Democrat James Buchanan. Fremont was born in Savannah, educated in South Carolina, and married Jessie Benton, the daughter of the powerful Sen. Thomas Hart Benton. Fremont's father had been a French dancing master who had wandered into the south. The Fremonts' sad story is told by Irving Stone in *Immortal Wife.*

What was Fremont's position on the western states?

Fremont became known as "the Pathfinder of the West." Brave and able, he explored western lands and blazed new trails for his country. Only 5'2" tall, he was hot-headed and impulsive, but he rendered great service.

He had moved west because he knew the value of new territory for this growing country. Though he was a southerner, he wanted the newly settled areas to come into the Union as free states, not slave states. Georgia's Howell Cobb and Herschel V. Jenkins, who both served as governors, recommended seceding if Fremont won the presidency in 1856; but he was defeated.

The secession idea was quiet for a little while after that, but not for long. Soon Abraham Lincoln would be nominated as the second presidential candidate of the Republican party. He would be elected and then would come a bloody war.

An Eatonton Teacher's Big Purchase

William H. Seward was responsible for the purchase of Alaska from Russia in 1867 for $7.2 million. He came to teach school at Eatonton in Putnam County when he was only 17 years old. He had left Union College in New York because his father had refused to pay for a pair of pants he had bought.

William H. Seward

In his diary he wrote: "On Jan. 1, 1819, I left Union College as I thought forever, and proceeded by stage with a classmate who was going to take charge of an academy in Georgia." Seven days later, he arrived by boat at Tybee near Savannah, delighted with the sunshine after New York's snow. Though his money was giving out, he took a stagecoach to Augusta. There his companion got a teaching job. Seward started walking to Eatonton.

What were Seward's experiences in Georgia?

He wrote, "I had only nine shillings and sixpence. My shirt was soiled by travel. My light cravat was even worse. I invested eight shillings in a neck clothe which covered my shirt bosom, and with one and six shillings left, I resumed my journey."

In a log cabin near Eatonton, he found a New York doctor and his family, and stayed with them. The next day, he got in touch with the school trustees. They hired Seward, even though his father wrote them threatening letters. This was the curriculum: Latin, Greek, Theoretical and Practical Mathematics, Logic, Rhetoric, Natural and Moral Philosophy, Chemistry, Geography, English Grammar, Reading, Writing, Spelling, "and such other subjects as are taught in northern colleges"!

Soon his sister wrote him that their mother was very ill. He asked the trustees if he might be relieved so that he could go home. They agreed. He wrote, "My successor came and was accepted. I took leave of my generous patrons and affectionate scholars and departed with a sadness I have seldom experienced."

Later Seward served in Lincoln's cabinet as secretary of state. The same crowd that plotted the assassination of Lincoln also planned to kill Seward. He was sick in bed when one of the plotters got inside his house, stabbed him about the throat and face but did not kill him. His wife Frances, who was an invalid, never got over the shock. She died two months later.

OTHER IMPORTANT PERSONALITIES

There were many individuals in this era important to the history of Georgia who were not politicians. In many ways, colorful politics diverts attention away from important accomplishments in other areas. And colorful politics tells us little about the great strength and courage of the many Georgians who lived in the 1800s. We will use three people to illustrate our point.

Dr. Long Discovers Anesthesia

Dr. Crawford Long, a physician who practiced in the quiet little town of Jefferson, is one of two Georgians to be honored by having his statue placed in the Statuary Hall in Washington. The other is his friend and University of Georgia classmate, Alexander Stephens, later vice president of the Confederacy and governor of Georgia.

Long noticed that people who had sniffed nitrous oxide, called *laughing gas* at the time, scarcely felt pain. Sometime later, Long observed that the use of sulphuric ether produced the same results. This was in 1842 and no one knew the dangers associated with the non-medical use of ether. Long began to think about what he observed and decided to experiment with sulphuric ether in a medical application. On March 30, 1842, he put some on a towel and let James Venable, who had a tumor on his neck that had to be removed, sniff it. As Dr. Long operated, Venable felt no pain.

How did Long discover anesthesia?

Nobody knows why this Georgia doctor did not put his discovery into print. By the time he did report it, he found that others claimed to have discovered it first. Yet records show that it was not until Sept. 30, 1846, that Dr. William Morton, a Boston dentist, used anesthesia with his patients. The U.S. recognized Long's accomplishment with a commemorative stamp.

Lafayette is Georgia's Guest

All America was excited in 1825 when the news came that the Marquis de Lafayette was coming on his second peacetime

Why did Georgians want Lafayette to visit the state?

visit to this country. Georgians wanted him to include Georgia in the American tour he was making. On Jan. 19, 1825, Lafayette notified Gov. George Troup that he would come to Georgia during his 4,000-mile journey. He arrived in Savannah March 19. In greeting him, Troup said, "90 years after Oglethorpe stood right on the spot where you are standing, 400,000 Georgians welcome you to Georgia."

The Marquis de Lafayette was a guest of Georgia in 1825.

In Savannah, Lafayette laid the cornerstone on the monuments for two of his old war comrades, Gen. Nathaniel Greene, and the Polish nobleman, Count Casimir Pulaski. Both had died in Georgia.

Troup invited Georgia's veterans of the Revolution to Milledgeville, then the capital, to greet Lafayette. Seeing Father Duffell, a Catholic priest from Twiggs County, Lafayette embraced him. He said, "I remember you. You helped carry me off the battlefield when I was wounded at Brandywine."

Georgians honored Lafayette not only for what he had done for their country, but for the courage he had shown in the French Revolution. Carlyle called him "the hero of two continents." On the 100th anniversary of his birth, Congress approved a stamp in his honor. Georgians named Fayette County and the towns of Lafayette and Fayetteville for him. LaGrange was named for his farm in France.

A Georgia Girl Makes the Texas Flag

In November 1835, Georgians who had volunteered to go help Texas fight for its independence from Mexico were marching from Macon to Columbus. When they passed through the little town of Knoxville, a 16-year-old girl named Joanna Troutman gave them a beautiful white silk flag which she had made, with one lone star in its center.

One of the volunteers, Lt. Hugh McLeod, wrote Joanna a letter from Columbus:

Miss Joanna:

Col. William Ward brought your handsome and appropriate flag as a present to the Georgia Volunteers in the cause of Texas and Liberty. I assure you . . . without flattery . . . it is beautiful, and with us its value is enhanced by recollection of the donor . . . Your flag will wave over the field of victory in defiance of despotism.

How did Texas get its flag?

Joanna's flag later became the Texas state flag, its colors reversed, with a white star on a blue field.

After Gen. Sam Houston defeated Santa Anna in April 1836, grateful soldiers sent Joanna a silver spoon and fork from the Mexican commander's possessions. There is a monument including her statue in the Texas capitol city of Austin. She was buried beneath it after her body was moved by Texas from her native Georgia.

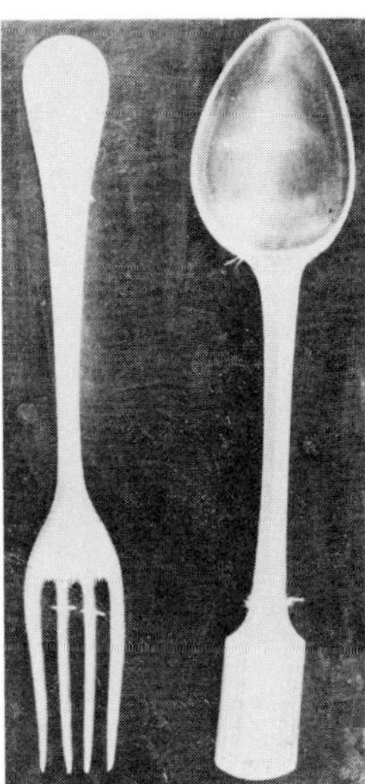

Joanna Troutman's silver.

For Extended Thinking

1. Can you justify moving Georgia's capitol from Louisville to Milledgeville?
2. What was Georgia's role in the War of 1812?
3. What was the average life span of Georgians in 1800 and why was this so?
4. What is the story of the first steamship to cross the ocean?
5. Why were the planters and frontiersmen so antagonistic toward each other?
6. What kind of person was John Clark?
7. What were George Michael Troup's views on politics?
8. Describe the Crawford loss in the race for the United States presidency.

Names, Terms and Concepts

War of 1812
Marthasville
William Seward
Joseph Henry Lumpkin
Federalist party
laughing gas
quarantine
"the era of the common man"
Marquis de Lafayette
Peachtree Road
"the Pathfinder of the West"
Joanna Troutman
Terminus

To Help You Study

1. What was John Clark's involvement with Milledgeville?
2. Tell about some of the health problems Georgians had in the early 1800s.
3. What two kinds of banks were started?
4. Discuss the attitudes of, and the differences between, the plantation owners and the up-country frontier farmers.
5. Who were the three most important political figures of the time?
6. What was the interesting discovery made by Crawford Long? How did he make it?
7. Did Georgians want Fremont elected president? Explain why you answered the way you did.
8. William Seward taught at Eatonton but he is famous for something else. What?
9. How did Georgia treat Lafayette and how has he been honored in Georgia?
10. How did Texas get its state flag?
11. What were the two ships named *Savannah?*
12. What was Georgia doing about railroads?

THE INDIAN STORY

CHAPTER 9

The Indian is not just a picturebook figure from history. When Columbus came, there were on the North American continent from one to three million Indians. About 25,000 lived in Georgia. By 1910, the Indian population had reached an all-time low of 220,000. The Indian is now one of America's fastest-growing minority. With a birth rate two and one-half times that of whites, the red man is no longer "the vanishing Indian." In 1970, Georgia had 2,347 Indians. By 1980 there were 7,619 living in the state.

The chief tribes in Georgia were the **Cherokees** and the **Creeks**. Among the smaller tribes were the Yamacraws, to which Tomochichi belonged. There were several groups of the Creeks. The Lower Creeks lived in middle and south Georgia, usually along the Flint and Chattahoochee rivers. They were friendly to the whites. The Upper Creeks lived in Alabama on the Coosa and the Tallapoosa. They were called Red Sticks and were hostile. An old story says that this name grew out of the fact that Tecumseh, the great Shawnee Indian leader, gave them a bundle of red sticks to count off the days before a council or a battle. A red stick was also supposed to point in the direction of one's enemies.

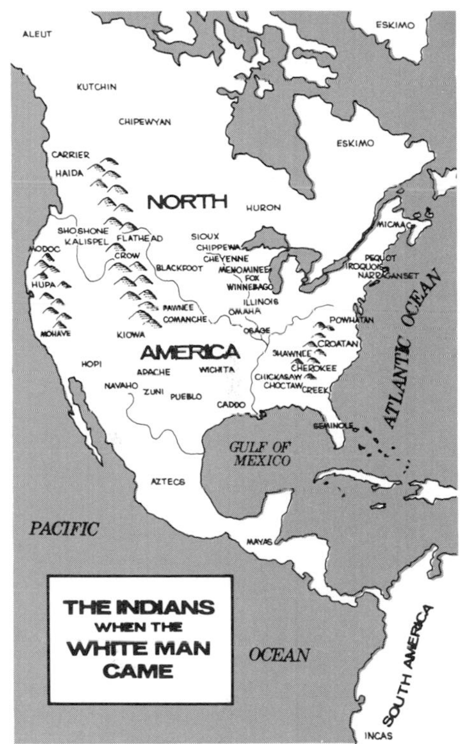

What is happening among Indians today?

The Cherokees lived among the north Georgia mountains. They achieved a higher degree of civilization than the Creeks. They resisted removal longer and carried their case to the white man's courts. The Cherokees, too, lost in the end and moved west to new homes.

Alexis DeToqueville, a Frenchman who wrote a wise book about America, said, "The Indians have unquestionably displayed . . . much natural genius. But they have been ruined by a competition they did not have the means of sustaining."

What were some Indian complaints against the white man?

The Indians said that the white men who brought them the horse and wheel also brought them whiskey, guns, smallpox and other ills. Sometimes Indians ceded lands to the whites willingly. At other times, they had to cede land to pay the big debts they ran up at trading stations and to compensate white settlers for damages. Sometimes the whites broke solemn treaties guaranteeing Indian holdings forever. Indian leaders resented seeing the white men come into their lands. One Cherokee chief criticized a young warrior for making a wagon. "Wagons mean roads, and roads bring the white man. Then our land will be gone, and the ways of our fathers will be changed," he said.

On the other hand, Georgians on the frontier begged the government to protect them from the Indians. On May 31, 1787, Creeks scalped two residents of Greene County and stole two slaves and 14 horses. Georgia soldiers stalked them and killed 12 Indians. Indian leaders demanded 12 white lives in return. Gov. George Mathews said, "We will deliver up none of our people, and if the Indians spill a drop of blood, we will lay their towns in ashes and sprinkle their land with blood."

What were white complaints against the Indian?

So the history of the Indian is a two-sided one. It is true that white settlers did suffer often from Indian hostility. It is also true that some white men wanted the Indians removed because they wanted the rich cotton lands of the Creeks and the gold lands of the Cherokees.

THE CREEKS

The Muscogean Indians who came to be known in Georgia and Alabama as Creeks were a hunting people. They hunted, fished, and traded their deerskins and other such things with the whites. The Creeks did some farming and knew about the plow.

Their most colorful festival was the Green Corn Dance, which began a new year for them. All of the cabins were painted red except those of the old men; these were painted white to symbolize age and virtue. In the center of the square a fire always burned. During the days of the Green Corn Dance, the Creeks pardoned all crimes except murder.

What happened at the Green Corn Dance?

These Indians never called themselves Creeks. That was the white man's name for them because they usually lived beside a stream. Like the other red men, they never referred to themselves as Indians either. The Creeks had white (peace) towns, and red (war) towns. Coweta was the leading war town, and Cusseta was the leading peace town. The chief of each town was called the mico. He was appointed for life and was always succeeded by a nephew. The military chief was called the Great Warrior.

Tecumseh Arouses the Creeks

Tecumseh, great chief of the Shawnees in the north, came to Georgia and tried to persuade the Creeks to join in his confederacy against the whites. He wanted Indians to reject the white man's ways and return to Indian customs. He urged them not to cede any more of their lands to the white men. "Sell our land?" he asked. "You might as well sell air and water. The Great Spirit gives the land and air and water, and they belong in common to us all. Do not sell the lands of our fathers. The dead will be grieved if you do. I can hear their voices wailing on the winds. They cannot rest in their graves." Nature itself helped Tecumseh. Comets, meteors, and even an earthquake occurred. The superstitious Creeks thought he caused them. When he left he said, "When I get home (to Ohio) I will stamp my foot and the earth will tremble." It did; it was an earthquake.

What were Tecumseh's purposes in coming to Georgia?

The trouble between the Indians and whites on the Georgia

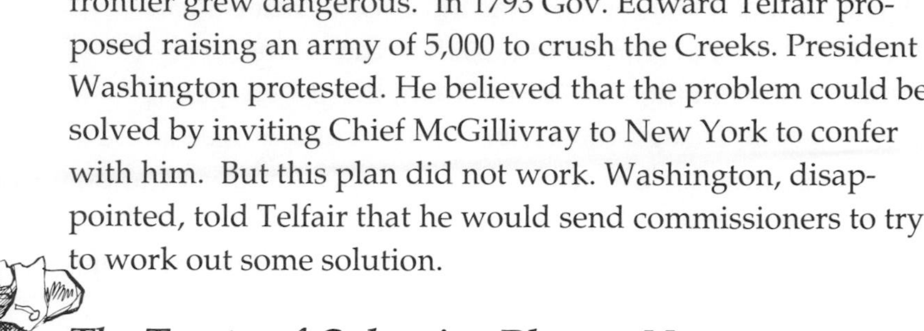

frontier grew dangerous. In 1793 Gov. Edward Telfair proposed raising an army of 5,000 to crush the Creeks. President Washington protested. He believed that the problem could be solved by inviting Chief McGillivray to New York to confer with him. But this plan did not work. Washington, disappointed, told Telfair that he would send commissioners to try to work out some solution.

The Treaty of Coleraine

The Treaty of Coleraine Pleases None

The commissioners met with both whites and Indians at a place called Coleraine, on the St. Mary's River six miles from the present Folkston. About 400 chiefs were there. Mico Fushatchee was their spokesman.

As head of the U.S. delegation, Washington sent Col. Benjamin Hawkins. As the treaty was being worked out, Gen. James Jackson presented a list of grievances of the white men against the Creeks for which he demanded money in damages. An old Creek chief replied, "I could fill many pages with 10 times that amount which the whites owe the Creeks." But finally, the Treaty of Coleraine was signed in 1796.

What were the main provisions of the Treaty?

The treaty established boundaries between the whites and Indians to run "from the Currahee mountain to the source of the main south branch of the Oconee, called by the whites the Apalatchee and by the Creeks, Tulapolka." The U.S. gave the Indians $6,000 and provided them with blacksmiths and tools.

But Georgians were not satisfied with this treaty. The lands they got were poor for farming and too far out on the frontier. It left the Creeks in possession of much of the most fertile farm land in the state, between the Ocmulgee and the Chattahoochee rivers. Each Indian was granted a square mile to live on and this, too, added to the discontent of the whites. So every few years, for the generation that remained of their life in Georgia, the Creeks would be forced to agree to a new treaty transferring more of their lands to the whites.

Hawkins Becomes U.S. Agent to the Creeks

Benjamin Hawkins

When Col. Benjamin Hawkins returned to Washington to report on the Coleraine Treaty, he told Washington that a permanent agent should be sent to live among the Indians in Georgia. "The Creeks and the other Indians can be controlled," said Hawkins, "but it would take a man of talent, and he would have to make the sacrifice of giving up his home and living permanently there in the wilderness among them."

Washington asked Hawkins himself to do this. He was a North Carolinian who had graduated from Princeton, served five times in Congress, and had once been Washington's interpreter. Accepting the appointment, he moved to Georgia with his fine library and other possessions.

He traveled among both Creeks and Cherokees for a time, learning about them. He then established the Creek Agency on the Flint River, on the stagecoach route between the present Columbus and Macon. At the agency, he entertained some of the great men who came this way. Moreau, a Frenchman, said that Hawkins was the most remarkable man he met in America.

Why did Washington appoint an Indian agent?

Hawkins spent most of his time helping the Creeks to farm better and to raise livestock. He planted 5,000 peach trees and experimented with new crops. He grew the biggest strawberries ever seen in the area. He taught Indian women to weave. This was much to the displeasure of their husbands, who thought their wives would no longer obey them if they became too smart. Hawkins was stern with the Indians but he was fair and considerate. He compiled a grammar for them.

Hawkins carried on an extensive correspondence with people all over the world, especially Thomas Jefferson. He sent the Empress of Russia a report on Indian dialects because she was interested in languages. One friend said, "Hawkins knows more about the Indians than any other man who ever scraped pen to paper." He looked out for the Indians' interests.

How effective was Hawkins?

Some white people resented Hawkins for this.

Hawkins had done much to keep peace between white men and red men. Then something happened in Alabama where the more aggressive Upper Creeks had been stirred up. This event brought the Creek question to a climax and caused more trouble in Georgia. It was the Ft. Mims massacre.

Georgia and the Massacre at Ft. Mims

Why did the Red Sticks want to fight?

The War of 1812 pushed the Indian problem to the background for a little while. However, it was during this war that the Upper Creeks, the Red Sticks of Alabama, who were supporting the British, attacked Ft. Mims. Stirred to a frenzy by the fanatical oratory of an Indian known as the Prophet, set against the whites by Tecumseh, and encouraged by the British to oppose all Americans, the Alabama Indians were ready for a fight.

At noon one day more than a thousand Creek Indians swooped down on Ft. Mims, near Mobile, attacking 500 whites, including women and children who had taken refuge

The Fort Mims Massacre

there. The leader of the Indians was William Weatherford, a follower of Tecumseh and a nephew of Chief Alexander McGillivray. In three hours of terror they killed nearly all the people in the fort. Only 12 escaped. About 400 Indians were killed or wounded. It was Aug. 30, 1813, the second year of the War of 1812.

When news of the Ft. Mims massacre spread, there was anger all over the country. The United States sent Gen. Andrew Jackson from Tennessee to quell the Creeks and to punish them. Georgia sent 3,000 soldiers to help. The Georgians assembled at Ft. Hawkins, near the present Macon. Their commander was Gen. John Floyd. Friendly Lower Creek Indians from Georgia under the leadership of halfbreed Chief William McIntosh went to help Floyd and his Georgians.

What was the reaction to the massacre?

Floyd captured two Indian villages in a daring daylight raid on Nov. 29, 1813. He and his men killed the Indian leaders, 200 of their followers, and burned 200 dwellings. The famous Indian fighter Davy Crockett fought in this battle. He said later, "We shot the Red Sticks down like dogs."

Jackson Defeats the Upper Creeks at Horseshoe Bend

Gen. Andrew Jackson picked Horseshoe Bend on the Tallapoosa River as the place to avenge the whites of Ft. Mims. In a seven-hour battle on March 27, 1814, the Red Sticks were finally defeated. Jackson forced them to sign a treaty ceding more of their lands. This included a 90-mile strip in Georgia that had belonged to Creeks friendly to Georgia—a total of 23 million acres.

This treaty turned some of the friendly Georgia Creeks into enemies. Some even fled to join the hostile Seminoles in upper Florida. After Horseshoe Bend, the Creeks were a broken and dispirited people. "Our lands are our life and breath," Mico Yahola said; "if we part with them, we part with our blood."

What resulted from Horseshoe Bend?

Governor Troup Insists U. S. Move the Indians

Why did Troup insist that the Creeks leave Georgia?

After the War of 1812 cotton prices went up. As a result, the white men looked with eager eyes on all that fertile land in middle Georgia that the Creeks still occupied. They were also frightened by the fearful massacre in Alabama. It could happen in Georgia, they told one another. Governor Troup pressed the federal government to carry out its 1802 promise to remove the Indians.

How did the Creeks respond?

Among the Creeks two factions grew up as to whether they should leave Georgia. The leader of the group favoring removal was a half-breed, Chief William McIntosh, a first cousin to Georgia's Gov. George Troup. Troup himself, of course, was for removal.

William McIntosh

McIntosh was a wealthy Indian, with a plantation called Lockchau Talafau in Carroll County. He lived there with his two Indian wives, Peggy and Susannah. In another home, about 50 miles away on the Tallapoosa River, lived his white wife Eliza and her children.

What happened at Indian Springs?

McIntosh played an unclear role in the final tragic years of the Creek Nation in Georgia. McIntosh believed that bit by bit, in one treaty after another, Indians had given to the whites lands that had been theirs for centuries. The federal government arranged a conference at Indian Springs, in February 1825. Only eight of the 56 Creek communities sent representatives. Even with the low turn-out, McIntosh signed a removal treaty that granted the last of the Creek lands in Georgia to the white man. In return the Creeks were to get equivalent land west of the Mississippi, plus a large sum of money.

Historians believe that for agreeing to the treaty McIntosh personally received both lands and money. In any case the Upper Creeks, the Red Sticks of Alabama, refused to have anything to do with it. At the treaty conference one of their chiefs warned McIntosh that if he signed the treaty he would die by the Creek Law of Pole Cat Spring. This chief urged his people not to accept the treaty.

"Brothers," he said, "the Great Spirit has met here with his painted children of the woods and with our paleface brethren. I see His golden locks in the sunbeams. You have been charmed and deceived by the double tongue of the snake McIntosh and by the paleface. Brothers, the grounds of our fathers have been stolen by our chief and sold by him to the paleface. Their gold is in his pouch. Brothers, the grounds are gone from us, and the plows of the paleface will upturn the bones of our fathers."

But McIntosh signed the treaty. The Upper Creeks, after a council session, decided to execute him. They met, formally heard the case against him, and condemned him to death under their Law of Pole Cat Spring. Chief Menewa took 170 Indians with him to carry out this sentence. They crept stealthily into the woods near McIntosh's inn, which was also his home, and waited through most of the night. They told James Hutton, an interpreter, to reassure any guests who might be there that they would not kill them. About three a.m. they set fire to the house. McIntosh fought as bravely as he could, but he was killed.

What happened to McIntosh and why?

The house containing the desk on which McIntosh signed the treaty is now a museum at Indian Springs. In front is the marker telling the story. The big rock from which the Indian shouted his warning is in front.

The Indian agent John Crowell told the new president, John Quincy Adams, that the Indian Springs Treaty had been obtained by fraud and that it was not valid. Adams agreed, and decided that a new treaty with the Creeks should be made. He ordered Georgia's Gov. Troup to stop surveying the Indian lands. But Troup was up for re-election and many of the people wanted those lands. They rallied around Troup in his contention that the Indian Springs Treaty was legal and that Georgia would insist on its terms. The campaign cry of the Troup people became "Troup and the Treaty." Troup even went so far in defiance as to threaten fighting. "Having exhausted our argument," he said, "we must stand by our arms."

What problems did Georgia have with the national government?

Troup called Secretary of War John C. Calhoun "the unblushing ally of savages" and warned him that if the federal government sent soldiers, Georgia would fight them as enemies and invaders. Meanwhile, the state went on with the survey and the lands were distributed. Out of this land the counties of Fayette, Henry, Monroe, and Dooly were eventually created.

The Creeks Leave

Even the Upper Creeks signed the Removal Treaty of March 24, 1832. The federal government guaranteed their safety in the west. After the last treaties were signed, the Creeks sent a delegation to explore the western lands that were to be their new homes. Some settled in Arkansas and some in Oklahoma.

Thus the Creeks were removed from the path of the whites in the southeast. About 23,000 had moved west. One old Indian said, "Now our people are on the road to disappearance; we are at the end of our trail."

But they built new lives in the west, lighted their ancient council fires, and recovered much of their old status and dignity as a people.

THE SEMINOLES ARE DEFEATED

Between the defeat of the Upper Creeks at Horseshoe Bend and the final Creek removal treaty of 1832, Georgia also had trouble with the Seminoles of Florida.

The **Seminoles** (their name means "separatist") were once part of the Creek Nation. In the early 18th century they broke away and moved south, occupying the Florida lands formerly held by the Appalachees. After the defeat at Horseshoe Bend many Creeks fled to join them in the Florida swamps. Other Georgia Creeks friendly to the whites were disheartened when

Gen. Jackson forced them to give up land that belonged to Indians who had actually helped him defeat the Red Sticks. They too joined the Seminoles, vowing never to cede another inch of their land.

Why did some Creeks join the Seminoles?

The Seminoles began to cause the white man much trouble. On Dec. 12, 1818, Secretary of War John C. Calhoun ordered Gen. Andrew Jackson to go to Florida and quell them and their Creek allies.

What did Calhoun decide?

Jackson came marching through Georgia on his way to Florida. As he went through Pulaski County he put three notches in the trees where he went along. This road came to be known as Three Notch Trail. Indians who lived in a village called Chehaw cared for his sick soldiers, and sent along with him 40 of their best warriors to help defeat the hostile Indians. About this time Gov. William Rabun of Georgia sent Georgia soldiers south where unfriendly Indians had been burning houses and destroying crops. Capt. Obed Wright was in charge of them, with orders to burn the towns of the hostile Indians. By mistake he burned the village of Chehaw and killed some of the Indians there. This led to an angry protest by Andrew Jackson to Gov. Rabun. The president of the United States ordered Georgia to turn Capt. Wright over to the federal marshal, but Wright escaped.

Osceola, the Seminole Leader

Trouble with the Seminoles continued for years. In 1832, at Payne's Landing, they were forced to sign a treaty agreeing to their removal to Oklahoma three years later. As 1835 approached more and more Seminoles repudiated the treaty. Under the leadership of their chief, Osceola, they determined to fight for their homeland.

Chief Osceola

Osceola, for whom Georgia's town of Ocilla was named, was the half-breed son of a white Georgian. He grew up around the camps of white soldiers and learned many things

What kind of person was Osceola?

about war. He became a warrior and a young chief. He was intelligent and, in some ways, humane. He forbade his warriors to kill women and children. "We are not making war on them," he said. But he was fierce and merciless to his enemies. The Seminole War, which was to last seven years, cost the lives of 1,500 U.S. soldiers. It was also the most expensive Indian war ever fought by the United States.

Adopting hit-and-run guerilla tactics Osceola succeeded in all but paralyzing the government forces. At length, in 1837, the American General Jessup induced Osceola to come to St. Augustine under a flag of truce for negotiations. When he arrived he was seized and thrown in prison, where, shortly, he died.

Andrew Jackson Defeats the Seminoles

The Seminoles were finally quelled, though they claim to this day that they never actually surrendered. In 1819, John Forsyth of Georgia, then U.S. Ambassador to Spain, helped buy Florida from Spain. Florida became a state in 1845. By that time, 11,700 Seminoles had been sent west. The small band that fled to the Everglades was still there.

What happened to the Seminoles?

Many of their descendants live there today. They grow most of the palms used in American churches on Palm Sunday. They also make totem poles and canoes. They live much as their ancestors lived. They are said to be the healthiest Indian tribe living today.

THE CHEROKEES

The Cherokees lived in upper Georgia in what they called the Enchanted Land. North Georgia is often referred to, even today, as Cherokee country.

Cherokee territory once spread over 40,000 square miles of

southwest Virginia, western North and South Carolina, eastern Tennessee, north Georgia, and northeast Alabama. Their capital was in Tennessee. They called themselves "The Principal People." They were the preeminent tribe of a group known as the Five Civilized Tribes, which included Choctaws, Chickasaws, Creeks, and Seminoles.

What kind of people were the Cherokees?

The Cherokees gave a surprisingly important place to women. They had a group of War Women, for example, who advised them about battles. Property passed through the female line. There was provision in their law for divorce. William Bartram described Cherokee women as tall, slender, erect, delicate, with cheerful, friendly faces and with grace and dignity in their movements. He found the Cherokee people grave, dignified and, when not busy with war, gentle and hospitable.

Their aged men were to them "the old beloved men." They had a saying, "The great chief is longest remembered for the time he helps the lame man across the stream." But the early Cherokees had been very warlike. A chief said, "If we make peace with the Tuscaroras, we will have to find somebody else to fight, for we cannot live without war. It is our favorite occupation."

The Cherokees Build a Nation

How did Sequoyah develop the alphabet?

The achievement of a Cherokee named Sequoyah in inventing an alphabet was almost miraculous. Yet this remarkable accomplishment was to hasten their expulsion from their lands in Georgia.

Sequoyah had been a crippled child. He became a silversmith and he noticed that white men signed the things they made. He believed he could devise written symbols to sign his silver wares. It took him 12 years working on pieces of bark, day after day, scratching curious markings. Some of the symbols are letters of the English alphabet turned upside

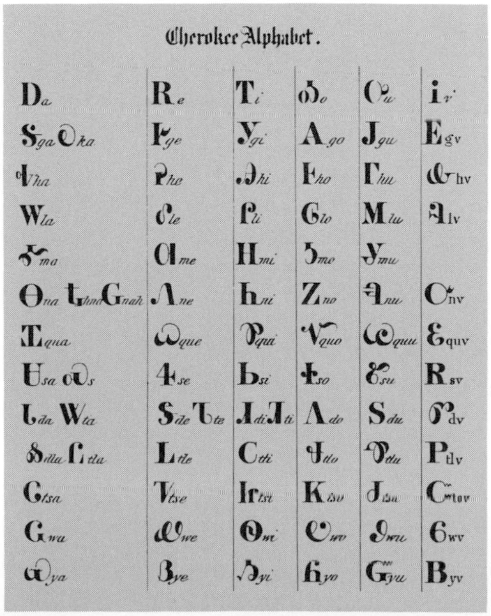

Cherokee Alphabet.

Ꭰ *a*	Ꭱ *e*	Ꭲ *i*	Ꭳ *o*	Ꭴ *u*	Ꭵ v
Ꭶ *ga* Ꭷ *ka*	Ꭸ *ge*	Ꭹ *gi*	Ꭺ *go*	Ꭻ *gu*	Ꭼ gv
Ꭽ *ha*	Ꭾ *he*	Ꭿ *hi*	Ꮀ *ho*	Ꮁ *hu*	Ꮂ hv
Ꮃ *la*	Ꮄ *le*	Ꮅ *li*	Ꮆ *lo*	Ꮇ *lu*	Ꮈ lv
Ꮉ *ma*	Ꮊ *me*	Ꮋ *mi*	Ꮌ *mo*	Ꮍ *mu*	
Ꮎ *na* Ꮏ *hna* Ꮐ *nah*	Ꮑ *ne*	Ꮒ *ni*	Ꮓ *no*	Ꮔ *nu*	Ꮕ nv
Ꮖ *qua*	Ꮗ *que*	Ꮘ *qui*	Ꮙ *quo*	Ꮚ *quu*	Ꮛ quv
Ꮜ *sa* Ꮝ *s*	Ꮞ *se*	Ꮟ *si*	Ꮠ *so*	Ꮡ *su*	Ꮢ sv
Ꮣ *da* Ꮤ *ta*	Ꮥ *de* Ꮦ *te*	Ꮧ *di* Ꮨ *ti*	Ꮩ *do*	Ꮪ *du*	Ꮫ dv
Ꮬ *dla* Ꮭ *tla*	Ꮮ *tle*	Ꮯ *tli*	Ꮰ *tlo*	Ꮱ *tlu*	Ꮲ tlv
Ꮳ *tsa*	Ꮴ *tse*	Ꮵ *tsi*	Ꮶ *tso*	Ꮷ *tsu*	Ꮸ tsv
Ꮹ *wa*	Ꮺ *we*	Ꮻ *wi*	Ꮼ *wo*	Ꮽ *wu*	Ꮾ wv
Ꮿ *ya*	Ᏸ *ye*	Ᏹ *yi*	Ᏺ *yo*	Ᏻ *yu*	Ᏼ yv

Sequoyah

down and others are Greek letters. In the end he had an alphabet of 85 symbols that represented every sound in the Cherokee language.

The Cherokee Council did not want this written language. Sequoyah took his small daughter, Ay-yo-ka, to help him convince the elders that their language could be written down so easily that a child could understand it. This turned the Cherokee country into one vast schoolroom overnight. The Indians sat around on stumps and fallen trees and learned the new alphabet. A spectacle salesman happened to travel through the country and many bought spectacles, to enable them to study the new alphabet. Some learned it in one day.

What was the response to the alphabet?

After the Cherokees learned their written language, they established a newspaper, the **Cherokee Phoenix**, at New Echota near Calhoun. The newspaper, printed in two languages, Cherokee and English, had its first issue on Feb. 21, 1828. The *Phoenix* was edited by Elias Boudinot, a bright young Cherokee who originally was named Buck Watie.

The Cherokees' newspaper served to inform and to unify

Office of the Cherokee Phoenix.

them. In 1827 they adopted a constitution providing for an elected chief and a bicameral legislature. This meant that the Cherokee Nation was organized in the style of the whites. It was not well received, however, by officials of Georgia's government. They did not like the existence of a separate nation within the borders of the state. In 1828, therefore, the Georgia legislature enacted a law extending the state's authority over the Cherokee Nation. The effective date was to be June 2, 1830.

Gold Discovered in the Cherokee Land

The discovery of gold hastened the Cherokee removal. Their mountain lands, not fertile like the Creek land, suddenly became desirable after gold was discovered in 1829. The discovery was made by Benjamin Parks, a farmer hunting deer near the Chestatee. He picked up a shining pebble that changed history.

What happened when gold was discovered?

Ten thousand goldseekers came swarming in, bringing about the nation's first gold rush. This was 20 years before the 49'ers swarmed to California. It also sealed the fate of the Cherokees.

A mint was set up in Dahlonega. The name "dahlonega" means "yellow metal." The town of Auraria became the center of the gold rush. After the mines began to give out, Georgia miners from Auraria went west and settled Auraria in Colorado, which later became Denver. Some went on to California. They had learned how to mine and pan gold in Georgia and they used these methods in the west. Many Georgians began to look with longing at the Cherokee lands. This song was sung in Georgia:

All I want in this creation
Is a pretty little wife and a big plantation
Way up yonder in the Cherokee Nation.

Finally the Indians elected John Ross chief. It was Ross who fought the desperate fight to keep the Georgia mountain country for the Cherokees. Ross was a brown-haired, blue-eyed man who was only one-eighth Cherokee. He was an avid reader of Jefferson's writings and helped design the Cherokee Nation and constitution on the principles of Jefferson.

The Supreme Court Decides Against the Cherokees

The Cherokees took several cases to the United States Supreme Court. Sometimes Chief Justice John Marshall and his associates decided for the Indians and sometimes against them. The trouble was that when the decisions were against Georgia, the state ignored them, backed up by President Andrew Jackson himself. "Marshall has made his decision," said Jackson, "now let him enforce it!"

How did the Court decide?

A Removal Bill passed Congress on May 24, 1830. Again the Cherokees appealed to the Supreme Court. On March 5, 1831, the Court handed down the decision that they were not a separate nation in the legal meaning of the term and could not bring a suit in the court.

Jackson Refuses to Help the Indians

In their desperation, the Cherokees sent Chief John Ross to Washington to appeal to their old war comrade, Andrew Jackson, who had become president of the United States. The Cherokees had helped Jackson defeat the hostile Creeks and the Seminoles. One of their chiefs had even saved Jackson's life at Horseshoe Bend.

What was Jackson's response?

However, President Jackson was not to be moved by the pleas of the Indians. He said, "You are not my friends. I have no friends. A curse upon all Indians." Then he said to Ross,

"Removal is best. We will guarantee your safety and peace in the west." Ross answered, "How can you protect us in the west when you can't even protect us now in our homes in Georgia?"

Chief Junaluska, the one who had saved Jackson's life at Horseshoe Bend, said, "If I had known that Chicken Snake (Jackson) would turn against our people, I would have let him die that day."

Andrew Jackson

Two Bitter Factions Under Cherokee Leaders

What were the two factions?

Just as they had among the Creeks, two bitter factions grew up among the Cherokees. One, led by Chief John Ross, was against the removal of the Cherokees to the west and fought it to the bitter end. The other, known as the Treaty Party, believed that removal was inevitable and favored ceding the lands to the whites under the best terms they could get. This group was led by Chief Major Ridge who, along with other Treaty Party members, said, "We cannot exist under the laws of the white man. Let us go west."

On Oct. 24, 1835, both groups met at Red Clay near Dalton, since they could no longer meet at New Echota, the Cherokee capitol. They signed an agreement to stop quarreling among themselves. The Treaty Party was instructed to get the best removal terms possible.

The Ridges and Boudinot Sign the Final Removal Treaty

On Dec. 29, 1835, the United States government met with the Treaty Party leaders of the Cherokees at their capitol, New Echota, and made a treaty with them about their removal to the west. Elias Boudinot, Major Ridge and John Ridge signed the agreement. For a large sum, the Cherokees gave up all their claims to lands east of the Mississippi River. "Our gold alone is worth more than this," Ross protested when he heard the terms. Most Cherokees agreed with Ross and felt they had been betrayed.

What were the terms of the Treaty?

The Cherokees were to get seven million acres beyond the Mississippi. This land was never to be included in any state. If they needed more land, the U.S. government agreed to sell it to them. The government was to protect them from foreign enemies and civil strife. The United States was also to assist their relocation to their new home and to maintain them for one year. This treaty was ratified by the U.S. Senate May 23, 1836. It gave the Cherokees two years to leave Georgia, until May 23, 1838.

Winfield Scott

On Friday, May 18, 1838, Georgia took possession of the Cherokee land. Although some 5,000 Indians had migrated, there were almost 20,000 who had not moved.

Gen. Winfield Scott, later a hero of the Mexican War, was commander of the U.S. Army which rounded up the Cherokees and moved them from their Georgia mountains. On May 17, 1838, he issued two official proclamations, one to his soldiers, one to the Cherokees. To his soldiers he recommended kindness, forebearance, and humility in dealing with the Indians. To the Cherokee Nation he pointed out that they had not fulfilled their obligation under the treaty of 1836 to move out within two years, and that he was there to see that they did so—humanely and peacefully if possible; by force if need be.

Many Die on the Trail of Tears

Then the army took the men from the fields, the women from their cabins, and the children from their play. It was hot summer weather when the round-up began. John Ross begged Gen. Scott to let them wait until cooler weather, promising that they would go peacefully then. Scott agreed, provided that they would leave on their 700-mile journey by Oct. 20.

In October, thousands of Cherokees gathered at Ross'

Landing on the Tennessee line. Others left from Rattlesnake Spring near Hiawassee. They were sad at leaving their beautiful mountain country in north Georgia.

But they had waited too long. The weather, cool at first, became freezing and wintry. They did not have enough blankets. There was much suffering. One Georgia officer said many years later that he had seen nothing in war as sad as this exodus of the Indians from Georgia. About 4,000 died on the westward journey. There was so much misery that it became known in history as the Trail of Tears.

What happened on the Trail of Tears?

Tsali Refuses to Go—and Is Shot

As the Indians started out on the Trail of Tears, many looked back at their little homes among the mountains. One Indian woman, the wife of Tsali, walked too slowly along the road. A soldier prodded her with his bayonet. Suddenly Tsali and his friends jumped the soldier and killed him. Then they all escaped into the mountains.

What did Tsali do and why?

The soldiers hunted and hunted for them. Many other Cherokees had stayed behind in the mountains also. Finally, the American commander sent a message to Tsali. He said that if the old Indian would come down with his sons and be shot, the government would let the remaining Cherokees stay in the hills undisturbed. Tsali thought this over, and he came down, with his sons. He and all but one of his sons were shot. The commander spared the youngest son, Watisunia, who was only a child. Many of the descendants of this remaining son of Tsali now live at Cherokee, N.C., on the Cherokee Indian reservation.

Boudinot and the Ridges are Killed

Like the Creeks, the Cherokees killed their leaders who had signed the treaty that ceded away their Georgia lands. Major Ridge and his son, John, and their kinsman, Elias Boudinot,

What happened to Cherokee leaders who signed the Treaty?

moved with the Cherokees to Oklahoma. The Cherokees had decreed death for these three, under the ancient laws of the tribe. They sent a war party to kill them.

Boudinot was helping a neighbor build a house. Three men came up and asked him for some medicine. Boudinot was in charge of the supplies. He started with the three men toward the house 300 yards away where the medicines were kept. Halfway there, they killed him. Then Major Ridge was dragged out of his house and shot. John was ambushed, killed and left dead on the roadside. It was June 22, 1839.

In the west, by 1846, the Cherokees had re-established their government, set up schools, and resumed the publication of their paper. They renamed the paper the *Cherokee Advocate* instead of the *Phoenix*.

John Ross became a leader of the Indians in the west. He helped heal the old factionalism and signed a treaty of friendship with the other group. They chose Tallequah for their western capitol on Sept. 6, 1839. Ross lacked the education or the eloquence of the Ridges but he had done his best for his people. He married a 17-year-old Quaker girl after the death of his wife Quatie. He was still alive when the Civil War broke out. He tried but failed to keep the Cherokees neutral.

So at last the Indians were driven from their ancestral lands. The red men who had hunted in the Georgia forests, fished in its waters, and crossed the old trails to make war or to trade had gone to the west.

CAN WE REALLY UNDERSTAND WHAT HAPPENED?

The story of these three great tribes in Georgia—the Creeks, the Seminoles and the Cherokees—is the setting for numerous thought experiments. You should think carefully about the experiences of individuals in these tribes. How do you think Tsali made the decision he made? In his view, the soldier had provoked the incident by prodding Tsali's wife with a bayonet.

Could Tsali have felt that he was not only being driven from his land but insulted and mistreated too? How do you think he decided to turn himself in, knowing that he would be shot? And don't you think it was especially difficult for him to turn himself in with his sons, knowing that they too would be killed?

Most historians are in agreement with the soldier who witnessed the event that the Trail of Tears was a very sad and tragic time in the life of a noble people. Suppose that you had been a teenage Cherokee fishing in the Chestatee River when the soldiers came for the roundup. What would you have felt? With whom would you have talked first and what would you have said? What would you have packed in the haste and confusion of the moment to take with you? Would you have felt bitterness toward the soldiers? Toward all white men?

In modern times, many Indian tribes have sought payment for old wrongs they felt were done them by white men. On August 13, 1946, Congress set up the Indian Claims Commission to act as a court to "settle all just and equitable Indian tribal claims against the U.S." Descendants of Georgia and Alabama Creeks sued for payment for the lands Andrew Jackson took from the friendly Creeks after Horseshoe Bend. The 700 descendants were awarded $3,573,810.

What was the function of the Indian Claims Commission?

Today there are no Indian reservations in Georgia. But in most of the counties along the northern border of the state live hundreds of people of part-Cherokee descent. A small group of Cherokees and Creeks live on Shell Bluff in Burke County. In many respects, the lot of Indians is becoming better. Their life expectancy is increasing because of better living conditions and better medical care. The education of Indian children is improving because they have better schools and they stay in school longer. Their economic condition is improving. However, their per capita income is still far below the national average. After years of difficulty, the outlook for Indian citizens is better than it has been since whites set foot on America 500 years ago.

For Extended Thinking

1. Why is the Indian story two-sided?
2. What was the response of the Creeks to Tecumseh?
3. Why did the Treaty of Coleraine please no one?
4. What was Benjamin Hawkins' life like among the Indians?
5. What were the forces, among both whites and Indians, that led to the removal of the Creeks?
6. Why do you think the Cherokees gave such an important place to women?
7. How did the Cherokees resist the efforts to take their land?

Names, Terms, and Concepts

Red Sticks
William McIntosh
Sequoyah
Lower Creeks
Indian Springs
John Ross
The Green Corn Dance
Law of Pole Cat Spring
Removal Bill of 1830
Mico
Three Notch Trail
Treaty Party
Treaty of Coleraine
Osceola
Trail of Tears

Names, Terms and Concepts (continued)

Creek agency
Seminole War
Tsali
Ft. Mims
The Enchanted Land
Indian Claims
Horseshoe Bend
The Principal People
Commission

To Help You Study

1. What were the chief tribes in Georgia?
2. What was Tecumseh's attitude toward whites?
3. Where did the Creeks live? Who was their chief?
4. What effect did an earthquake have?
5. Tell your opinion of Benjamin Hawkins and what he did.
6. What happened at Ft. Mims and what was its effect?
7. What happened at Horseshoe Bend?
8. Were the Seminoles and the Creeks related? Who was the leader of the Seminoles?
9. What attitudes did the Cherokees have about learning to read?
10. What type of government did the Cherokees develop?
11. What do you remember about Auraria and Dahlonega?
12. What is your opinion of the Trail of Tears?

GEORGIA AND THE CIVIL WAR

CHAPTER 10

What was the Civil War? How did Georgia get into it? What happened here and what difference did it make?

The Civil War is sometimes called The War Between the States, a term some southerners prefer because it implies a war between two separate nations: the United States and the Confederate States of America. But one of the most important issues of the war was the question of whether or not states could secede, or withdraw, from the United States. And the answer given by the war was a definite "No!" Thus the war was a civil war between two factions of the same nation. Robert E. Lee referred to it as the Civil War and the term has now become almost universally accepted.

Gen. Robert E. Lee

What kind of war was the Civil War?

In order to understand the full impact of the Civil War, it should be remembered that it was not only a war of Americans against Americans, but of friends, neighbors and sometimes families against their dearest ones. Most Georgians, even those who were slow to favor secession, were for the Confederacy once it was established. But there were in north Georgia, especially in mountainous Union and Pickens counties, those who kept the United States flag flying throughout the war. Some families were like that of the Wilkes County man, Judge Garnett Andrews, who was loyal to the Union but whose children were passionately for the Confederacy.

How divisive was it?

Not only was the Civil War the most divisive war in American history, it was also the most deadly. Nearly as many men died in the Civil War as have been killed in the other eight wars the nation has fought combined. In the Civil War, 618,152 Americans died. In the other seven wars, over 646,000 died: 4,435 in the American Revolution; 2,260 in the War of

How many were killed compared to other wars?

1812; 1,733 in the Mexican War; 2,446 in the Spanish-American War; 116,563 in the first World War; 407,828 in the second World War; 54,246 in Korea; and 56,886 in Vietnam. In the Civil War, the North used 2.5 million soldiers and lost 360,000. The South had a million fighting and lost 258,000. Georgia sent 125,000 and lost more than 25,000—more than any other state in the Confederacy. The 3.5 million men who fought in the Civil War made other wars seem small. In the Battle of Fredericksburg alone, 200,000 men were fighting. Even at Waterloo, where Napoleon was defeated, only 170,000 men fought. The magnitude of the Civil War is still hard for Americans to grasp. As you think about Georgia and the war, you should not let these large numbers keep you from understanding the experiences of individuals. Events are important ultimately because they affect people.

BACKGROUND OF THE CIVIL WAR

As with any complex event, there was no one thing that caused the war. Many events, one after another, increased the bitterness and differences between the North and South. The 1850's had been a particularly violent decade. It was during this period of highly unsettled conditions that some historians find the initial wedges of separation driven between the two regions. Differences over slave states and free ones, of whether or not to buy Cuba, the decline of the established Whig Party and the emergence of Know Nothingism were features of the 1850's that set the stage for secession. But above all these events, economic discontent in the South and slavery were the triggers that finally resulted in secession.

What caused the war?

The economy of the North had exploded with development—a situation some historians refer to as the "**expansionist North**." Many individuals in the South were very skeptical of that development. The economy of the South was based on

What economic factors contributed to the war?

agriculture, not industry. This condition led many to believe that the South was economically dependent on the North for manufactured products. As early as 1837, a group of Georgians met in Augusta "to attempt a new organization of our commercial relations with Europe." It was thought that direct trade relations with Europe would break the dependency of the South on northern goods. This goal, along with the steamship line, was not realized.

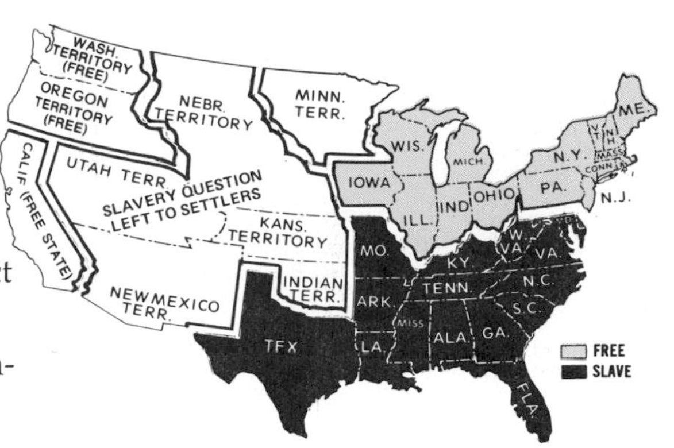

The United States in 1854

The northern expansion was supported by the national government. Northern capitalists, for example, obtained a monopoly over the shipbuilding business and trade between American ports. The northern fishing industry received a subsidy from the national government. New England manufacturers obtained a very favorable protective tariff. Again, this led many in the South to believe that there was a conspiracy between northern capitalists and the national government to exploit the South. In a speech before the Georgia Senate in 1860, Robert Toombs argued that the national government had no sooner been organized than "the Northern States evinced a general desire and purpose to use it for their own benefit, and to pervert its powers for sectional advantage, and they have steadily pursued that policy to this day." He concluded that the national treasury had become "a perpetual fertilizing stream to them and their industry, and a suction-pump to drain away our substance and parch our lands." In other words, Toombs and a number of other influential people in the South believed that the North had conspired with the federal government to drain the South of all its wealth. This feeling of economic exploitation was a powerful factor in the movement toward secession.

How did the nation support northern economic interests?

In addition to the economic situation, slavery in many ways was the crux of the problem. The historian Bruce Catton says, "Slavery was not the only cause of the Civil War, but it was the one cause without which the war would not have taken place." The South thought that a state should have the right to decide about slavery. Thus, the slavery question was also the political question of states' rights.

The Slavery Situation

Georgia had been the only original colony to forbid slavery. At the national level, Congress passed an act in 1807. It made bringing slaves into the country after Jan. 1, 1808, illegal. The Northwest Ordinance of 1787 had forbidden slavery in that territory.

How did slavery evolve in the South?

Most of the slaves were in the South because they worked in the cotton, rice and indigo fields. But slavery was expensive. It took one slave all day to separate a little cotton from the seeds. Then Eli Whitney invented the cotton gin and cotton became a money-making crop. This meant that more land and more slaves were needed to work in the fields. About 70,000 slaves were imported each year. By 1860 southerners owned four million. Some southerners moved west to get more land. The northerners feared that slavery would spread throughout the west. Slaveholders would then control Congress.

Many southerners had begun to feel that slavery was morally wrong but they were caught up in an economic system. They could not afford to lose the great amount of money they had invested in slaves. No way could be found to reimburse them. Besides, what would happen to four million black people uneducated and unprepared for freedom?

Some had suggested that the slaves be freed and established in a colony in Africa named Liberia. Alfred Cuthbert, a Georgia slave owner for whom Cuthbert was named, not only freed slaves. He paid their way to Liberia.

The Missouri Compromise Delays War

The question of slavery in the west first received national attention in 1820. Missouri wanted to come in as a slave state.

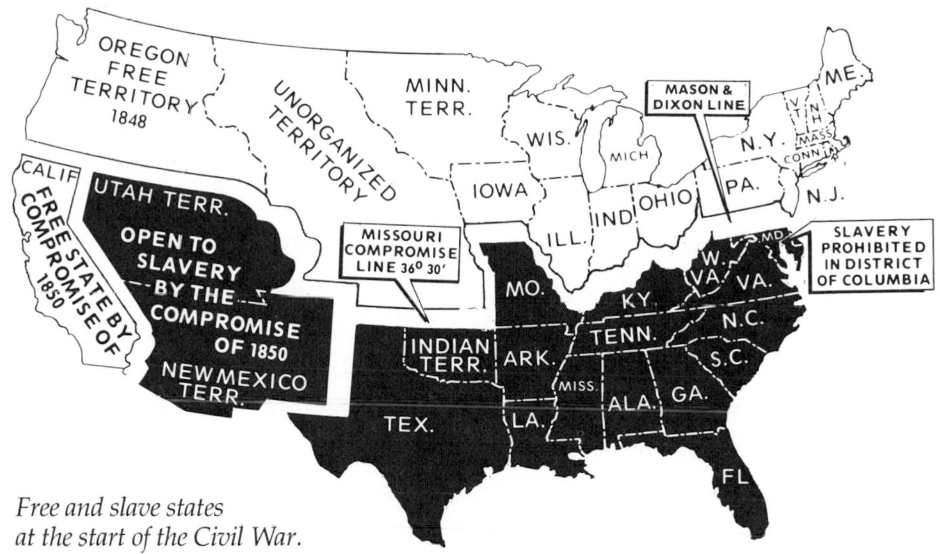

Free and slave states at the start of the Civil War.

There were then 11 slave states and 11 free states and, naturally, the North objected. Henry Clay proposed a compromise that said Missouri could come in as a slave state but that there could be no more slave states above the latitude of her southern border. It was just at this time, too, that Maine wanted to separate from Massachusetts. It came in as a free state. That kept the balance at 12-12 and enabled the Missouri Compromise to be accepted.

What was the problem requiring the Missouri Compromise?

The Missouri Compromise only postponed the showdown. Thirty years later the issue of slavery in new territories again threatened the Union. In 1850 Henry Clay worked out a new compromise over the admission of California as a free state. In this effort, Georgia played a significant role. There were three Georgians then in Congress: Alexander Stephens, Robert Toombs, and Howell Cobb. Georgia and the other slave states sent 157 men to a conference in Nashville, Tenn., to discuss the plan. Georgia's support became known in Congress as "The Georgia Platform." It said, "We do not like all the terms of this 1850 Compromise, but to keep the nation intact, we will go along with it. However, if the North continues to be aggressive, we will rescind our approval and the Union could possibly be dissolved."

What role did Georgians play?

Harriet Beecher Stowe

The nation rejoiced. Many felt that Georgia had made the 1850 Compromise possible. But the very things Georgia had warned the nation about happened.

The abolitionists became more furious than ever about slavery. In 1852 Harriet Beecher Stowe wrote *Uncle Tom's Cabin*, a novel about slavery. It helped hasten the Civil War. When Lincoln eventually met Mrs. Stowe, he said, "So this is the little woman who started a big war." When Georgia's Robert Toombs met her, he told her she did not know the facts or understand the situation.

How did the North and South compare in strength?

There were 33 states in the United States when the Civil War began. The North had 22 states with almost 22 million people. The South had 11 states and not quite nine million people. Of these, 3.5 million were black slaves and 260,000 were free blacks. There were also 429,501 slaves in the Union states.

Both sides thought the war would be short. Lincoln just asked soldiers to volunteer for three months. Seward, his secretary of state, said, "If I don't settle things in 60 days, I will give you my head for a football!" A southern leader said he would mop up with his handkerchief all the blood that would be spilled.

GEORGIA GETS INTO THE CIVIL WAR

Georgia faced the question of whether or not to secede from the nation it had helped found to become part of a new nation, the Confederate States of America. Some Georgians wanted to do this, others opposed it. At the end of the decade of the fifties the times were tight with tension.

What was Georgia like in 1860?

In 1860, Georgia had a total population of 1,057,286 people, half of them black. On the coast where the big plantations were, 80 per cent of the population were blacks. Georgia was a prosperous state. Its bountiful harvest of cotton and other crops, its growing industry, its state-owned property, such as the Western and Atlanta Railroad, made it one of the most promising of all the Confederate states. The war would take a terrible toll. Along with Georgians who were killed, the state would lose three-fourths of its property in the conflict. Sherman's March to the Sea would destroy over a hundred million dollars worth.

What was Georgia's law on importing slaves?

In 1798, Georgia passed a law forbidding importation of slaves for sale. In spite of this, it took 60 years for the the last slave ship to dock at Jekyll Island. Ironically, it was flying the colors of the New York Yacht Club! It was Nov. 28, 1858, and the ship brought a load of young boys in their teens. The mess kettle of this ship stands in front of Jekyll Museum, with this inscription: "This kettle from Slave Yacht *Wanderer* used for feeding the slaves landed on Jekyll Island, Nov. 28, 1858. Yacht owned by Charles A. L. Lamar of Savannah." Lamar was not on the *Wanderer* at the time. As a result he was later acquitted of violating Georgia's law. He became a colonel in the Confederate Army and ran the blockade for the South.

Mess kettle from the Wanderer.

Georgia Votes to Secede from the United States

What actions did Georgia take to secede from the Union?

Joseph Emerson Brown was born a poor boy but through diligent work became a millionaire. He also became governor of Georgia in 1857. He was a dark horse candidate that few people knew. Robert Toombs, traveling in Texas, asked "Who's Joe Brown?" He was elected governor of Georgia four times and served as the "war governor."

The Georgia legislature was in session when news of Lincoln's election came to the state. On Gov. Brown's recommendation the legislature appropriated a million dollars to prepare Georgia for the war. A part of the money was to pay for a special convention to meet in Milledgeville on Jan. 16, 1861, to decide whether Georgia would secede from the Union. It was a cold January day when the 297 delegates elected to serve in the convention arrived in Milledgeville. A few urged

A statue of Governor and Mrs. Joseph E. Brown.

that Georgia think long and carefully before seceding. Most were excited over the prospect of secession.

How did the leaders feel?

How did the leaders stand? It was an odd alignment. Alexander Stephens was against secession. His closest friend, Robert Toombs, was an ardent secessionist arguing that "we can whip the Yankees with cornstalks." Gov. Joe Brown was urgently for secession. He was a strong states' rights man. That deep conviction would often put him at odds with the Confederate president.

How did Georgia secede?

Actually, what the convention did was simply to rescind the 1788 ratification of the Constitution of the United States. This was the wording of the Ordinance of Secession:

An Ordinance To Dissolve The Union Between The State Of Georgia And Other States United With Her Under A Compact Of Government Entitled "The Constitution Of The United States."

We, the people of the State of Georgia, in convention assembled, do declare and ordain that the ordinance adopted by the people of the State of Georgia, in convention assembled, on the 2nd day of January, in the Year of Our Lord 1788, whereby the Constitution of the United States was assented to, ratified, and adopted, and also all Acts of the General Assembly ratifying and adopting amendments of the said Constitution, are hereby repealed.

We do further declare and ordain that the union now subsisting between the State of Georgia and other states, under the name of the United States of America, is hereby dissolved and that the State of Georgia is in full possession and exercise of all those rights of sovereignty which belong and appertain to free and individual states.

The vote was 208 to 89. Judge Eugenius Nisbet asked that even those who had voted against the resolution sign it. All of them did so. Alexander Stephens, who had been in opposition, stood loyally behind his state once the vote was taken.

Free states

Slaveholding states which did not secede

Slaveholding states which seceded before April 15, 1861

Slaveholding states which seceded after April 15, 1861

Georgians in the Organized Confederacy

By Feb. 1, 1861, six states had seceded from the Union: South Carolina, Georgia, Alabama, Mississippi, Louisiana and Florida. These six sent delegates to Montgomery, Ala., to organize the Confederate States of America. They elected as president Jefferson Davis of Mississippi, then serving as U.S. Senator from Mississippi. Leaving the Senate, he said, "Gentlemen of the North, a war is to be inaugurated, the like of which men have not seen."

Alexander Stephens of Georgia was elected vice president. He had been in Congress and had known Lincoln there. He had begged Georgia not to rush into secession but to wait and see what Lincoln did. Stephens' closest friend, Robert Toombs, was elected secretary of war. Toombs would have preferred to have been secretary of treasury. Many did consider him a financial genius. Toombs became bored with a cabinet job and soon resigned to take an active command on the battlefield.

Stephens was sent to Virginia to persuade the state to secede. He promised that the capitol would be moved to Richmond. When Virginia seceded, that move was made. One by one, the other southern states seceded and joined the original six. Virginia, Texas, Arkansas, Tennessee and North Carolina brought the total to 11 states. Four slave states, Maryland, Missouri, Kentucky and Delaware, remained in the Union. However, many men from two of those states fought with the South. As a result, the Confederate flag has 13 stars, although 11 states officially seceded.

Alexander Stephens

How were the Confederate States of America organized?

Who were its officials?

Why did the Confederate flag have 13 stars?

THE WAR YEARS

The capsule story of the war is simply that the South fought valiantly for its homes, its beliefs and its way of life. Only twice did the South invade northern territory; at Antietam and

Jefferson Davis

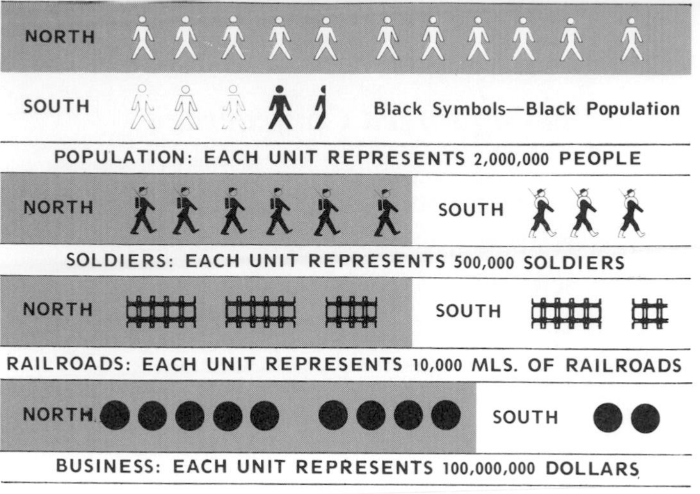

Strength of the North and South at the Outbreak of the War--1861.

What was the North's strategy?

Gettysburg. For the rest of the war, the Confederates were fighting on their own soil. The North aimed, as Gen. Grant put it, to "get control of the railroads and the rivers. Then face 'em and fight. Wear 'em down." Thus the North pursued a two-part strategy. The first part was to split the Confederacy in two. Sherman did this by his march through Georgia. The second part was to wear the South down by ceaseless fighting in the upper South, which Grant did against Lee.

The War in 1861

What happened at Fort Sumter?

Of the first year's events, the opening of the war at Ft. Sumter was the nearest to Georgia. Georgia's Robert Toombs, though an ardent secessionist, warned the Confederacy that firing on Sumter would be fatal. "It will unloose on us a swarm of hornets that would sting us to death, and start such a war as the world has never seen," he said. Gen. Beauregard, in command of Confederate forces in Charleston, ordered the firing to start at 4:30 on the morning of April 12, 1861. It kept up all day long, and through the next night: 33 hours. The Confederates fired 3,000 shells at the 12-foot walls. The heat at the fort was so intense that the men inside had to wrap wet rags around their faces to survive. Not a man on either side was killed in the shelling.

The fort's commander, Robert Anderson, surrendered at 2:30 p.m. Saturday, April 13. The Confederates allowed him to fire a 50-gun salute to the United States flag. Two of his gunners were killed in an explosion in this salute. Anderson tucked his flag under his arm and marched out with his men as his band played. The long, bloody war had started.

When the news spread over the South there was much rejoicing. Bells rang and torchlight parades were held. In Atlanta, they burned Lincoln in effigy.

The South had believed that European nations would readily support the Confederacy. "Cotton is king!" cried the South. A newspaper reporter from England, William Howard Russell, traveled through America writing about the war for his paper. He heard time and again in the South, "Your country will have to recognize our government because your looms will be empty, your factories will close, your workers will starve without cotton."

Why did the South think it had European support?

It did not happen. In the first place, England had a good supply of the South's cotton already on hand from the bumper crops of the two preceding years. Moreover, England's workers had read Harriet Beecher Stowe's *Uncle Tom's Cabin*. They were not enthusiastic about aiding an economy dependent on slaves. Also, they had been told by their leaders that if the South won, slavery would spread.

Why did England proclaim neutrality?

When the blockade of the southern coast from Virginia to Texas was at its height, Queen Victoria proclaimed England's neutrality as "between the two belligerents." Thereafter British merchants could legally buy from and sell to the South as well as the North. But the queen's act was far from the recognition the South wanted and needed.

The War in 1862

Lincoln had difficulty with the position of general-in-chief of the Union army in the initial year of the war. Actually, three

What kind of man was Grant?

What were some important battlefield events?

Why did the Great Locomotive Chase take place?

different men, Scott, McClellan and Halleck, served in that position. In 1861, a West Pointer named Ulysses S. Grant, who had left the army, reenlisted. Grant had never really found himself and had failed at several things in civilian life. He was an odd and silent man. He liked cucumbers for breakfast, sometimes drank a lot, and wore plain Army fatigues instead of the splendid regalia that many generals wore. After he captured several forts, Lincoln said, "I can't spare this man. He fights."

Several important battlefield events occurred in 1862. The South lost its brilliant Gen. Albert Sidney Johnston, who bled to death of battle wounds. The battle of the famous ironclads, the *Merrimac* and the *Monitor*, was also in 1862. The Federals captured Ft. Pulaski in Georgia, Corinth in Mississippi and Memphis in Tennessee. The South won the Seven Days' Battle near Richmond, the second Battle of Bull Run or Manassas, and Fredericksburg. At the Battle of Antietam a Maine regiment lost 700 of its 900 men in seven minutes, and a North Carolina regiment was completely wiped out. But neither side won.

During 1862, one of the most dramatic incidents of the Civil War, the **Great Locomotive Chase**, took place on April 12, 1862, at Kennesaw near Marietta.

The North planned to attack Chattanooga. They did not want the city to get help or supplies from Atlanta during the attack. The Western and Atlantic Railroad was a main line of supply. A daring Union spy, James J. Andrews of Flemington, Ky., said he could get into Atlanta, capture a train and drive it to Chattanooga. On the way, he proposed to burn bridges, cut telegraph wires and twist the rails behind him. In that way, the Confederates could not use the railroad to help Chattanooga. "I'll succeed or leave my bones in Dixie," he said.

On April 12, 1862, the anniversary of the firing on Ft. Sumter, the *General*, a locomotive, pulled out of the Atlanta train station before daylight. It hauled three freight cars, a baggage car, and several passenger coaches. In the coaches were Andrews and his 24 raiders disguised in civilian clothes. By morning, at a stop called Big Shanty seven miles north of Marietta, Andrews and his men hijacked the train. Capt. William A. Fuller, the conductor, witnessed the hijacking and ran after the train on foot. He had chased the train for three miles when he met some workers with a hand car. Later Fuller found a rickety old locomotive named *Yonah* and chased Andrews to Kingston. Andrews had been delayed in Kingston for an hour by trains coming in the other direction.

What happened during the chase?

Andrews' men filled up their boxcars with cross-ties and rails and threw them out to obstruct the pursuing locomotive. Fuller removed them, but when he came to places where the railroad was torn up, his locomotive was useless. He and his crew ran on foot to within three miles of Adairsville. There they commandeered an engine named *Texas* from a freight train. There was no time to turn it around, so they ran it backward all the way to Adairsville. Beyond Calhoun they came in sight of Andrews. There was a hot race for a few miles. Andrews dropped more cross-ties and rails. He even uncoupled his freight cars to block Fuller. But Fuller's men removed the obstructions in their path. At Resaca the *Texas* drove the *General* onto a siding. Both engines left this place and raced on toward Ringgold. There Andrews' Raiders, knowing they could be captured, jumped off the train and fled into the woods.

They were later captured. Andrews and seven of his men were hanged in Atlanta on June 7, 1862, at the corner of Peachtree and Ponce de Leon—just nine days before Andrews was to be married. Six others escaped from prison and made their way to federal lines.

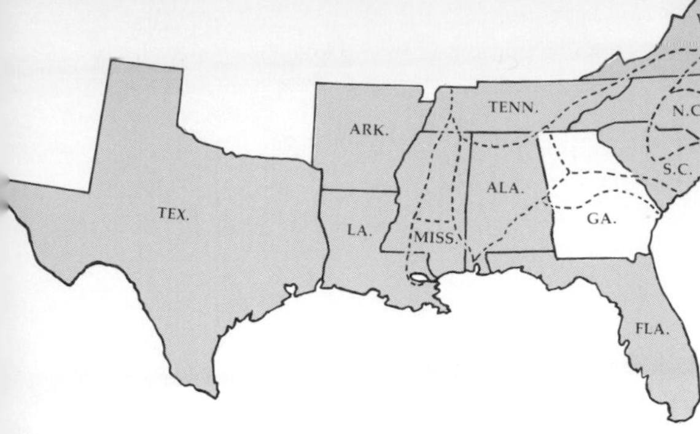

Railroads of the Confederacy

The *General* was regained by Georgia after a long case in the courts. It is now on exhibit at the Big Shanty Museum in Kennesaw. The *Texas* has long been on exhibit at the Cyclorama in Grant Park in Atlanta.

The War in 1863

Why was 1863 the beginning of the end of the Civil War?

The year 1863 was a crucial one in the Civil War. Among other things, Lincoln issued the **Emancipation Proclamation**. It was designed to free the slaves in the Confederate states effective Jan. 1, 1863.

In this year, the federals burned Darien, Georgia's Scotch Highlander town on the Altamaha. The South won at Chancellorsville, but paid the terrible price of the death of Stonewall Jackson. He was mistakenly shot by his own men. Grant took Vicksburg, Miss., in an important battle that meant that the North controlled the Mississippi River.

This year marked the beginning of the end for the Confederacy. Two events especially concerned Georgia. The first was when Lee was driven back from Gettysburg. An argument has gone on for years about whether Georgia's Gen. James Longstreet had caused it by his delay in bringing up troops. Gettysburg was one of the few battles fought in the North. It was also one of the world's bloodiest battles.

Later, Lincoln made a five-minute speech in which he said few people would notice and nobody would remember what he said there. But he was wrong. Lincoln's speech was the Gettysburg Address. Although many of his own people and the press made fun of it, those who came after thought it was one of the finest collections of words ever uttered. It is now inscribed in thousands of history books and on the back of Lincoln's statue. The statue was carved by Daniel Chester French out of Georgia marble.

The second event was the most terrible battle ever fought on Georgia soil. One of the worst in the Civil War, it was fought

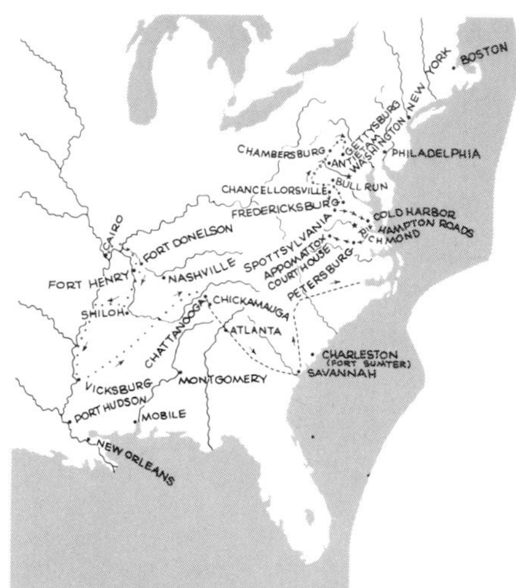

Campaigns of the Civil War

- Sherman's March
- Grant's Western Campaign
- Lee's Northern Invasion
- Grant's Eastern Campaign

Cabin of the Widow Snodgrass at the Chickamauga battleground.

The battleground at Chickamauga.

at **Chickamauga** in northwest Georgia on Sept. 19 and 20, 1863. The Union Army of the Cumberland was commanded by Maj. Gen. William S. Rosencrans. The Confederate Army of Tennessee was led by Lt. Gen. Braxton Bragg. Chickamauga is an old Indian word said to mean "the place of death." It was the place of death for 34,000 American soldiers. The South won, but at a terrible price.

Everybody expected Bragg to follow the defeated federal soldiers on to Chattanooga and keep pounding them until he made his victory complete. But he seemed unable to believe that he had won a victory. Gen. Ulysses S. Grant had been sent to rescue the Union Army at Chattanooga. He decisively defeated Bragg in a battle that lasted three days, from Nov. 23 through Nov. 25, 1863. This defeat drove the Confederates back into Georgia. In a few months a schoolteacher named Sherman would step over the Georgia line from Tennessee and Georgia would never be the same again.

The Georgians who died at Chickamauga are honored in the monument which stands on the Chickamauga Battlefield.

Why was the Battle of Chickamauga so decisive?

The War in 1864

In March 1864, Lincoln appointed Grant general-in-chief of the United States Armies. Gen. William Tecumseh Sherman took over his previous command. Grant and Sherman sat down at Ringgold and talked about how they could most effectively conquer the South. Sherman proposed that he split the Confederacy in two by marching through Georgia to the Atlantic Ocean. This would also cut off the "breadbasket" of the southern army and drastically limit its food supply. Grant was finally persuaded that it might work. He told Sherman he would talk the plan over with Washington and send him a telegram later.

What plan was worked out by Grant and Sherman?

After Bragg was defeated at Chattanooga he was replaced by Gen. Joe Johnston. Johnston took his troops to Dalton and set up winter quarters. A soldier wrote, "I am mity tired of this here war!"

In Virginia, Lee and Grant fought wearily through the long, hot summer in the Wilderness Campaign. Grant would lose 34,000 men in 16 days.

Early in May, Grant sat down on a log in Virginia. He took a pencil and wrote a telegram to Sherman at Chattanooga. The telegram gave Sherman permission to split the Confederacy in two by marching through Georgia. This would enable Sherman to get behind Lee's armies in Virginia while Grant fought Lee from the front.

Sherman was tall, nervous and red-haired. He chain-smoked cigars. He had once painted the Georgia mountains with his brushes. On May 5, 1864, Sherman's army walked down the mountain into Georgia, heading toward Atlanta and the sea.

What enabled Sherman to move quickly into Georgia?

Sherman, coming into Georgia, found the Snake Creek Gap pass unguarded by the Confederates. Records of the war do not reveal why it was unprotected. This made it possible for him to move swiftly into Dalton and later to win the battle at Resaca.

Sherman was determined to fight his way to Atlanta, destroy the city, and march to the sea, destroying Georgia as he went. He had 97,987 men. Just 25 miles down into Georgia ahead of him was Gen. Joe Johnston with 50,000 men. Johnston knew he was badly outnumbered. He believed the best thing to do was to retreat slowly, making Sherman's advance as costly as possible to the federals.

What was Johnston's plan?

Johnston moved to Resaca. There Gen. Leonidas Polk joined him with 24,000 more men. After three days of skirmishing, he moved on to Cassville. From there Johnston fell back behind the Etowah River at Allatoona Pass. Sherman struck out for Atlanta. The men marched down roads so dusty that the dust all but blinded and choked them. Then the skies darkened and it began to rain. It rained and rained and rained, for 17 days. Men trudged through mud and wagons bogged down in the mire.

Johnston moved to intercept. The two armies clashed at Pumpkin Vine Creek and New Hope Church, near Dallas in Paulding County. The terrible two-day battle was fought in the rain, on May 25-26, 1864. It was like a spectacle out of some grim old drama. Lightning flashed, thunder roared, and the woods were lighted with such pine torches as would flame in the rain. In the kitchens of the little houses around the battlefield, the amber glow of lamplight shone as surgeons flashed silver knives amputating limbs of men whose lives they hoped to save. Through the wet woods, the moans and groans of the wounded and dying could be heard between the awful claps of thunder.

What happened at Pumpkin Vine Creek?

After the bloody fighting around Dallas, the armies moved east to the mountains near Marietta. Here were Pine Mountain, Lost Mountain, and Kennesaw Mountain—all fortified by the Confederates. Most Civil War battles just lasted a few days. The battle of Kennesaw Mountain in Georgia lasted a month. Sherman kept attacking Hood's forces there and lost many men. The mountain paths were piled with the bodies of blue-clad soldiers who died. Sherman finally withdrew.

Johnston moved to the north bank of the Chattahoochee River. Sherman sent troops around and got between him and

Atlanta. Sherman later wrote of these maneuvers, "I always thought Johnston missed his chance here. He lay comparatively idle while we got control of both banks of the river above him." Georgia was alarmed that Johnston would not fight. Leaders in the state asked Davis to replace him. General J. B. Hood was named as commander. Sherman was delighted since he considered Johnston the most able of the southern generals.

Battle of Atlanta at the world-famous Cyclorama

On Sept. 2, 1864, Sherman was in Atlanta. Hood's men fought desperately to save the city. A Union officer, Capt. George Pepper, wrote, "The Rebels fought with a fierceness seldom if ever equalled. They stood firm as a rock though our artillery cut them down. No life was worth a farthing now . . ." Some in Atlanta asked Sherman to show mercy to the people. Sherman felt that the worse one could make a war, the more quickly it would be over. Sherman gave orders to set fire to the city on Nov. 15, 1864. Then he cut loose from his Allatoona supply lines and headed toward Savannah. He and his army lived off the country until he could get to his supply ships at the seashore.

How did Sherman get around Johnston?

Why did Sherman burn Atlanta?

Sherman divided his marching men into two lines. Each

line sometimes divided for foraging supplies or for off-path destruction. The two lines of march were planned to go by Milledgeville, then the state capital, and by Macon. His men ate what they could, and destroyed the rest. They poured out syrup, ruined the meat in smokehouses, burned cotton in the field, and set fire to many houses. They often destroyed fine furniture, looted homes, and frightened women and children. They destroyed hundreds of miles of Confederate railroads. Sherman wrote General Halleck, "If the people raise a howl against my barbarity and cruelty, I will answer that this is war and not a popularity contest. If they want peace, they and their relatives must stop the war."

What were Sherman's routes to the sea?

Andersonville National Historic Site.

In another part of the state, near Americus, **Andersonville prison** was opened. It received its first prisoners in February. By war's end, 49,485 prisoners had been sent there, without shelter and with little food and no medicine. More than 13,000 prisoners died. Whose fault was it? The United States government tried and hanged the doctor, Capt. Henry Wirz, who had been commander of the prison. But the argument about the treatment of northern and southern prisoners goes on forever: 22,576 died in southern prisons; 26,436 in northern prisons.

As it became apparent that the Confederacy was about to fall, Davis tried desperate measures. Lincoln and Seward agreed to meet his representatives, including Vice President Alexander Stephens of Georgia, on a boat at Hampton Roads to talk about peace. But Lincoln would not hear of any peace on grounds less than total surrender and the maintenance of the Union.

What were the conditions at Andersonville prison?

What were the first peace efforts?

When this peace effort failed, Davis held a mass meeting on a snowy day, Feb. 6, in Richmond. He told his people that the peace effort had failed. But he still urged them to keep up their hopes that the South could win. On March 18, 1865, the Confederate legislature adjourned. Most of them knew in their hearts that they would never convene again. Davis' cabinet continued to meet, since Davis believed that there was still hope for the Confederacy.

Sherman's army entering Savannah.

Lee's dispatches grew darker. He could hold the lines only a few days longer. Davis had sent his family away. At St. Paul's Episcopal Church an usher brought Davis a note. It was from Lee. The fall of Richmond was a matter of hours. Davis got up and walked out of the church. Davis and his cabinet left Richmond. They would hold their last session in Georgia in the town of Washington.

THE WAR ENDS

Where did Lee surrender?

By April 1865, it was clear to most southern leaders that the South was about to be defeated. It was outnumbered four to one. It was blockaded so that it could not sell its cotton or get needed supplies from England.

On April 9, 1865, Grant went to meet Lee at **Appomattox Courthouse**. There Lee surrendered. Grant allowed the southerners to keep their horses and mules to make their spring planting. He also sent Lee's hungry men food. After the surrender had been signed, Lee mounted his horse Traveller and went home.

Five days after Lee surrendered, John Wilkes Booth, an

actor, shot Abraham Lincoln in Ford's Theater. The president, his wife, and some friends had gone to see a play entitled *Our American Cousin*. The next morning Lincoln died, on a bed in a house across the street from the theater. Fanatics in the North immediately charged Jefferson Davis with involvement in the murder. Posters were issued offering rewards for his capture.

$100,000

REWARD!

IN GOLD.

Headquarters Cav. Corp.,
Military Division Mississippi,
Macon, Ga., May 6, 1865.

One Hundred Thousand Dollars Reward
in Gold, will be paid to any person or persons who will apprehend and deliver **JEFFERSON DAVIS** to any of the Military authorities of the United States.

Several millions of specie, reported to be with him, will become the property of the captors.

J. H. WILSON,
Major-General, U. S. Army,
Commanding.

Lincoln's death was a tragedy for the South, for he had compassionate plans for its treatment. His theory was that they had never really been out of the Union. As early as 1863, he had offered to recognize any state in which ten percent of the 1860 voters petitioned for it. This would include a pardon to any southerner who took the oath of allegiance to the United States. He said to his aides, "Let 'em up easy!"

What were Lincoln's plans for the south?

Jefferson Davis was arrested near this Irwinville home.

Mrs. Jefferson Davis

Alexander Stephens Goes to Prison

Alexander Stephens was at his home, Liberty Hall in Crawfordville, playing a card game with his friends. Some

What happened to Stephens?

one told him that federal officers had arrived in town. "I expect they have come for me," he said.

Quietly, he had his servant pack his bags. In 15 minutes he was on his way to prison in Ft. Warren, Boston Harbor. The frail little Georgian was a sick man. He was released from prison on Oct. 12, after a five-month stay. The war did not end his career. He was elected to the U.S. Congress and served a brief time as governor of Georgia.

Stephens' statue is in the front yard of Liberty Hall, where he is buried. On the statue is his favorite saying, "I am afraid of nothing . . . but to do wrong."

Robert Toombs

Robert Toombs an Exile

Big, colorful Bob Toombs went to his white-columned home in Washington, Ga. One day federal Gen. Wilde came to arrest him. Mrs. Toombs invited the officer and his soldiers into the parlor. She kept them talking while her husband escaped out the back door. Finally suspicious, the federals threatened to burn the house unless Toombs appeared and submitted to arrest. "Then you will have to burn it," said Mrs. Toombs. They searched the whole house.

What was the career of Toombs after the War?

The son of a neighbor took Toombs' horse to him in the woods. Toombs rode off with the young lieutenant and spent some weeks riding over Georgia, hidden by friends. Then he sailed for Cuba and to Europe in July. He sold his lands in Texas because he needed money in his exile. "I eat an acre a day," he wrote. Sad and lonely, and grieving for a daughter who had died, Toombs came home. He went to talk with President Andrew Johnson and was allowed to return to Georgia unmolested.

Historical marker at the home of Robert Toombs.

Toombs became a power in Georgia politics again. He was to be the guiding genius in the 1877 revision of the Georgia Constitution. Toombs sat there with his unlighted cigar, his linen duster, and sometimes his brown straw hat, and spoke his mind. "Listen to Toombs talking," said a friend, "and him with no more vote than a chicken." His civil rights had been taken away until he swore allegiance again to the United States. He never did.

"Have you asked them for a pardon?" inquired a friend.

"A pardon? I've done nothing to ask forgiveness for—and I haven't pardoned them yet!" he shouted.

To this day he is known as Georgia's "Unreconstructed Rebel."

Sherman After the War

Perhaps the most astonishing post-war career was that of the despised Sherman. He actually became a champion of the South which he had ruined. He came back to Atlanta as a guest!

What was Sherman's attitude after the War?

Sherman not only visited Atlanta, he lectured all over the country, and was in great demand. A friend said, "His last 25 years was just one long chicken dinner." He also wrote his memoirs. He wrote:

> I confess without shame that I am sick and tired of fighting. Its glory is all moonshine. Fighting men want peace. Only those who never heard shot nor shriek nor groan of the wounded and dying, cry aloud for more blood, more vengeance, more desolation. I know the rebels are whipped to death and I declare before God that as a man and soldier, I will not strike a foe who stands unarmed before me. Brave men never attack the conquered, nor mutilate the dead.

Sherman despised the adulation of crowds. "Read history. Read Coriolanus," he said. "You will see the true measure of popular applause. Vox populi, vox humbug." He died in February 1891 at age 71.

THE WAR AND THE CIVILIAN GEORGIAN

How did the war affect civilians?

The war is an endless storehouse for a number of thought experiments. History tends to concentrate more on the participants in and especially the leaders of any event. Therefore, it would be well if you thought long and carefully about the civilian "nonparticipants." Though not fighting, they were affected deeply and personally.

Listen to the words of a woman near the end of the war. Mary Boykin Chesnut wrote in her diary, "How grateful I was today when a friend sent me a piece of chicken . . . my pantry is empty . . . I have no wood to burn . . . and cannot afford sackcloth to wail in . . . Enough! I will write no more." Think carefully and analytically about the hardship that women experienced. Try to understand the grief and sadness that was theirs as they heard of the death of a husband or son, or of the deep sorrow they felt as they watched their homes burn.

In Rome, there is a monument to the women of the Confederacy. The inscription on it was written by Woodrow Wilson:

> To the women of the Confederacy, whose fidelity, courage and gentle genius in love and in counsel kept the home secure, the family a school of virtue, the state a court of honor, who made of war a season of heroism, of peace a time of healing, the guardians of our tranquility and of our strength.

Was Wilson exaggerating or was he accurate? Think about the role of women during the Civil War. Listen to the words of an Atlanta girl, Carrie Berry, who wrote in her diary while Sherman was in the city:

> We could not sleep because we were afraid the soldiers might set fire to our house. They behaved very badly, I thought, going around setting people's houses on fire. Wish I could go to school. We are having all holidays. I work at home

> and sleep if mosquitoes don't bite too much. Soldiers pace back and forth but orderly. We are all in so much trouble. Mamma is so worried. Papa does not know where to go. We had stewed chicken. It is a dark rainy day. The last train has left. We are obliged to stay now.

This girl was ten years old when she wrote those words. How do you think she felt? Do you sense that she was frightened? Brave? What would have been your feelings and thoughts had you watched Atlanta burned by Sherman's soldiers?

The toll of the war was indeed high in terms of the numbers of soldiers killed and wounded. Add to that the suffering and anguish of unknown millions of civilians from both the North and the South. When you do, the ultimate costs of the war begin to surpass the imagination.

For Extending Thinking

1. Did everyone in Georgia support the Civil War?
2. Evaluate the complex factors that caused the Civil War.
3. Discuss Georgia's laws on slavery and describe the slavery situation in the state at the beginning of the Civil War.
4. Describe the actions leading up to Georgia's secession from the Union.
5. Imagine yourself a participant in the Great Locomotive Chase. What would you have experienced?
6. What strategy did Grant and Sherman work out? Did it prove effective?
7. How did the war come to an end?

Names, Terms and Concepts

a civil war
Ordinance of Secession
Chickamauga
expansionist north
Ft. Sumter
Snake Creek Gap Pass
Missouri Compromise
Battle of Antietam
Battle of Pumpkin Vine Creek
states' rights
The *General*
Henry Clay
The *Texas*
Kennesaw Mountain
the Georgia Platform

Names, Terms and Concepts (continued)

Andersonville Prison
Harriet Beecher Stowe
Appomattox Courthouse
Gettysburg Address
Unreconstructed Rebel

To Help You Study

1. Discuss the meaning of the terms "The Civil War" and "The War Between the States."
2. Do you think the Civil War was bad? Do you think there was anything good about it?
3. Discuss the secession convention, its activities and the results.
4. One Georgian held a high office in the Confederacy. Who was he and why was it unusual for him to get the office?
5. Do you think it was smart for the Confederates to fire on Ft. Sumter?
6. What do you think of the Battle of Chickamauga? Which side won? Did the victors take advantage of the enemy's defeat?
7. What was the most important event of the war in 1864?
8. Do you think Sherman did right in burning Atlanta and a 60-mile wide path to Savannah?
9. Tell about the role and condition of women in the war.
10. Do you think Davis and Stephens should have been put in prison? Why?

CHAPTER 11

ASHES AND PRIDE

THE BEGINNINGS OF MODERN GEORGIA

When the fighting ended in April 1865, Georgia found itself almost prostrate. Land was half its pre-war value. Most of the railroads had been destroyed; Sherman had torn up over 300 miles of them. There was little money and no credit. The state cancelled taxes for the years 1864 and 1865. There was so little food that Kentucky sent Georgia a hundred thousand bushels of corn in 1866. People had few seeds to plant for new crops. Cotton, once a dollar a pound, was four cents. There were few farm tools, no slaves to work the land, and little machinery. The towns and cities were swarming with people who had fled from farm to factory seeking jobs that did not exist. Robert E. Lee advised the South to work with the North, do the best they could, and cooperate with the inevitable.

What were the conditions in Georgia after the Civil War?

THE DARK DAYS OF RECONSTRUCTION

On June 17, 1865, President Andrew Johnson appointed James Johnson as provisional governor of the state. He was a Columbus lawyer who had fought against secession and had taken little part in the war. Johnson took office in July. He immediately ordered elections for delegates to a constitutional convention to meet in Milledgeville in October. The convention was to meet the requirements for readmission to the Union, adopt a new constitution and elect a governor. Governor Johnson told Georgia leaders that they must abolish slavery and repudiate their war debt. This was necessary to

What did Governor Johnson tell Georgia it would have to do?

The restored Governor's Mansion at Milledgeville.

reestablish the state's credit and because Georgians held many Confederate bonds. Georgia then thought it was ready for readmission to the Union.

But it became clear by the end of 1865 that the fanatical abolitionists in Congress were determined to overrule President Johnson's conciliatory policy and punish the South. They claimed that by trying to secede, the states had returned to the status of territories. This, they argued, placed them under the jurisdiction of Congress. They insisted that military rule be established. They argued that no state could re-enter the Union until it gave blacks the right to vote.

What was the position of the radical abolitionists?

The South was divided into five military districts. Georgia was in the third, with Florida and Alabama. On March 30, 1867, Gen. John Pope arrived to take command. The military commanders were directed to register those who were to be allowed to vote. Many blacks could, though they had little preparation. Few white people were allowed to vote. No one who had been a Confederate leader or owned $20,000 worth of property could register. In May, Pope closed the University of Georgia when a student at graduation annoyed him with a speech.

Congress set up a committee to investigate the situation in the South and to decide what should be done. President Johnson vetoed the harsh measures that resulted from the investigation. Congress passed them over his veto. President Johnson and the Congress began to have severe conflict. Congress passed the 1867 Tenure Law forbidding the president from firing even the members of his own cabinet. Johnson fired Secretary of War Edwin Stanton on Aug. 5, 1867. For this he was impeached by the House of Representatives. Only one vote saved him from being convicted by the Senate. Even though he escaped removal from office, much of the president's power was gone.

What were the positions of the president and congress?

Governor Jenkins Saves Georgia's Money

Gov. Charles Jenkins was in office when the convention met to adopt the new 1868 constitution. That document finally abolished imprisonment for debt in Georgia—a strange law to have existed in a state that had been colonized in part out of sympathy for debtors in Britain.

The convention cost $40,000. When Gen. Pope demanded this money, Gov. Jenkins refused to pay it. Gen. George Meade, who succeeded Pope, also demanded the money. When it was not paid, Meade removed Jenkins from office. Jenkins hid the executive seal, took the $426,704.42 from the state treasury to a bank in New York for safekeeping, and went to Nova Scotia. Four years later, when he returned the money, the Georgia legislature gave him a replica of the seal with the words *In arduis fidelis* (faithful under difficulties) inscribed thereon. The seal is visible in a big painting of Jenkins that hangs in the State Capitol in Atlanta.

How did Jenkins save Georgia's money?

Bullock Elected Governor

The constitution was approved in April 1868. Rufus Bullock of Augusta was elected governor. Gen. Meade left Georgia, leaving Bullock in charge. Bullock's regime was notoriously extravagant and corrupt. He was forced to resign and left Georgia. He was later indicted and returned to face trial, but he was never convicted.

Georgia was finally readmitted to the Union on July 15, 1870, and obtained control of its own government again. In 1877, President Rutherford B. Hayes removed the last of the federal troops from the South.

SOME GEORGIANS ADAPT, SOME LEAVE

When were the last federal troops withdrawn?

When Georgians got their government back, they were not all in one accord. Some adapted well while others responded negatively. At least one group actually left the state.

What was the condition of blacks after the Civil War?

Blacks After the War

During the Civil War, most blacks stayed on the farms carrying on their work. Their situation changed after the war was over. Many of the plantations had been destroyed and others neglected. Many blacks simply began to work for wages or a share of the crops. Georgia finally adopted the Fourteenth and Fifteenth amendments to the United States Constitution, guaranteeing their citizenship and voting rights. Some, influenced by carpetbaggers, joined in the political organizations that began to grow up in each state.

How the Ku Klux Klan Began

The Ku Klux Klan came into existence almost by accident. Six young veterans near Pulaski, Tenn., had been attending a masked party just before Christmas and were returning home. They and their horses were disguised in white bedsheets. Blacks they met on the road were frightened by the strange sight, thinking them to be the ghosts of Confederate dead. Immediately some southerners believed that they had found an effective way to control blacks.

How and why did the Ku Klux Klan develop?

The name Ku Klux originated from the Greek word *kuklos*, which means circle. Soon the Ku Klux Klan was organized and spread over the southern states. Gen. Nathan Bedford Forrest was said to have become Grand Wizard. This was not proved at the 1871 congressional investigation of the Klan. Lee himself had declined to be the Klan's leader. After the war Forrest moved to Memphis and went into the railroad business. He began organizing Klan units throughout the South at the same time. In Georgia, Gen. John B. Gordon was the reputed head of the Klan.

Statue of Gen. Nathan Bedford Forrest.

Improved education slowly reduced the Klan's power and it became unacceptable to most Georgians. The original Klan was formally dissolved in March 1869.

2,000 Confederates Move to Brazil

Many people in the South felt they could not adjust to defeat and the rule of the federals. About 2,000 of them moved to Brazil, which did not abolish slavery until 1888. Most were farmers who introduced the plow, harrow and better farming methods into the community. They also introduced pecans and watermelons, especially the melon called Georgia Rattlesnake.

What happened to the Georgians who went to Brazil?

Some of these people returned to the South; others died and are buried in Brazil. In April 1972, Gov. Jimmy Carter was on a Latin American tour. He visited a cemetery where confederates are buried, some 80 miles from Sao Paulo, Brazil. The largest number of them lived in a town called Americana, Brazil. Their descendants today speak Portuguese as well as

English. They go back to the little chapel with the cemetery for services every three months. A Confederate flag hangs over the pulpit. But the leaders say, "We have stopped fighting the Civil War."

Gov. Carter carried several copies of *This Is Your Georgia* with him on his Latin American tour. He gave copies to officials in each of the nations he visited.

Henry Grady Leads the Way

Henry W. Grady

Many people worked to build a better Georgia on the ruins of the Civil War. The clearest voice was that of a newspaper editor named Henry Grady. He did much to heal the old hurts and unite the state again.

Henry Grady was born in a four-room cottage in Athens on May 24, 1850. As he grew up, one of his playmates was a girl named Julia King. Later, writing about her, he said, "I fell out of my baby carriage trying to reach out to Julia in hers. When she was 12 and I was 14, I asked her to marry me. I said, `If you will say "Yes," wear a yellow dress to the picnic and wave a handkerchief at me.'"

When they grew up, they married. Their home was in Atlanta, where Grady became editor of the *Atlanta Constitution.* A member of his staff was Joel Chandler Harris, the creator of the Uncle Remus tales. Grady attracted the attention of the nation with his stories about the earthquake that shook the South and almost demolished Charleston, S.C. So, later, he was listened to as he wrote and spoke on what the South should do about rebuilding into prosperity and greatness. He urged his people not to sit mourning about the past, but to face the future believing that it could be bright.

One speech dramatically focused attention on Georgia's need to manufacture its own products. He argued that the state should use its resources and not let them be sent out to enrich the owners of factories in the North. This is what he said:

> I attended a funeral in a Georgia county. It was a poor, one-gallused fellow. They buried him in the midst of a marble quarry; they cut through solid marble to make his grave; yet the little tombstone they put above him was from Vermont. They buried him in the midst of a pine forest, but his pine coffin was imported from Cincinnati. They buried him within touch of an iron mine, but the nails in his coffin and the iron in the shovel that dug his grave were from Pittsburgh. They buried him in a New York coat, a Boston pair of shoes, a pair of breeches from Chicago, and a shirt from Cincinnati. Georgia furnished only the corpse and a hole in the ground.

What was Henry Grady's message to Georgia?

On Dec. 13, 1886, Grady went to New York to speak at a banquet at the old Delmonico's Restaurant. One of the guests was Gen. William Tecumseh Sherman, who had burned Atlanta. Grady said,

> I want to say to General Sherman, who is considered an able man in our parts, but kind of careless with fire, that from the ashes he left us in 1864, we have built a brave and beautiful city in Atlanta, that we have caught the sunshine in the brick and mortar of our homes, and have builded therein not one ignoble prejudice or memory.

Grady died on Dec. 23, 1889. Seven thousand people came to his funeral. The *New York Tribune* said, "Never was a private person so universally mourned."

A monument to Henry Grady.

INDUSTRY AND AGRICULTURE DEVELOP AGAIN

There were nearly 50,000 fewer people in Georgia after the war than when it began. Many had been killed, some had moved to other states, and a few had gone to South America or Europe.

How much did Georgia develop between 1870 and 1900?

The period between 1870 and the end of the century is sometimes referred to as a 30-year depression. Many Georgians had a hard time making a living. But Georgia's population doubled in those 30 years to 2,216,331. The number of factories doubled too and their output actually tripled. Georgia's products of field, farm and forest became more important than ever. So the experience of this era is very mixed indeed. Benjamin Hill described it as "one of those rare junctures in human affairs where one civilization ends and another begins."

How did the expositions help Georgia?

In 1881, there began the first of several expositions that brought more than a million visitors to see Georgia products and talents. The Liberty Bell was brought from Philadelphia. A replica of it now stands on Capitol Square. When men in the North and elsewhere saw what was possible in Georgia, they began to invest more money in the state. The expositions had paid off.

The break-up of the plantation system brought many workers into the towns. Along with this, the establishment of factories encouraged the growth of towns and cities. Along the fall line, where the rivers created water power, Augusta, Columbus and Macon became centers for the manufacture of textiles. Textiles began to bring more money into the state. In addition, there was a growing market for Georgia's bountiful lumber supply.

Georgia had more railroads than any other state except Texas. These railroads connected the state with the north and the west. The work on the railroads brought many white laborers from other countries.

Men seeking ways to make a living took to the gold mines again. In 1880, more than a million dollars' worth of gold came out of Georgia.

There was more than gold in the hills. Former Gov. Joe Brown added coal mining to his many other business enterprises. The state also had stone, especially granite and limestone. And it was just beginning to discover that its marble was beautiful enough to provide many of the world's finest buildings and statues. Daniel Chester French used 28 blocks (some weighing 40 tons) to carve the brooding statue of Lincoln in the memorial in Washington, D.C. In the capital, too, the Folger Shakespeare Library, the Pan American Building and the Corcoran Art Gallery are among the structures built of Georgia marble. As the century came to an end, the world had learned about the beauty of Georgia marble.

Georgia's current industry would astonish and gratify those early promoters like Henry Grady.

A NEW CAPITOL AND A NEW STYLE POLITICS

The powerful social forces that were working to stimulate industry and agriculture were also affecting government and politics. The last 30 years of the 1800's were times of great political division within the state. Some, like Henry Grady, wanted the monied men of the north to invest in Georgia. Farmers thought that northern capitalists, and the Georgia leaders who worked with them, devised benefits for the factory workers but not for the farmers. This sentiment was to result in the growth of farm groups and political parties strong enough to change the situation.

How did economic development cause division in the State?

Atlanta: The New Capitol

When they ratified their new constitution, the people of Georgia also voted to keep their capitol in Atlanta where it had been during the Reconstruction era. As a railroad center, Atlanta was becoming more and more the center of the economic life of the state, and a gateway to the southeast as well.

Why was Atlanta chosen as Georgia's capitol?

In 1883, the legislature authorized the construction of a new capitol building. When the bids were opened, the lowest bid designated Indiana limestone as the building material. The next bid specified Georgia marble. Many Georgians were later to lament that the exterior of the capitol was not built of Georgia marble! The legislature had appropriated one million dollars for the construction of the new building. When it was finished, $118.43 was left over.

The building was completed in 1889. Inside, there are the offices of the governor and the two legislative chambers. On the fourth floor is an interesting museum with displays depicting the life and products of the state. In the rotunda under the golden dome is Statuary Hall. Here are found marble busts of many great Georgians of the past. Around the walls are dozens of portraits of great Georgians of yesterday and today.

The statue on top of the golden dome is called "Miss Freedom." Some mistake her for a replica of the Statue of Liberty. The steel statue is 15 feet tall and holds a torch in one hand and a sword in the other. Beneath her feet is the gold-washed dome that began glistening in 1959 with gold from Dahlonega. It again glistened brightly in 1981 when it was replated once more with gold from Dahlonega. Two new state office buildings have been completed near the capitol.

The Bourbon Triumvirate

Three men, Joe Brown, John B. Gordon, and Alfred Colquitt, wielded great influence after the war. They were dubbed the **Bourbon Triumvirate**.

Joe Brown had been arrested after the South lost the war, and sent to prison. After he came back, he advised Georgians to work with the northerners. He himself joined the Republican party. "I didn't leave the Democratic party; it left me," he said. This made him very unpopular.

What was Joe Brown's role in Georgia politics?

Gov. James Johnson made Brown Chief Justice of the Georgia Supreme Court. He soon resigned to become president of a railroad. Brown became a rich man. In alliance with Colquitt and Gordon he wielded tremendous political power. Deep in his heart, Brown keenly felt his repudiation by the people whom he had led through the war. It was always his ambition to be politically accepted by his people again.

When John B. Gordon suddenly and unexpectedly resigned from the United States Senate in 1880, Gov. Alfred Colquitt appointed Brown to fill the vacancy. Many Georgians were indignant. One city tolled the bells, as if mourning for the dead. Many people charged the "Bourbon Triumvirate" with "trading," particularly when Gordon got a $14,000 job with Brown's railroad. But all three denied it.

Gen. John B. Gordon was the first Georgia governor to occupy the new state capitol in 1889. He had been elected in 1886. It was a very strange election.

Gen. Benjamin Hill had died and a statue of him was to be unveiled in Atlanta. (This statue now stands in the capitol.) The aging Jefferson Davis came from his home in Mississippi, with his daughter Winnie.

Henry Grady, who was in charge of arrangements, had Gordon meet the Davises in Alabama and ride on the train with them to Atlanta. Davis, whom crowds swarmed to see, was too feeble to speak. He let Gordon speak for him. In Atlanta, he rode in a coach drawn by six white horses. About 1,000 old soldiers marched behind, and 6,000 school children threw flowers in his path.

Thousands came to the unveiling of the statue. The many Confederate veterans who were there were touched at the sight of their old military leaders, Davis and Gordon. As the ceremonies began, Gen. James Longstreet arrived from his home at Gainesville, and the three leaders had a touching reunion. The crowd went wild.

This launched a campaign for governor which Gordon won. Confederate veterans, some of them with only one arm or leg, helped at the polls. Gordon made a good governor.

How was Gordon elected governor?

The third man in the trio of power was Alfred Colquitt. He was the son of a wealthy Georgia planter. Both father and son were preachers. A graduate of Princeton, he served as a soldier in the Mexican War and as a major general in the Confederate Army. In 1877 Alfred Colquitt defeated Jonathan Norcross for governor by the biggest majority that Georgia voters had ever given a governor.

The Bourbon Triumvirate rescued Georgia from the Carpetbaggers and the Scalawags. However, they dominated Georgia politics for so long that many began to feel that the state needed to be free from them. The first real revolt against their power was in a Congressional race. It foreshadowed the farmers' revolt in the 1890's.

The Farmers' Revolt and the Independents

There was tremendous power in the farm vote in Georgia. In 1888, Georgians organized a branch of the Farmers' Alliance, which had started in the west earlier. It was an organization dedicated to improving life on the farm. Farmers soon came to realize that in politics lay the power to make these improvements. They developed a strong core of Independents in revolt against the regular Democrats.

What was the Farmers Alliance?

The Independents were led by Dr. and Mrs. William H. Felton of Cartersville. The initial warnings of political discontent came when Felton opposed the regular Democratic nominee for Congress. This was in the district around Cartersville known as the Bloody Seventh.

Felton had the help of a remarkable wife, Rebecca Latimer

Felton, who grew up in Decatur. She attended the academy at Madison, where she graduated at 17 with first honors. The commencement speaker was W. H. Felton, a doctor-lawyer-farmer. A year later, they were married. Settling on their farm in the Etowah Valley, they became a powerful team in Georgia life and politics. They wrote letters, edited a paper and made political speeches.

What positions did the Feltons take?

The Feltons were strongly opposed to the convict lease system. Under that system, farmers, manufacturers and others could lease prisoners from the state. Sometimes they were paid less than a dime a day. The leased convicts were frequently starved, overworked, and badly housed. Many became ill and died.

The Feltons were outraged by this degrading system. They joined Tom Watson's powerful voice in opposing it. It was not until years later—in 1908—that the convict system was abolished.

In 1881, prodded by the Feltons, the Independents turned to the aging Alexander Stephens as a candidate for governor. He had served his state for many years and the people loved him.

The home of Alexander Stephens, Liberty Hall in Crawfordville.

The kitchen at Liberty Hall.

But Stephens accepted the Democratic, not the Independent, nomination for governor. The Feltons and other Independents were furious. Mrs. Felton never wrote to him again.

What was the significance of Stephens' election as governor?

In the election Stephens defeated the Independent candidate. The Independents never recovered from this blow. But they had forced the regular Democrats to accept most of their platform for reform. In this way, the Independents broke the power of the Bourbons.

After her husband died, Mrs. Felton kept up her activities. These included lending her talents to politicians whom she favored, among them her friend Tom Watson. By the late century she was crusading for women's rights. Until 1879, for example, a woman who worked had no legal right to her own pay. Any employer who refused to turn it over to her husband or father, if asked, could be made to pay double!

What were Mrs. Felton's continuing activities?

In 1899, when she was 65, Hoke Smith hired Mrs. Felton to write for his *Atlanta Journal*. For 20 years thereafter rural readers were powerfully influenced by her advice about how to improve their homes, rear their children, and vote. Politicians feared her and courted her favor. She was sarcastic about the "ring of rich Bourbon politicians in Atlanta, and the courthouse ring in the rural counties."

In 1922, when her friend Tom Watson died, Gov. Tom Hardwick appointed the 87-year-old woman United States Senator for one day. Rebecca Felton was the nation's first woman senator.

Tom Watson and the Populist Party in Georgia

What were the achievements of the Populist Party?

The Farmers' Alliance and the Independents gained control of the legislature. Among their achievements were better education, pensions for Confederate widows, and programs for agriculture. Their greatest achievement, however, was their forcing the old Democratic party to adopt many of their proposals.

Many farmers realized that some state problems were also national problems. Things like railroad monopolies were plaguing the entire nation. One state could not cure the evils by itself. This was the era of great fortunes, of great power exercised by men who sought wealth and position. A new movement called the Populist Party, or the People's Party, was organized in 1892. Many Democrats, Independents and Alliance members joined the new party. It advocated free coinage of silver, a graduated income tax, and government ownership of railroads, telegraph and telephone lines.

Grover Cleveland became the first Democrat to be elected president since the Civil War. But the Populists were not happy with the Democratic program. Watson had been elected to Congress in 1890, with early Populist backing. They put him on the national ticket for vice president and later for president. He lost, but he remained a power in state politics in Georgia for many years and a potent force in Congress.

Watson thought that Georgia's Democratic leaders helped northern industrialists exploit Georgia for their own profit. He believed that the natural alliance of southern farmers was with the farming west and not with the manufacturing east. He also had something of a personal grudge against the aristocrats. He and his family had a hard time making a living after the war, and his brother once worked as a sharecropper on a farm. Tom Watson waited one Sunday morning until this planter rode into town on his horse, then took the man's own whip and horsewhipped him.

What were Watson's views on political strategy?

The statue of Tom Watson in Capitol Square in Atlanta shows him making one of his fiery speeches. It records on the base that he was "the father of the R.F.D." Thousands of followers were passionately devoted to him and he wielded as much power as any politician who ever lived in Georgia. But it is likely that he will be longest remembered for launching the Rural Free Delivery of mail. The original R.F.D. is marked in Georgia. It was in Warren County near Norwood.

EDUCATION AND THE ARTS

Why was education a problem for people in the post war period?

Little in the post-war story is more thrilling than what was happening in education and the arts. Most schools and colleges had closed while teachers and older students went to war. In the last days of the Confederacy, even 16-year old boys were fighting.

Education was a real problem for parents in the post-war years. Families who had sent their children to private academies in Georgia rarely had the money for their tuition and board. Confederate money was worthless and there was little or no credit.

Orr as "The Father of the Public Schools"

How did Georgia's public school system come into being?

The federals designed a system of public school education in 1866, but it had not gone into effect. The 1870 legislature set up free schools for the children of both races. The Bullock regime substituted worthless bonds for the school money and the plan could not be financed.

Finally, after Gov. James M. Smith took office, he appointed a new state school commissioner in 1872. He was Gustavus J. Orr, a graduate of the University of Georgia. Orr became known as "the father of the Georgia public school system."

In 1872, the state legislature voted that half of the Western and Atlantic Railroad rentals should go to finance the public schools. The money was diverted to other purposes. Finally, in 1873, the Georgia public school system was actually launched. The Constitution of 1877 provided for elementary schools, but not high schools. Vocational education began to appear in the schools, inspired years earlier by Benjamin Franklin in Philadelphia, who had given a push to more practical studies.

The Colleges Were Making Progress Too

The colleges also found it necessary to broaden their educational offering. The state provided a scholarship of $300 a year for each veteran under 30. He had to promise to teach in Georgia a year for each $300 he received.

In 1862 Congress passed the Merrill Land-Grant Act to open college careers to students interested in agricultural and mechanical pursuits. In that year Georgia was in a war. In 1866 the legislature appropriated $2,000 to put up a "mechanical and agricultural college" which could get funds under the federal law. Georgia obtained a grant of $243,000, and the land-grant college was finally set up in Athens. It was named "The Georgia State College of Agriculture and the Mechanical Arts." It was eventually absorbed into the University.

What was happening in land grant colleges?

PTA Founded by Georgia Woman

Mrs. Alice McClellan Birney was living in Washington, D.C., when her third child was born. She thought how little she really knew about children, how urgently parents needed to know more and to band together to help all children. "All children are our children" was later to become a PTA theme.

Who founded the PTA?

Mrs. Birney interested Mrs. Phoebe Randolph Hearst, the wealthy mother of newspaper tycoon William Randolph Hearst, in her ideas. These two women launched the National Congress of Parents and Teachers to help make the world a more comfortable and happy place for children. This was in an era when little children often worked 10 to 12 hours a day in factories.

In a schoolyard in Marietta, Alice Birney's home town, is a sun court to her memory. At Oglethorpe University in Atlanta is Phoebe Hearst Hall. Each year on Feb. 17, these two women are honored by millions as the PTA celebrates Founders Day.

Sidney Lanier—Georgia's First Great Poet

Sidney Lanier

Sidney Lanier was Georgia's first top-ranking poet, often spoken of as "the Poet of the South." He was born on Feb. 3, 1842, in a house that is still standing in Macon. Later, he clerked in the Lanier Hotel in Macon, which belonged to his family.

During the Civil War, Lanier was taken prisoner when the ship *Lucy* was running the blockade with medical supplies. He was carried to the prison at Point Lookout, Md. He smuggled a five-dollar gold piece into the prison under his tongue. He also took his flute. Released, he walked most of the way home. But he had contracted tuberculosis and did not have long to live. He died Sept. 7, 1881, at 39. Somebody had just brought him a handful of morning glories, a flower that he loved.

Lanier's poems that Georgians know best are two about Georgia: *The Song of the Chattahoochee*, and *The Marshes of Glynn*. Lanier County and Lake Sidney Lanier were named for him.

What famous poems did Lanier write?

The birthplace of Sidney Lanier in Macon.

Joel Chandler Harris and the Uncle Remus Tales

Joel Chandler Harris

Joel Chandler Harris, a writer who became world-famous, was born in Eatonton on Dec. 9, 1848. He worked in the print shop of a planter named Joseph Addison Turner. Turner published a paper called *The Countryman*.

Henry Grady of the *Atlanta Constitution* had read some of his writings. He asked Harris to come by to see him the next time he was in Atlanta. Harris found Grady riding with his children on the merry-go-round at the fair. They met and became fast friends.

While associated with the *Constitution*, Harris wrote the whimsical stories of Brer Rabbit and Brer Fox and the other animals who could talk. Many famous people came to his home, Snap Bean Farm, to visit Harris. He once refused to let the postman put mail in the mailbox. A wren was nesting there and he did not want her disturbed.

What stories did Harris write?

Blind Tom Bethune, a Georgia Pianist

Outside Columbus, on the Macon road, there is a grave with an astounding story behind it. It is the burial place of Thomas Greene Bethune, known also as Thomas Wiggins.

Gen. James N. Bethune's daughters noticed that sometimes a tiny blind black boy would sing along with them in perfect harmony. The big surprise came when Tom was four. The Bethune sisters had been playing the piano for guests. After the party was over, they heard melodies from the piano. The child, scarcely big enough to reach the keyboard, was playing like Mozart. The Bethunes took him to a music teacher in Columbus. The teacher refused to take Tom as a pupil. "You cannot teach genius," he said. "This world has never seen anything like that blind Negro child."

How did Tom Bethune start as a pianist?

Young Bethune began giving concerts when he was eight.

He also composed music. For 20 years he played to appreciative audiences throughout America and Europe. During the Civil War, he played for both sides. Willa Cather put him into her book *My Antonia*, in which he is called Blind d'Arnault.

THE CENTURY MOVES TO AN END

The last decade of the century was known in America as the Gay Nineties. But there were many things that were far from happy. The world would soon be moving into a century that would bring many new problems. Up from Mexico across the Rio Grande River a tiny insect called the boll weevil was crawling to topple King Cotton. And almost predictive of the next century, America found itself again in war.

Georgia in the Spanish-American War

What was Georgia's role in the Spanish-American War?

The United States went to war with Spain. Theodore Roosevelt, later to be president, led the Rough Riders in a charge up Cuba's San Juan Hill. Georgia's Gen. Joe Wheeler, of Civil War fame, also fought in the Spanish-American War. Camp Chickamauga, on Georgia's old Civil War battlefield near Chattanooga, was used by the U.S. as a central place of mobilization and supplies. Georgia became a mustering-out center for soldiers of this war.

When America defeated Spain, Georgia held a victory celebration, a Jubilee attended by President McKinley. Brass mortars captured at Santiago, Cuba, are on Capitol Square in Atlanta now.

Georgia at the Beginning of the 20th Century

The 1900 census showed that 2,216,331 people were living in the state. When the century opened, Georgia was still a rural state. It would change to an urban state in a half century.

Think carefully and analytically about Georgia in the 19th century. The century had seen the Indians removed from Georgia. It was the time Georgia and the nation experienced the terrible Civil War. But the state came through the war and reconstruction. Industry was developing, providing for higher levels of prosperity for all Georgians. Textiles, the oldest of the industries, was well established. Education was making progress and public schools were added to the state plan. Roads were getting better and railroads were increasing their business. While the boll weevil was making its destruction felt, a black genius teaching chemistry at Tuskegee Institute was finding hundreds of products possible from peanuts and potatoes. Automobiles were coming in. Electric lights were beginning to shine in homes and offices. And people were marvelling that the Wright Brothers had actually flown an airplane successfully at Kitty Hawk.

What important things were happening at the turn of the century?

So engage in this thought experiment. You are in Atlanta on New Year's Eve, December 31, 1899. It is three weeks after your 62nd birthday. Fireworks are being shot and people are laughing, dancing and having a good time. In spite of the noise and fun, you become a little dreamy. What do you think would be your basic thoughts and feelings about the century that is coming to a close? How many good times do you think you would remember? What difficulties and hurts do you think would still be clearest in your mind?

And what about the 20th century to come? How do you think you would view it? With anticipation and hope? With skepticism and despair? Do you think it would have been possible at all to have sensed the great changes that the 20th century would bring?

As the group sang *Auld Lang Syne* that night, would you have looked backward with pride and forward with hope?

For Extended Thinking

1. What were the demands placed on Georgia by the national government after the Civil War?
2. How did the various groups in Georgia adapt after the Civil War?
3. Who was the opposition to the Bourbon Triumvirate?
4. How did Georgia establish its public school system?
5. What was happening in art and literature during the post-war period?

Names, Terms and Concepts

military districts
Bourbon Triumvirate
Gustavus Orr
Charles Jenkins
Farmer's Alliance
The Poet of the South
kuklos
Independents
Joel Chandler Harris
Henry Grady
convict leasing system
Tom Bethune
Miss Freedom
Gay Nineties
Rebecca Felton

To Help You Study

1. Tell what you think Reconstruction means.
2. What did Gov. Jenkins do that helped his state?
3. Blacks faced unusual problems after the Civil War. Discuss some of their problems and how they handled their newly-won freedom.
4. Describe briefly the work of Henry Grady.
5. Where are some of the places Georgia marble is used? Why was it not used to build the state capitol?
6. What was the Bourbon Triumvirate? Who were the three men that made it up?
7. Who were the Feltons and what contributions did they make to Georgia politics?
8. What does "populist" mean?
9. Name two poems written by Sidney Lanier.
10. Why is Joel Chandler Harris famous?
11. Thomas Wiggins became Tom Bethune. Tell why he is famous.
12. What was Georgia's role in the Spanish-American War?

CHAPTER 12

GEORGIA IN THE EARLY 20TH CENTURY

No one could have predicted at the celebration in Atlanta on December 31, 1899, what the 20th century would hold. Invention would follow invention in almost dizzying fashion. These inventions would change American life styles and the American workplace. Economic prosperity would reach heights no one could have dreamed. At the same time, the century would experience an economic depression deeper than the nation had ever known. Great possibilities and immense problems seemed always to run hand in hand. Fearful wars, the atom bomb, nuclear power, pollution and population explosions would stir men's minds. All those things raised the question of how to deal with the great changes the 1900's would bring.

THE PEOPLE AND THEIR DAILY LIVES AND WORK

What were the conditions on Georgia's farms?

Georgia was still a rural state early in the 20th century. Most people lived and worked on farms. Many people who lived in rural areas did not own their farms. Very few of the thousands of former slaves would have owned land. Many whites lost their land as a result of the Civil War. Also, many had not previously owned land because of the plantation system. These non-landowning farmers, both black and white, became **sharecroppers**. Landowners did not have the money to pay farm workers but they had to have workers to plant and harvest the crops. Non-landowners in the rural areas needed

What was the basis of the sharecropper system?

work. Thus owners provided the land, non-landowners provided the labor and both shared the crop. These economic facts, more than anything else, are the basis of the sharecropper system.

What type of credit developed?

Along with the emergence of sharecropping, a form of credit developed that was very important to the lives of many people. There were very few banks in Georgia. The ones that did exist did not have much money. As a result, storekeepers began to advance food and farm supplies to farmers in return for a share of their crop. A similar system arose in many textile mill towns. Lacking money but needing workers, the mills often paid in **script**. This was a certificate that could be used at the company-owned store to buy food and clothing. Some workers felt that the mills abused this system and took advantage of the workers. This was because the only place the script could be used was in the mill store. The country store owners were often taking substantial risk. They provided food and farming supplies in advance and on credit. If the cotton crop failed or the boll weevil destroyed the crop, the store owner and the sharecropper both were hurt.

Many things affected the lives, health and jobs of the people in the early 20th century. Several of them helped shape Georgia as we know it today.

Georgia Enacted Health Laws

Certain diseases had plagued Georgia from the beginning. The colonies had malaria and smallpox. Yellow fever had been a plague along the coast. The poverty of sharecroppers meant that their meals were mostly corn meal, meat and molasses. This made them subject to pellagra. Hookworm was also rampant in many areas of the state.

By 1903, Georgia had established a state board of health. Local health departments and local boards of health were set up also.

In 1914, health laws were made stronger. Water was analyzed for purity. Slaughterhouses were inspected. The purchase of drugs was restricted to prescriptions. Nurses were required to register. Mosquito-breeding lands were drained. Quarantine laws were passed in an attempt to control contagious illnesses. All of these things did much to improve the public health situation in the state.

What public health steps did Georgia take?

The Convict Lease System was Abolished in 1908

Georgia built its first penitentiary in 1819 at Milledgeville. After the Civil War, that prison could not hold all the prisoners. The state then started the convict leasing system. In this system, the state leased convicts to certain companies. The convicts worked in fields, mines, forest and on the railroads. By 1877, over a thousand convicts worked for various companies.

The convict leasing system was one of the evils the Populists had protested. By the turn of the century, more and more people in the state were growing concerned and angry about the situation. A legislative committee appointed to investigate the convict camps found that nothing was being done to rehabilitate the prisoners. Instead many became even worse criminals. Convicts were very inhumanely treated in some camps. For example, in some camps, men, women, and boys were chained together.

What forces opposed the convict leasing system?

The issue was a very explosive one. The chairman of the committee to investigate the prisons, Robert Alston, was shot and killed in the state capitol by Edward Cox. Cox managed the plantations of John B. Gordon where convicts worked.

In 1908, the state passed a law that forbade any private hiring of the state's convicts. Those who were not sent to the prisons at Milledgeville were sent to counties to do road work. But the chain gangs, as these units were called, in some counties became very bad. Later in the century more improvement would be made. However, the problem of prison overcrowding is one that Georgia still faces today.

High Freight Rates Handicapped Georgia

What was the problem with the freight rates?

Freight rates in the south were so high in the first half of the century that they put a burden on those who had to ship their products. The railroads had what they called a "density formula." It required southern shippers to pay higher rates. The railroads claimed that it would cost more to handle freight in the south than in the north and east. This kept some manufacturers from locating their plants in Georgia.

Several efforts were made to get the railroads to end the unfair practice. During Hoke Smith's governorship, the legislature set up a Railroad Commission. The idea was to tighten control over the railroads that caused the trouble. Gov. Ellis Arnall entered suit in 1944 against twenty-one railroads. He asked for fifty-six million dollars in damages to Georgia because of the high freight rates. But it was not until 1952 that the state got relief. In that year, the Interstate Commerce Commission ordered equalization on rates on all railroads east of the Rocky Mountains.

The Boll Weevil Toppled King Cotton Off His Throne

Cotton had long been king in the south. Georgia's Sea Island cotton, a long staple variety, had been brought to the state during the colonial period. It could grow only along the coast. When Whitney invented the cotton gin, the short staple upland variety could be grown anywhere. It was also very profitable. The south was soon shipping millions of bales of cotton to Europe and to the north. The crop became very important. Some argue that the south had built a whole culture on it. Certainly slaves had been bought to work in the cotton fields.

The boll weevil helped change all that. The tiny insect had crawled up from Mexico into Texas. It had spread across the states by the beginning of the 20th century. This tiny creature multiplied by the millions and left misery and poverty in its path.

The tragedy of the boll weevil had a brighter ending than the farmers could have imagined. The weevil taught farmers what the agricultural colleges had been proclaiming: that dependence on just one crop was not sound agricultural practice. Farmers learned to grow more of other crops. They began planting corn, peanuts, soybeans, truck crops for the vegetable markets, tobacco and others.

Why was the boll weevil so important?

Peanuts Paid Off in Georgia

When the boll weevil taught Georgia farmers not to depend on one crop, peanuts became a paying crop. At Tuskegee Institute in Alabama, Dr. George Washington Carver discovered over 300 uses for the peanut. He developed over 118 uses

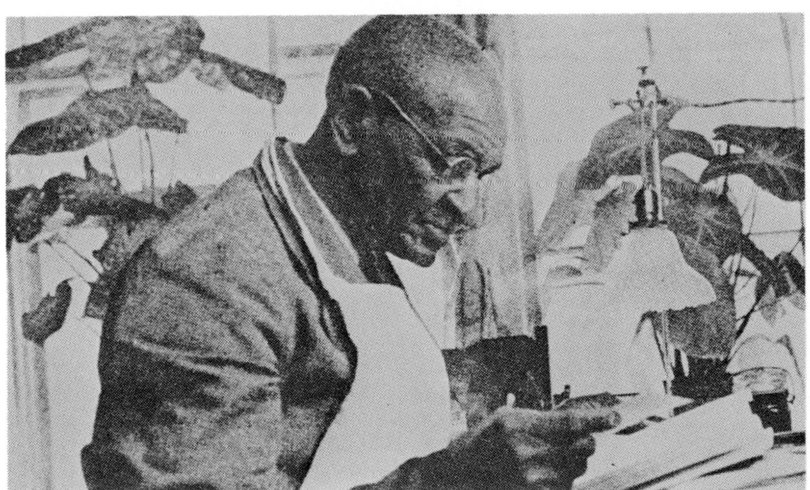

George Washington Carver

How did peanuts become an important crop?

for the sweet potato. At the Birmingham Research Institute of the South, another scientist found a way to keep the oil from collecting on the top of the jar of peanut butter. This discovery made peanuts an even more marketable crop. Southwest Georgia became a major peanut processing area. Factories were set up to roast and toast them. Assembly lines turned out jars of peanut butter to be marketed throughout the world. Soon the peanut industry became a multi-million-dollar business.

Dr. Charles Holmes Herty

Tall as a Georgia Pine

Why was Herty's invention important?

Charles Herty, born in 1867, began experimenting with pine trees in 1902. After developing the Herty Turpentine Cup, he began experimenting with a method to make paper out of pine tree pulp. Up to that time, most paper made of pine pulp was too sticky to use in printing newspapers. Dr. Herty's experiments were successful. Soon worn-out Georgia cotton lands were being planted with pine seedlings. By mid-century, Georgia ranked second only to California in the value of lumber products. Paper companies moved into the state and bought pulpwood. In pulpwood, Georgia led the nation.

Pine was not the only important tree. Gum, oak and pine were the principal woods for furniture. Other woods provided the raw materials for over three hundred products. These include paint, varnishes, synthetic rubber, adhesives, soaps and disinfectants, inks, dyes, plastics and many others.

What were Wilson's connections with Georgia?

GEORGIA AND WORLD WAR I

The years from 1912 through 1929 are often called the Wilson Era. Wilson, believed by many to be one of America's great presidents, had close ties to Georgia. He lived in Augusta as a little boy, had an uncle who taught in a Georgia

President Woodrow Wilson

college, married a Georgia girl and practiced law in Atlanta. It was Wilson who guided the nation during the terrible years of World War I. Not all Georgia leaders agreed with Wilson. Nearly all of them respected his ability and admired his courage.

World War I began when a fanatic shot and killed an Austrian archduke. Germany, Austria, and Turkey went to war against England, France, Italy and Russia. Wilson tried hard to keep America out of the war. But Germany announced its intention to sink on sight all ships that entered the European war zone. Following that threat, four American ships were sunk off the Dutch coast. Wilson asked Congress to declare war in a speech in which he said, "The world must be made safe for democracy. We have no selfish ends to serve." Georgia's delegation in the House of Representatives backed Wilson and voted for war. Georgia's Senators, Hoke Smith and Thomas Hardwick, disagreed with Wilson. On April 6, 1917, war was declared by the Congress. At the time of the declaration of war, German submarines were already near Georgia's coast. The millionaires on Jekyll Island had to desert their vacation retreat because of them.

The first Mrs. Wilson, Ellen Louise Axson.

Why did America get into World War II?

Georgians, like most Americans, rallied behind the war effort. Civilians joined with the military to support the war. Where there had been about 300 Red Cross chapters in the state before the war, there were soon over 3,000. They sent thirty million surgical dressings to Europe. Georgians were buying bonds in the Liberty Bond campaigns. Atlanta was the bond headquarters for eight southeastern states.

Fort Oglethorpe and Fort McPherson were two of the fourteen sites in the nation chosen for training camps. It was during this time also that the nation bought Fort Benning, Camp Gordon and Camp Wheeler. Fort Benning spreads over many acres in Chattahoochee and Muscogee counties. After having served as a camp during World War I, it was made permanent in 1922. Fort Benning was soon to become the world's largest infantry school. Soldiers from all over the world have trained there.

How was Georgia important to the war effort?

After much fighting, Germany and her allies were defeated. Though the United States was in the war for just nineteen months, American participation had made an important difference. The Allies in Europe had all but exhausted their resources, money and men in fighting the Central Powers. The United States had four million men in arms. Two million of them were sent abroad. Gen. John Pershing insisted that U.S. soldiers fight as an American army and not be put under European officers or into foreign units.

STATE POLITICS IN THE EARLY 20TH CENTURY

Voters get intensely interested in national elections. But nothing equals the color and character of the exciting campaigns Georgians wage for state offices, especially governors.

The Populist Party Weakens

What happened to the Populist Party?

In 1902 Gov. Joseph Meriwether Terrell defeated the Populist candidate for governor. The Populist candidate got only 5,000 votes. This showed that the strength of the Populist party in Georgia was nearing its end.

Why were A & M schools established?

Gov. Terrell is remembered especially for his crusade to get district agricultural and mechanical schools established. Georgia had only 64 accredited high schools in 1906. Only 12 of these had four years of education to offer. The academies were disappearing. There was need for schools to bridge the gap between the elementary schools and the colleges. Eventually, 12 A & M schools were set up. These were considered a part of the College of Agriculture at Athens. Agricultural education eventually became a part of the university itself. As vocational agriculture courses were set up in the high schools, the A & M schools began to disappear from the scene.

Smith-Brown Campaigns for Governor

Early in this century the Hoke Smith-Joe Brown campaigns for governor divided Georgia into two excited factions for a decade.

Hoke Smith, owner of the *Atlanta Journal,* had been secretary of the interior in President Grover Cleveland's cabinet. Born in North Carolina, he was a young lawyer in Atlanta at the same time as Woodrow Wilson.

Brown, known as "Little Joe" Brown, was the son of Joseph Emerson Brown, Civil War governor of Georgia. He was a brilliant student, graduating with first honors from Oglethorpe. Because of poor eyesight he gave up law and took a $40-a-month job on the railroad his father owned. In 1904 Gov. Terrell appointed him railroad commissioner. Gov. Hoke Smith fired him from that job. Brown then defeated Smith for governor. A depression was haunting the state and nation. Brown's slogan was "Hoke and Hunger—or Brown and Bread."

What was Brown's platform against Smith?

Smith and Brown opposed each other again in 1910 for the governorship. Smith won. In 1912 Little Joe Brown was re-elected governor of Georgia. So you can see that the two had great appeal to the Georgia voters. Not since the old days of Troup and Clark nearly 100 years before had there been such fierce political battles for the office as those of Hoke Smith and Joe Brown.

The Last Confederate to be Governor

Nathaniel Edwin Harris joined the Confederate Army at 16. Afterwards he entered the University of Georgia with money

What was the last election in which an ex-Confederate soldier held the balance of power?

borrowed from Alexander Stephens. He was a classmate of Henry W. Grady.

After he graduated he taught and then went to Macon to practice law. He was elected governor in 1915 with the backing of his fellow Confederate veterans. This was the last election in which the veterans held the balance of political power. Harris was the last Confederate veteran to serve as governor of Georgia.

Among Harris' accomplishments was his part in the founding of Georgia Tech. He served as chairman of the Board of Trustees for 30 years. He signed more than 15,000 diplomas. Harris was also able to establish a pension for Confederate veterans.

The Leo Frank Murder Case

Leo Frank, a New York man of the Jewish faith, had come to Atlanta as manager of a pencil factory. On Memorial Day 1913, a 14-year-old girl named Mary Phagan, who worked there, went by to get her pay and never came out again. She was found murdered in the basement. Frank was convicted of her murder. However, the evidence against him was mostly circumstantial and there was much doubt of his guilt. Judge Arthur M. Roan, who presided at the trial, said that Frank's innocence "had been proven to a mathematical certainty." The case made headlines all over the world.

What happened in the Leo Frank case?

Feeling was so intense that Frank was not in the courtroom when the jury brought in its verdict against him. There was danger that a mob would kill him. He was sentenced to be hanged. His lawyers appealed the case. Gov. John M. Slaton was not convinced that Frank's guilt had been proven. He commuted the sentence to life imprisonment. He knew the danger he would encounter, but he did it anyhow. He and his wife were living at their beautiful home called Wingfield, in

Buckhead. The Governor's Mansion was being repaired. A mob of 3,000 quickly gathered around the house. Slaton's friends went to protect him and state police were called out. Later the Slatons left on a trip around the world. When Slaton later ran for the U.S. Senate he was defeated.

Frank was taken to the state prison in Milledgeville. An old convict tried to cut his throat. A mob took Frank out of prison one midnight. They took him back to Cobb County and hanged him as near as they could get to the grave of Mary Phagan. Many books and ballads were written about the Leo Frank case. The latest is Harry Golden's *A Little Girl Is Dead.*

What happened to Frank?

In 1916 the state was still aflame with the repercussions of the Frank case. Hugh Dorsey, who had prosecuted Leo Frank, was elected governor.

The County Unit System

A far-reaching measure passed by the legislature during Dorsey's administration was the **Neill Primary Act**. It went into effect in 1920 and affected Georgia government for many decades.

The Neill plan provided for a primary election in each county. A primary is an election in which the political parties determine their candidates for each office. The key point was that it made it mandatory that each representative to the state convention cast his vote in accordance with the majority vote of the primary. This meant that each county's vote was cast as a unit. It worked like this: the eight largest counties had six unit votes each; the next 30 counties had four unit votes each; the remaining 121 had two unit votes each. In 1960, the three smallest counties combined had 6,980 people. Yet their combined six unit votes equaled the six unit votes of Fulton, which had 566,326 people. Because of the county unit system, Georgia state government was dominated by the rural areas for

How did the county unit system work?

Why was the county unit system important?

years. Urban areas did not gain equal power until 1962. This was a result of the U.S. Supreme Court case Baker vs. Carr that required "one man, one vote."

THE CRASH THAT ENDED THE ERA

What happened in the financial crash of 1929?

On Black Monday, October 29, 1929, the financial crash that ended the era began. Stock prices fell drastically. Many factories closed while others cut production. Thus workers in them were fired or had their wages cut. Real estate values declined and construction almost stopped. Banks closed, wiping out the life savings of a number of people. By 1932 more than ten million Americans were out of work and soup lines were commonplace in the cities.

Why was there poverty in a land of plenty?

What caused the Great Depression? Many factors contributed to it. For one thing, the nation was on a wild jag of prosperity. Installment buying had lured many people into debts they could not repay. The nation's businesses were selling to Europe on credit. Economic experts were warning that the debts could not be paid. Few people paid attention to them. It was the F. Scott Fitzgerald age of loud music and louder voices. A generation was reacting against the hard days of the war.

Another major reason for the depression was that America was producing more than it could sell. The country was able to produce enormous amounts of manufactured goods and agricultural products. It could not sell them all. Foreign trade had declined after the war. This was partly due to the high tariff America had put on foreign goods coming into this country. Within this country, many Americans could not afford to buy things. We have already described how most farmers were broke and had to have a special kind of credit from the country stores. Those who worked in the factories made very low wages. A woman who worked a fifty-hour week in a textile mill could expect to make $2.29 for the entire week. These low wages coupled with high unemployment meant that domestic consumption simply could not equal America's ability to produce. Thus there existed the peculiar spectacle of want and poverty in a land of plenty. The era of jazz and gaiety had given way to a time of hunger and despair.

This is a good place for two thought experiments. Imagine yourself on a Georgia farm in 1930, one year after the stock market crash. What do you think your situation would be? Was the depression a force which would have significantly altered your life? Is it true that people on the farms could just kill another chicken or pick more butter beans and things would not be so bad because they had plenty to eat? In what ways would you have felt the depression?

Now imagine yourself a young person in Atlanta in 1930. Your father has been laid off from his job in the mill. What do you think your situation would be? Would the depression be a force which would significantly alter your life? How would your family manage? How would it get food and pay for essential things like medical services? Could you stay in school? In what ways would you have felt the depression?

The truth is that very few Americans and very few Georgians escaped the impact of the Great Depression. And in that crisis, many joined in turning to a new leader with deep and personal ties to Georgia. That leader was Franklin Delano Roosevelt. He was the president who led the country through its deepest depression and most dangerous war.

For Extended Thinking

1. What was the life of rural Georgians like at the start of the 20th century?
2. Who were some of the leaders in the development of agriculture in Georgia?
3. What was Georgia's role in WorldWar I?
4. Why did the Leo Frank case cause so much conflict in Georgia?
5. What were the major factors causing the Great Depression?

Names, Terms and Concepts

sharecroppers
Charles Herty
Neill Primary Act
script
Fort Benning
primary election
chain gangs
A & M schools
county unit system
Railroad Commission
Leo Frank
Black Monday
George Washington Carver

To Help You Study

1. What problems did Georgians living in the rural areas face? Were most of them landowners?
2. What kinds of things were done to solve the problem of money and credit in both the rural areas and the cities?
3. How did higher freight rates on the railroads affect Georgia?
4. What was the importance of the work of George Washington Carver to Georgia?
5. How did the invention of Charles Herty affect Georgia farming?
6. What were the important military bases in Georgia during World War I?
7. Who was the last Confederate soldier to be elected governor?
8. What were the Smith and Brown campaigns for governor like?
9. What was the county unit system and how did it affect Georgia politics?
10. Discuss the Leo Frank murder case.
11. How did the Great Depression affect Georgia?

CHAPTER 13

THE GREAT DEPRESSION AND WORLD WAR II

The years from the 1929 crash up to 1950 are often referred to in Georgia as the years of the Roosevelt impact. Actually, most Georgians had known Franklin Delano Roosevelt long before he came to the state in search of relief from polio. They had known him as assistant secretary of the Navy during the Wilson administration. A majority of Georgians cast their vote for him when he was the vice presidential candidate of the Democratic Party in 1920. A number of things are memorable about the Roosevelt years in Georgia.

The Famous "Unfinished Portrait"

Franklin Delano Roosevelt

Whether your grandparents liked Roosevelt or not, you will find that they remember him clearly. He was elected to the presidency four times, more than any other individual. He used the power of the president to do many things in the area of domestic policy. And he was president during World War II. Most people remember personal things about FDR most vividly. If you can, talk with some older individual about FDR's Fireside Chats, his smile, his cigarette holder and his dog named Fala.

Why are people likely to remember FDR?

Roosevelt came to Georgia in 1924, the same year Woodrow Wilson died. From 1924 to 1945 when he died at Warm Springs, Roosevelt was a vital part of Georgia life and politics. He learned a lot about Georgia people by driving around the back roads of Meriwether County in his specially-equipped automobile. He loved to drive to the top of Pine Mountain and sit quietly on Dowdell's Knob. He built a "little white house"

The Little White House

that would take on new meaning after he became president and world leader. The Little White House was to bring Georgia to national and international attention for a quarter of a century.

THE NEW DEAL

In his acceptance speech on his nomination for president, Roosevelt said, "I pledge you, I pledge myself, to a new deal for the American people. Let us all here assembled constitute ourselves prophets of a new order of competence and of courage." Roosevelt's words, "new deal," caught the imagination of the press and public. His administration was known thereafter as the **New Deal**.

What was Georgia like during the Great Depression?

The Depression of the 1930s affected Georgia more than it did the nation as a whole. In our thought experiment in the last chapter, we had you think on what the depression would have been like had you lived in the country and then what it would have been like had you lived in the city. Had you lived in the country, you would have found that large numbers of people were no longer able to make it on the farm and had to move to the city. In 1920, there were 310,732 farms in Georgia. By 1940, near the end of the Great Depression, there were 216,030. Georgia had lost nearly 100,000 farms. The number of people living on the farm declined sharply also. In 1920, 206,954 people lived on the farm; in 1940, only 129,850 did so. The farming practices changed drastically also. In 1920, farmers planted 4,332,000 acres of cotton in Georgia. By 1940, they were planting only 1,935,000 acres of the crop that was once king. During the Great Depression dramatic changes occurred in agriculture.

The movement of Georgians from the farm to the city was in many ways like going from the frying pan into the fire. The cities were experiencing high levels of unemployment. There were not enough jobs for the people who already lived there, much less for the large influx of population from the rural areas of the state.

The New Deal was based on the belief that the national government should help both individual citizens and business firms. Previously, it was thought that the government should let the economy alone, a view known as *laissez faire*, to run its course whatever that might be. Thus there were many in both the nation and Georgia who disagreed strongly with the actions that Roosevelt took.

What change in the role of government occurred in the New Deal?

The New Deal was a multifaceted program. A number of the policies were designed to help people get back to work. The Civilian Conservation Corps (CCC) hired many thousands of men to work in national forests, state parks and at planting trees. And yes, they also planted some of the kudzu you see in Georgia. They thought it would prevent soil erosion. The National Youth Administration (NYA) gave young people in college jobs so they could continue to pay for their education. Individuals in the Public Works Administration (PWA) worked on projects like dams, post offices, bridges and libraries. The Works Progress Administration (WPA) hired people for the widest range of jobs—from ditch digging to writing books and painting murals.

What were the major programs of the New Deal?

Along with programs to put people back to work, the New Deal contained a number of programs for agriculture and business. The Agriculture Adjustment Acts (AAA) set acreage allotments on controlled crops to reduce the amount that was planted. Under this policy, a farmer was limited in the number of acres that could be planted in cotton, peanuts or any of the other controlled crops. In return for not planting as much as he wished, the farmer got price supports for his products. Soil conservation programs, credit to tenants to buy farms, and credit for storage and marketing of crops were other things the New Deal did to assist farmers. It was during the New Deal that the Rural Electrification Administration (REA) was established to make cheap electricity available in rural areas. Many rural areas in Georgia are still served by the REA.

What program had the biggest impact on Georgia?

Under the New Deal, American business and industry attempted to set reasonable working hours and wages. The National Industry Recovery Act (NRA) was an effort to end cutthroat competition in which the company that worked its employees the longest hours at the lowest pay made the most profit. When the NRA was declared unconstitutional, the New Deal turned to the Fair Labor Standards Act (FSLA) to accomplish the same purpose. Through this and other programs, the New Deal raised wages, shortened hours, and prohibited child labor.

So far as its immediate impact on Georgia and neighboring states is concerned, the biggest project in the New Deal was the Tennessee Valley Authority (TVA). The goal of the TVA was to conserve and develop the resources of the Tennessee River and its tributaries. Thus the TVA built dams to control floods, built fertilizer plants to aid agriculture and promoted industrial development in the states of the Tennessee valley.

These "alphabet agencies," and more, did bring about many changes in Georgia. Hiking trials in the mountains were built by the CCC. There are many public buildings, roads and bridges that were constructed by the WPA. The national government still has an extensive farm program in place. And if you put money in the bank, the federal government will guarantee that deposit up to a certain limit. Roosevelt was very familiar with economic problems in Georgia since he observed them firsthand. He once said that the south was "the nation's No. 1 economic problem." Ironically, it was World War II more than the New Deal that brought economic growth to Georgia. Unfortunately, it was to bring a lot of sorrow also.

GEORGIA AND WORLD WAR II

Georgians began to read of an Austrian house painter named Schickelgruber, later known as Adolph Hitler. Hitler dreamed of great conquest. Germany was still resentful of the Versailles peace treaty which had placed a heavy burden on them for World War I. It paid little attention to Hitler at first. With his little mustache and his emotional rantings, he was a rather comic figure. He served time in jail and wrote his book *Mein Kampf*, or "My Struggle." His infamous Nazi Party started with only seven men. Gradually, Hitler gained power in Germany. He rebuilt the army. Most important, Hitler persuaded Germans that they should build their nation into new strength and conquer the world.

What were the conditions in Germany?

When he felt strong enough, he marched into small nations and took them over. In 1939, Hitler and Stalin of Russia divided Poland between themselves. Poland had been guaranteed protection by England and France so those two countries went to war against Germany.

America tried, as in World War I, to remain neutral. On December 7, 1941, Japan bombed the United States fleet at Pearl Harbor in Hawaii. Instantly, Roosevelt was on the radio condemning Japan's treachery. He called December 7 "a day that will live in infamy." America was at war and Georgia was a part of it.

How did America get involved in the war?

Georgians turned to war work as they had in World War I. Shipyards in Savannah and Brunswick made Liberty Ships. War factories turned out bombers.

During World War II, more than 300,000 Georgians served in the armed forces. Of that number, 6,754 lost their lives. Georgia also furnished many military leaders in the war. Gen. Edward P. King was leader of the forces on Bataan. Col. Robert Lee Scott was with the China air force and wrote *God Is My Co-Pilot*. Gen. Courtney Hodges led the forces across the Rhine River. Admiral J. H. Towns commanded the Pacific Fleet's air force. Rear Admiral W.A. Ashford commanded the carrier *Midway*. Gen. Lucius Clay served as military governor of the Occupation Zone in Germany after the war. In the national congress, Representative Carl Vinson was the influential chairman of the

What was Georgia's role in World War II?

Naval Affairs Committee. He was later to be chairman of the Armed Services Committee of the House. Senator Richard B. Russell became chairman of the Armed Services Committee in the Senate.

New military installations were placed in Georgia and officers and soldiers were trained in those already established. Fort Benning, the world's largest infantry school, was an important site. Fort McPherson in Atlanta, Camp Gordon in Augusta and Camp Stewart in Hinesville were also already permanent posts. The Navy set up some of its training operations at the University of Georgia. In all, the Army had more training fields in Georgia than in any other state except Texas.

Georgia buzzed with the activity of workers getting planes and other things ready for the military effort. The Bell Bomber Plant in Marietta brought 20,000 workers to the site. In Macon, another 15,000 worked at Warner Robins. Returning soldiers found Georgia more industrialized, urbanized and prosperous than it had been before the war.

Roosevelt was elected to an unprecedented fourth term in 1944. He had been to Yalta on the Black Sea for a conference with Churchill and Stalin. When he returned to the United States, he came to Warm Springs to rest. His friends and neighbors were shocked to see how tired he looked. He was sitting for his portrait, which was being painted by Elizabeth Shoumatoff, when he suddenly put his hand to his head and complained of a headache. In a few hours, he was dead.

Where did Roosevelt die? What took place then?

Roosevelt had been widely loved and fiercely hated. Few Americans and few Georgians were neutral toward him. But on that day, April 12, 1945, the nation mourned his death. Graham Jackson was a black musician who had performed often for the president. He played Dvorak's *Going Home* on his accordion as the train carrying Roosevelt's body pulled out of Warm Springs station. As the train moved through Georgia, thousands gathered along the track to view it. The Little White House that Roosevelt loved so much is now a national shrine in his memory.

STATE POLITICS IN THE ROOSEVELT ERA

The two decades of the Roosevelt era were a period of vast social and economic change in the state. The political leadership of Georgia had to deal with complex social, economic and political forces at work. Their problem was largely that of helping Georgians to plan changes in social structures, economic activity and political ideals.

Russell Streamlines Georgia's Government

Richard B. Russell

Richard B. Russell, Jr., son of Chief Justice Richard B. Russell, Sr., of the Georgia Supreme Court, became governor in 1931. He was one of 13 children. He grew up in Winder and graduated from the University of Georgia at nearby Athens.

Russell was elected to the legislature in 1921 and soon became Speaker of the House of Representatives. He was elected governor on a platform of "the 3 R's": Reorganization, Redistricting, and Refinancing. He was 31 years old, the youngest governor in the nation. Russell said to the legislature:

> One of the crying needs of Georgia is a complete, thorough overhauling of state government. We have boards, bureaus, departments and commissions almost too numerous to name . . . The citizens of this state are more interested in your efforts to reorganize our administrative machinery than in any other measure.

What was Russell's plan for Georgia government?

Other governors had recommended reorganization but this was the first time it was actually done. With the help of the legislature, Russell reduced the 102 bureaus, departments and commissions of state government to 18. The trustees of all the separate colleges were abolished. A single board of regents was named for the whole university system. By 1972 however, the state government had grown—again—to over 300 units!

What were Russell's accomplishments in the Senate?

In 1933 Russell was elected to the United States Senate—one of the first to have the advantage of radio for reaching the people. In Congress he went on to national fame as a statesman. He launched the national school lunch bill. He became chairman of the powerful Armed Forces Committee of the Senate. He achieved a reputation as a brilliant orator and a skillful parliamentarian. In 1948 he was seriously considered for nomination by the Democrats for President. Russell served as adviser to many Presidents. He was one of the most powerful men who ever served in the U.S. Senate.

The Man From Sugar Creek

What was the basis of Eugene Talmadge's support?

"I may surprise you, but I will never deceive you." These words are carved in stone on the monument to Eugene Talmadge on Capitol Square. When he spoke, Talmadge usually took off his coat, showing the red suspenders which came to be his political trademark. He paid special attention to the rural voters. Talmadge often said that he did not care about getting the vote of any county where a streetcar ran. When he was elected governor, he brought his cow to graze on the lawn of the Governor's Mansion. Yet this well-educated man could also attract urban and corporation support. It is often said that Talmadge dominated Georgia politics for two decades.

Eugene Talmadge was born at Forsyth on Sept. 23, 1884. He graduated from the University of Georgia in 1907 and opened law offices in McRae in Telfair County. Soon he married a widow, Mrs. Mattie Peterson. They ran their farm at Sugar Creek and campaigned all over Georgia. "Miss Mitt" was to see both her husband and son become governors of Georgia.

Talmadge became governor of Georgia in 1933, the same year that Roosevelt became president. He had a turbulent career as governor. He did not always agree with President Roosevelt's New Deal. In 1936 he was re-elected, carrying all but three of Georgia's 159 counties.

Statue of Governor Eugene Talmadge.

Talmadge had spectacular battles within the state. The legislature adjourned in 1936 without passing an appropriations bill. The treasurer and the comptroller refused to pay out any money without legislative authorization. Talmadge fired them, and ran the state by executive decree. He called out the National Guard to protect the state treasury. He also used soldiers during a 1934 textile strike to "protect men in their right to work," he said. Some strike leaders were put in barbed-wire stockades. This caused him trouble with labor.

What problems did Talmadge face?

Yet through all his difficulties Talmadge kept his hold on the hearts of Georgia's rural supporters. They flocked in droves wherever he spoke, called out, "You tell 'em, Gene," and swarmed to shake his hand. Even though Georgia supported Roosevelt, it also gave Talmadge enough support to be elected governor four times.

Talmadge was finally defeated by those who did not like it when his actions resulted in the University's losing its accredited status. At that time students could not vote but their parents and friends could. Talmadge was defeated for governor in 1942 by Ellis Arnall of Newnan.

Georgia First to Give Eighteen-Year-Olds the Vote

A student from Georgia Tech came by Gov. Arnall's office to congratulate him before leaving for the Army. The student said, "I'm not old enough to vote, but I am old enough to fight." Gov. Arnall said to Georgians, "If our youngsters are old enough to fight and die for their country, they are old enough to vote." Arnall gave 18-year-olds the right to vote by using his power to issue executive orders. He then led a successful effort to include 18-year-old voting in the 1945 constitution. Georgia became the first state to do this.

Since you will be 18 years old soon, this is a good place for you to do a serious thought experiment. In 1971, the U.S.

constitution was amended to give all 18-year-olds the right to vote. How have 18-year-olds exercised that right? Do most or only a few of them vote? What difference have they made in politics and government? On an individual level, how interested are you in politics? Do you plan to vote when you are 18? The basic thing you should keep in mind as you think about these questions is that being granted a right brings responsibilities. The right to vote carries with it the responsibility to exercise that right. As the old saying puts it, you are free to decide for whom you will vote, but you should vote.

What did Arnall accomplish as governor?

Arnall accomplished many things as governor. The 1945 Georgia constitution was adopted during his administration. He appointed 23 Georgians to draft a new constitution to replace the 1877 constitution, which had been amended 301 times.

During Arnall's term, the poll tax was abolished. "No man should have to pay to vote," said the governor. Arnall brought suit in federal court to establish fairer freight rates charged by railroads. There had been much talk of cruelties in Georgia prisons and a state board of corrections was established.

After Arnall went out of office, he became an attorney for film producers in Hollywood. His home was in Newnan. He wrote books, the most widely-read being *The Shore Dimly Seen.*

The Three-Cornered Fight for Governor

Eugene Talmadge ran for governor again in 1946. He was elected but died before he took office. After the death of governor-elect Eugene Talmadge, a three-cornered fight for governor occurred. Two men, Herman Talmadge and Melvin Thompson, each claimed the office of governor. Arnall, the incumbent, was determined to turn over the office only to the properly chosen successor. This, he believed, was Thompson, the new lieutenant governor.

Eugene Talmadge had been ill during his campaign. Some of his supporters had foreseen the possibility of his death. They had written on the ballot the name of his son. Eugene Talmadge received 143,279 votes, Herman Talmadge 675 write-in votes, and Carmichael 669 write-in votes. The new constitution specified that the lieutenant governor should succeed a governor. However, it said nothing at all about whether he could succeed a governor-elect. The matter went to the legislature. On Jan. 5, 1947, the legislature voted 161 to 87 that Herman Talmadge was the rightful governor. Arnall refused to turn the governor's office over to Talmadge. Then the Talmadge supporters took over the governor's office and executive mansion, barring Arnall from both. Arnall called this a "coup d'etat."

How did the three-cornered fight occur?

On Jan. 19, 1947, when Thompson was sworn in as lieutenant governor, Arnall resigned the office of governor. He believed that Thompson was his duly qualified successor. The matter went to the courts, while Talmadge held the office of governor for 67 days. On March 19, 1947, the Georgia Supreme Court ruled that the legislature had exceeded its authority in electing Herman Talmadge. Talmadge deferred to the court's decision. Thompson became governor.

The election of 1946 was the first in which Georgia blacks had been allowed to vote in the primary. A primary is the pre-election in which a political party chooses its candidate to run in the general election. During the years in which Georgia was a one-party state, winning the primary was equivalent to election. The reason was that there was rarely a candidate to oppose the Democratic nominee. Blacks had voted in the general election but not until this election in the primary. The U.S. Supreme Court had decreed that they must be allowed to vote also in the primary election. The matter had reached the Supreme Court through a case brought by Primus King, a Columbus black, in 1945.

Why was it important that blacks be allowed to vote in the primary?

Melvin Thompson Buys Jekyll Island for the State

What did Thompson do as governor?

Melvin Ernest Thompson had to work hard to get his education. He waited on tables and at other jobs to put himself through Emory University. He went to the University of Georgia, obtained a master's degree, and became an educator.

Thompson served as executive secretary to Gov. Ellis Arnall. In 1946, he was elected lieutenant-governor. He became governor in 1947, by decree of the Supreme Court.

He did all he could for education. He also promoted Georgia's highway program. He backed a conservation program to "Keep Georgia Green." Thompson bought Jekyll Island for the state. It caused much argument at the time, but turned out to be a great benefit to the state. Vacationers from many states go there to relax and enjoy the beauty of the sand, surf and sunshine.

GONE WITH THE WIND

MARGARET MITCHELL

Greatest best-seller of our century—
the modern American classic already read by over 20,000,000 people.

WHAT ELSE WAS HAPPENING IN GEORGIA?

So much was going on during these years in Georgia! Even Nature seemed active. In 1936, a tornado struck Gainesville, killing 200 people and doing millions of dollars worth of damage. Destructive storms hit other places but Gainesville suffered the worst tragedy.

Many positive things were happening too, particularly in the area of the arts and education. Georgia had produced some good writers from the first. In this era, however, the nation was astonished when Georgia began to blossom with writers who were praised throughout the world. Margaret Mitchell, the tiny Georgia-born author of *Gone With The Wind*, wrote the big novel that made the Civil War real to the world. Published in 1936, it became an immediate best-seller and won

A portrait of Margaret Mitchell.

her the Pulitzer Prize. The world premier of the movie version was held in Atlanta. It drew huge crowds, including Vivian Leigh and Clark Gable, who starred in the film. Flannery O'Connor wrote short stories and novels about the grotesque in mankind. She achieved world acclaim. Some consider O'Connor the greatest of Georgia's writers.

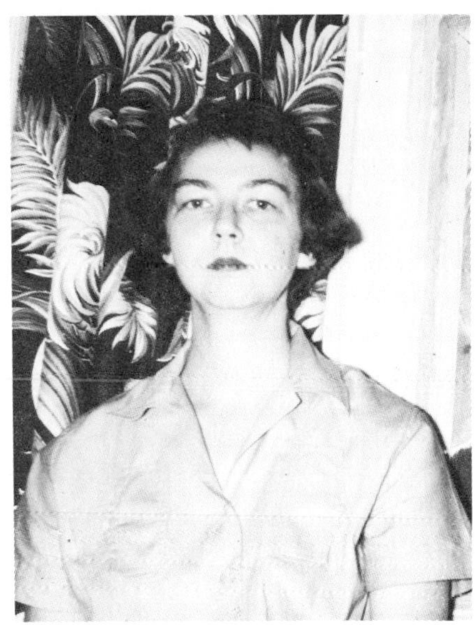

Flannery O'Connor

Two Georgians wrote plays that had runs on Broadway that placed them in the top four of all time. Erskine Caldwell's *Tobacco Road* ran for 3,182 performances, the second-longest run of any play. Anne Nichol's play *Abie's Irish Rose* ran 2,328 performances, the fourth-longest run in Broadway history. Though appreciation of his work was slow to grow in Georgia, Caldwell attained world fame for his novels and plays. These were usually about people who were sometimes derisively referred to as "po' white trash."

Among the many other writers who attained fame were Caroline Miller (who also won a Pulitzer Prize for her *Lamb in His Bosom*) Carson McCullers, Davenport Stewart, Lillian Smith, Vinnie Williams, Genevieve Holden, Celestine Sibley and Tommy Wadelton. You should read as many of these books as you can and familiarize yourself with these important Georgia authors.

Who were some of Georgia's famous authors?

Great advances were also made in education. Dr. Mauney D. Collins became state school superintendent in 1933 and served to 1958. He served in that office longer than any other man and led public school education in many advances and improvements. During his tenure in office, Georgia achieved better salaries for teachers, built more school buildings, began the free textbook program, expanded vocational education, started the school lunch program, extended the length of the school term and established Georgia's educational television network. Many of these things are simply taken for granted today.

What progress was made in the public schools under Collins?

Advances were being made in higher education also. Enrollments in the private colleges increased. The public colleges and universities were organized into one system, the University System of Georgia, in 1931. A single board of regents was established to govern the system. Georgia State College was started in an old downtown garage in Atlanta. It was to grow into Georgia State University and promised to become one of America's great urban universities. A Science Center for the University of Georgia and a nuclear reactor for Georgia Tech helped gear Georgia up for the Space Age. Georgia was becoming a more educated state.

The Atlanta Stadium

Who were some of Georgia's famous sports figures?

During these years many national and worldwide records were being attained by Georgians in various sports. Robert Tyre Jones, Jr., became the world's greatest golfer. Bobby, as he was called (a name he hated), won four great golf championships. He was for years the focus of the Master's Tournament and the great golf center in Augusta. Tyrus Raymond Cobb of Royston became one of the sports world's most famous personalities. Many regard Ty Cobb as the greatest baseball player who ever lived. He played in 2,805 games and was noted as a stealer of bases. He stole 866 bases, including 96 in a single season. Jackie Robinson, who was born in Cairo, Georgia, became the first black player in the big leagues. He attained fame with the Brooklyn Dodgers and later the New York Giants. Robinson was named to the Baseball Hall of Fame in 1962.

Trappist monks of the Benedictine Order came in 1944 to build a magnificent abbey and monastery near Conyers in Rockdale County. Their very appearance was strange to Georgians. The silent, brown-clad monks looked like figures out of the Middle Ages, studying, praying and working as silent as the falling snow. Trappists have taken vows of silence. Georgians soon became good neighbors to the gentle monks.

What Was Ahead?

Mid-century marked the last years before the ruling of the U.S. Supreme Court which would change a long-time way of life. The decision in Brown vs. Board of Education, handed down in 1954, affected education, politics, government, social relations, and nearly every other facet of living in the south.

Change was at hand. But much of it was already emerging, even before the court decree. And not all of it was related to the race question. Much was the result of new technology, especially that which mechanized farms.

Ahead was what many people believe is the most interesting period of Georgia's entire history—from mid-century until now.

For Extended Thinking

1. How did the New Deal programs affect Georgia?
2. What was Georgia's role in World War II?
3. What was the "three-cornered fight" for governor and how was it settled?
4. Who were some Georgia writers who attained fame during this period? Can you think of any reasons why Georgia produced such great writers?

Names, Terms and Concepts

Little White House
TVA
New Deal
Mein Kampf
Erskine Caldwell
laissez faire
Melvin Thompson
Ty Cobb
acreage allotment
Margaret Mitchell
Jackie Robinson
Flannery O'Connor

To Help You Study

1. What is the significance of the Little White House at Warm Springs? Why did Roosevelt begin to visit Warm Springs?
2. What were some of the main programs in the New Deal?
3. What was the most important New Deal program to Georgia and its neighboring states?
4. What was Russell's main accomplishment as governor? Did it last?
5. Who was the man from Sugar Creek? What was his political trademark?
6. Who gave 18-year-olds the right to vote in Georgia? How was this made permanent?
7. What did Gov. Thompson buy for the state?
8. Who were the world-famous Georgia authors who wrote plays that had long runs on Broadway?
9. What Georgians gained fame as great sports figures during this era?

CHAPTER 14

THE MODERNIZATION OF STATE POLITICS

As Georgia moved into the last half of the 20th century, many changes were coming to the state. Some, such as the changing patterns of racial relations, were convulsive and painful. But most of the people concerned with the changes were doing their best to meet them with courage, intelligence and dignity.

What changes were taking place in Georgia's population?

The tremendous farm-to-city movement was causing many changes in government. In 1950, the state had over four million people. For the first time more of them lived in urban places than in rural areas. To make the situation more complex, great suburbs were developing around the larger cities in the state. This development sometimes involved towns which were already incorporated. At times, the suburbs simply "grew out of nowhere." As a result, the state saw the emergence of metropolitan areas. In 1990, Georgia had eight metropolitan areas. These were Atlanta, Chattanooga, Athens, Albany, Columbus, Macon, Augusta, and Savannah. (The presence of a metropolitan area called "Chattanooga" indicates that many such areas are multi-state in nature.) The largest of those metropolitan areas was Atlanta with 18 counties. These changes are startling for a state that was almost wholly rural when the century began.

GEORGIA'S POLITICAL LEADERSHIP

The last half of the 20th century had been ushered in with the much-disputed three-cornered race for governor. While some governor's races were hotly contested, the state was not to experience another such election in the rest of the century.

Herman Talmadge

Talmadge and the Minimum Foundation Program

Herman Talmadge served as governor from January 1949 to January 1955. He was born on Aug. 9, 1913, at the Talmadge farm at Sugar Creek. After graduating from the University of Georgia, he practiced law with his father in Atlanta before going into the Navy as a volunteer in 1941. He was discharged 52 months later as a lieutenant commander.

During his administration, the Minimum Foundation Program of Education was financed by a three-cent sales tax. This was the greatest single boost that education has had in Georgia. Schools and colleges were greatly strengthened.

What did Herman Talmadge accomplish as governor?

When he left office, he returned to private law practice. In 1956, he decided to become a candidate for the U.S. Senate. Walter F. George, who had been senator, decided not to run again because of poor health. Talmadge was elected and joined Sen. Richard B. Russell in the U. S. Senate.

Talmadge became chairman of a Senate committee important to Georgians, the Agriculture Committee. Damaging publicity, including a divorce, tarnished the magic of the Talmadge name in the Georgia voter's mind. After barely surviving a tough Democratic primary, Talmadge lost his Senate seat to a Republican, Mack Mattingly. Mattingly became the first Republican elected to the U.S. Senate from Georgia in 107 years. He was defeated in 1986 by Democrat Congressman Wyche Fowler.

Gov. Vandiver and the Integration Crisis

"A governor of Georgia was born yesterday," said Vandiver's father on July 4, 1918. And it was true. The quiet young Samuel Ernest Vandiver, Jr., of Franklin County became governor in 1959. He had been adjutant general of Georgia and lieutenant governor. He had experience in politics, since he managed the campaign of Herman Talmadge for governor. Vandiver was a governor when Georgia was in the painful process of deciding how to cope with the Supreme Court decision which declared segregated schools unconstitutional.

The most convulsive changes that came to Georgia were those which made a difference in the racial patterns of more than 100 years. In 1954 the U.S. Supreme Court in the case of Brown vs the Board of Education of Topeka, Kan. outlawed segregation as "inherently unequal." Black children had long gone to school in makeshift buildings. In many instances black schools had inadequate libraries, lunchrooms and laboratory facilities. After the Supreme Court decision, the state, in meetings that included both races, worked out legal designs for the education of all Georgians.

What was the Brown vs Board of Education decision?

There were other laws and Supreme Court decisions that affected Georgia's racial customs. Among these were the 1957 civil rights legislation prohibiting the prevention of persons from voting. This act also created a Civil Rights Division in the Department of Justice. The 1964 Civil Rights Act prohibited discrimination in public accommodations and in federally financed programs. It set up the Equal Employment Opportunity Commission. In 1965 came the Voting Rights Act. It authorized the U.S. Attorney General to appoint federal examiners to register voters when necessary. The 1968 Housing Act prohibited discrimination in the sale or rental of most housing.

Vandiver had allowed the people to express their opinions on integration to a commission which held hearings around the state. The people told the commission they wanted to keep their schools open. Georgia's black children began to be admitted to both public schools and universities. The first two blacks admitted to the University of Georgia were Charlayne Hunter and Hamilton Holmes. Hunter became a reporter for the *New York Times* and the Public Broadcasting System. Holmes became a doctor. But private schools and academies, predominantly white, began to spring up all across the state.

Lester Maddox

Maddox as Governor: 1967-71

Lester Maddox, Georgia's 75th governor, had known poverty in his childhood in Atlanta. He had dropped out of school, gone to work, married and, with his wife, built up a successful restaurant, The Pickrick. He closed it when new federal laws decreed that he must serve blacks. He believed in segregation and he maintained his right to operate his private business as he saw fit. In 1966 he ran for governor.

What was Maddox's position on the race question?

He had little money for his campaign and often tacked up his own signs, "This Is Maddox Country." He promised to give what he described as "the little people" more voice in their government.

What happened in the Maddox-Callaway race?

In the general election Ellis Arnall received 52,831 write-in votes. This prevented either Maddox or Howard "Bo" Callaway, the Republican candidate, from having the required legal majority. The matter went to the General Assembly. Callaway had received the most votes in the general election but it was a different story in the legislature. Most of the legislators were Democrats and felt that they were obligated to support the party nominee, Maddox. A joint session of the legislature was held on January 10. By a vote of 182 to 66, it confirmed Lester Garfield Maddox as governor of Georgia.

Maddox was already known far beyond Georgia because of his refusal to serve blacks at his restaurant. He appeared on TV talk shows and his picture was on the cover of the *New*

York Times Magazine. Maddox received about five times as much mail as previous governors. He was a controversial figure but he was able to identify with thousands of Georgia voters.

Georgia and America's Two "Limited Wars"

Woodrow Wilson referred to World War I as the "war to end all wars." No such optimism existed with regard to World War II. Almost as soon as World War II ended, the world found itself in the Cold War. The Cold War was not really a war in the battlefield sense of the term. It was a period of very poor relations between the United States and the Soviet Union. These strained relations did break out into war on two occasions. These wars were the Korean War and the Vietnam War.

What is the Cold War?

The Korean War started on June 24, 1950. North Korea, backed by the Soviet Union, invaded South Korea, backed by the United States. A resolution passed by the United Nations Security Council on the same day condemned the invasion. It called for nations to provide support in resisting the invasion. On June 27, 1950, President Truman announced that he had ordered U.S. air and sea forces to support South Korean troops. Truman said, "This is the toughest decision I ever had to make."

How did the U.S. get involved in Korea?

Leaders in the United States spoke of the Korean War in different ways from previous wars. They talked about a war of containment. By this they meant that the objective of the war was to keep North Korea contained to its own territory. Leaders also spoke of the war as a limited war. This meant that the war would be fought only on Korean territory. It also meant that no atomic weapons would be used.

How did U.S. leaders see the war?

The Korean War was far from limited in the number of soldiers that it involved. Many nations sent troops. The United States sent more than the rest. In total, 5,720,000 American soldiers served in Korea. Of that number, about

34,000 were killed in battle. There were 75,000 Georgians who served in the military during the Korean War. Of those, 523 were killed.

How did Georgia contribute?

Several Georgians played important roles in the United States Congress during the Korean War. Walter Franklin George was one of the most respected and powerful senators at the time. At one time, Franklin Roosevelt had tried to purge Sen. George as too conservative. The people of Georgia would not let anyone tell them how to vote. They sent George back to the Senate. Sen. George's son was killed during World War I. As a result, his heart reached out to understand a bigger world. He made moving speeches in support of the United Nations. He said to his Georgia neighbors, "You are today a part of the world. You cannot separate yourself from the rest of Georgia, the rest of the nation, from the rest of the world." Sen. George died on August 4, 1957.

In the House of Representatives, a Georgian was setting a record for serving longer than anyone else. Carl Vinson, of Milledgeville, was elected in 1914. He served in the House until he retired in 1965, at age 81. Vinson served as chairman of the powerful Armed Services Committee. He was an important figure in a number of defense decisions. Vinson became known as the "father of the modern Navy." In 1973, on Vinson's 90th birthday, President Nixon announced that the next nuclear-powered aircraft carrier would be named the *Carl Vinson*. Vinson became the only living American to have a major warship named in his honor. Congressman Vinson died in 1981.

What did Vinson accomplish? How was he honored?

Dwight Eisenhower ran for the presidency on a platform of ending the Korean War. After he won the presidency, Eisenhower successfully negotiated a peace settlement. It was signed on July 27, 1953, and brought the Korean War to an end. Gen. Mark Clark signed for the United States.

United States involvement in the Vietnam War began gradually. War had been going on in Vietnam for a long time before the United States entered the fighting. United States involvement began during the Eisenhower presidency. So as the Korean War was ending, the United States was getting into the Vietnam War. Most historians date America's entrance into the "shooting war" as August 4, 1964. This was the day President Johnson ordered attacks against North Vietnam. It had attacked American ships in the Gulf of Tonkin.

How did the U.S. get involved in Vietnam?

The Vietnam War involved more Americans than the Korean War. In all, 8,744,000 Americans served during the war. Of these, nearly 47,000 were killed. Many Georgians were among those who served and died. There were 228,000 Georgians who served in the Vietnam War. Of these, 1,703 were killed.

How many Georgians served in Vietnam?

During both the Korean War and the war in Vietnam, Georgia provided an important part of the training base for American soldiers. Fort Benning is the home of the infantry. During both wars, it trained infantry soldiers and paratroopers in all branches of the Army. The Army's only Ranger training school was and still is at Fort Benning. Fort Gordon was the Army's signal school and military police school during both wars. Fort Gordon was also a place for basic training for new soldiers. It was among the first places to train soldiers specifically for conditions in Vietnam. A "Vietnam village" was built at the fort. It was used to train thousands of soldiers who were on their way to southeast Asia.

How was Georgia important in training soldiers?

Dean Rusk

A Georgia native, Dean Rusk, was secretary of state during the Kennedy and the Johnson presidencies. This meant that he was a high-ranking government official through most of the Vietnam War years. Rusk believed that the United States should study all of its options. He was not convinced that our nation was making the right decision by getting deeper and deeper into the war. In a time when some in government were calling for a censorship of news about the war, Rusk said, "Unless we are in a formal state of war with censorship here (in Washington), there is no point in having censorship (in

What were Rusk's ideas?

Vietnam). Here is where most of the leaks come." When Rusk left the government, he returned to Georgia. He became a professor of international and corporation law at the University of Georgia.

Some people describe the Vietnam War as "the media war." It was the first war that was widely televised live into American homes. Americans saw the tragic scenes of battle. Along with other things, this meant that the Vietnam War became unpopular. Demonstrations against the war were held. The growing unpopularity of the war was one of the factors that resulted in the signing of a ceasefire on January 27, 1973. Since then, Americans have become more sensitive to Vietnam War veterans. A national monument has been built. Georgia has a Vietnam monument, as do several cities in the state.

What is meant by the media war?

A Former Georgia Governor Becomes President

In 1971, James Earl Carter became the 76th governor of Georgia. His ancestors had lived in the state for 200 years. After service in the state legislature, he ran for governor in 1966. He came to know the people of Georgia as few politicians know them. He made nearly 2,000 speeches. He rose early in the morning to shake hands with and talk to workers coming off the early shifts. He stopped by hundreds of fields to talk with fellow farmers. Carter did not win in 1966 but began immediately to work on his 1970 campaign. In that year, he won the Democratic nomination for governor and went on to win the general election.

What was Carter's early political experience?

Under Gov. Carter significant improvements were made in the condition of prison inmates. Counselors and educational programs were quadrupled and treatment programs were increased 150 per cent. He also made a determined effort to bring more qualified blacks into state government, from clerks and typists to policy-making positions on state boards. The public school systems were integrated in fact. Civil and racial incidents subsided dramatically. State patrol assistance for

What improvements were made when Carter was governor?

Jimmy Carter, President of the United States, 1977-1981.

Jimmy Carter with his mother, Miss Lillian.

civil disorders was reduced from 1879 man-days in 1970 to only seven in 1973.

After the 1972 Dem ocratic Convention, Gov. Carter began to give serious consideration to the possibility of running for the presidency in 1976. Increasing numbers of Americans began to doubt the wisdom of fighting a war in Vietnam. The Watergate scandal was making headlines almost daily as more and more top government officials were implicated. Faith in our national leadership was shaken. President Nixon was forced to resign and his vice president, Gerald R. Ford, became president. Conflicts of interest and other indiscretions of congressmen were aired. Inflation was rampant, and petroleum products were costly and in short supply. The people were ready for a change and Jimmy Carter knew it. He made the decision to run.

What were the national political developments that encouraged Carter to run?

Gov. Carter was relatively unknown to the average American when he announced for the presidency. Even some Georgians ridiculed the idea. After all, the last man to be elected president from the Deep South was Zachary Taylor, and that was in 1848! Taylor had been a hero of the Mexican War and widely known at the time. "Jimmy who?" became an oft-heard question.

What political victories put Carter as the front runner?

The first state to name delegates to the Democratic Convention was Iowa, in caucuses, on January 19. Carter surprised the political observers by winning an impressive 2-to-1 victory over Sen. Birch Bayh, his closest rival. The first primary was held in New Hampshire in February 1976. When the votes were counted, Carter led all contenders and won 15 of the 17 delegates. Carter was suddenly a man to be taken seriously. He was no longer "Jimmy who?"

March was the decisive month. Gov. Wallace had strong support in Florida and in 1972 had overwhelmingly carried the state. But Carter emerged from the contest with 36 delegates to Wallace's 26. Illinois, followed by North Carolina, went for Carter. Those states clearly established him as the Democratic front-runner for the nomination.

What was the extent of Carter's convention victory?

Old-line Democrats began to worry. Carter was a man who owed them nothing, a man over whom they had no control. If he should win the nomination, they did not know if they would have influence with him. Carter kept winning, and one by one his competitors dropped by the wayside. When the Democratic Convention convened in New York's Madison Square Garden in July, there was little doubt that Jimmy Carter would get the nomination on the first ballot. When the vote was tallied, Carter, needing 1,505 to win, received 2,238.5. At a news conference later, Carter announced his choice of Sen. Walter F. (Fritz) Mondale of Minnesota for vice president.

What was Carter's inauguration like?

Inauguration Day, January 20, dawned on a snow-covered Washington. Spirits were bright. Spectators started gathering at the Capitol in the early morning hours to witness the swearing-in ceremony at noon. A chorus of students from Atlanta University, accompanied by the U.S. Marine Corps Band, sang *The Battle Hymn of the Republic*. An estimated 350,000 people were there. Jimmy Carter placed his hand upon the Bible his mother had given him and took the oath of office. A 21-gun salute sounded. For the first time a Georgian was president of the United States, the nation's 39th.

The Carter administration tried to solve many of the nation's problems. A Department of Energy was created to attempt to halt the shortage and the rising prices of energy. A Department of Education was created as a separate department. It attempted to solve the problems of educating the nation's youth by making more federal money available to school systems.

President Carter's most notable achievement may have been the peace accords, or treaty, he worked out between Israel and Egypt. It lessened tensions in the strife-torn Mideast. Egypt's President Anwar Sadat and Israel's Prime Minister Menachem Begin each came to Plains in 1981, to visit former President and Mrs. Carter. Both lauded Carter for his role in seeking peace in the Mideast. Shortly after his visit to Georgia President Sadat was assassinated. Carter represented President Reagan at the funeral services.

Some serious problems occurred during the Carter term. The price of gasoline soared. The cost of heating and cooling homes, offices and factories skyrocketed. Inflation increased, rising to nearly 20 per cent per year, the highest since right after World War II. In the midst of inflation, high interest rates handicapped business and industrial growth enough to produce a recession, with thousands jobless.

Then an event occurred that was to turn public opinion in Carter's favor for a few months. The new revolutionary government in Iran allowed a group of militant "students" to take over 60 Americans at the U.S. embassy in Tehran as hostages. This action, in part, was a response to the United States admitting the Shah of Iran for medical treatment.

But nothing Carter tried to do to secure the release of the hostages seemed to have any effect on the Iranian authorities. In April 1980 a military attempt to rescue the hostages ended in failure in an Iranian desert.

The skill that won the presidency for Jimmy Carter was not able to solve many of the problems that beset the Georgian's

President and Mrs. Jimmy Carter walk down Pennsylvania Avenue in the Inaugural Parade.

What were President Carter's most important achievements?

What problems developed in Carter's administration?

presidency. The first Georgian since the Civil War to serve as president was destined to be the first incumbent president since Herbert Hoover to lose a re-election campaign. Former President Carter returned to Plains. He maintains offices in Plains and in Atlanta. The Carter Center at Emory University attracts important individuals from around the world to discuss how to solve world problems.

A THOUGHT EXPERIMENT

You and Your Civic Responsibility

What kind of political leadership does Georgia need in the future?

There have been several governors since Jimmy Carter. We have talked about many of the 78 men who have served as governors of Georgia in the past. Now we want you to think carefully and analytically about who will be governor in the future. Who will be the leadership of Georgia in the future? What kind of individuals will they be? What programs and policies should they support to make Georgia a better state in which to live? Other states have elected females and blacks to their governorships. Do you think Georgia will? What special difficulties, if any, do you think a female or black would face in running for the governorship of Georgia?

Now think carefully and analytically about your responsibilities as a citizen of Georgia. After all, it is from among you that the future leaders of the state will come. In a democracy, citizens have certain responsibilities. We call these responsibilities "civic obligation." A citizen is obligated to obey the law. He or she is obligated to vote and to pay taxes that are lawfully imposed. What about the obligation to run for public office? Are you interested in running for the city council? For the state legislature? Even for governor? If so, how do you think you should prepare yourself? What types of talents and competencies do you think you will need? If you are not interested in running for public office, why not? What then is your obligation to support those who do run and are elected? Think carefully about these important questions.

IMPORTANT CHANGES IN STATE POLITICS

Along with the programs of governors, a number of basic changes were taking place in state politics. We will review the most significant of them.

The Emergence of Two-Party Politics

Georgia, like most southern states, had long maintained the **Solid South** Democratic pattern in voting. The Republican Party to many Georgians was the party of Lincoln and their Civil War conquerors. Georgia voted so consistently Democratic that the Republicans, few in number, did not put up candidates. Georgia lost out in national elections also. The Democrats never nominated a Georgian for high office, knowing that the state would vote Democratic anyway. The Republicans did not waste a nomination on Georgia for the same reason.

What effect did "Solid South" voting have on Georgia politics?

Over time, more and more Georgians became Republicans. Some switched from the Democratic Party because they believed the national party was out of touch with their interests. Young executives moving from the north with the new industries were often Republicans. Native Georgians whose incomes increased and who moved to the suburbs also had a tendency to join the Republican Party.

Why did the Republican Party gain strength in Georgia?

In 1970 the Republicans held their first statewide primary. Hal Suit, former news director for WSB-TV, became the Republican nominee for governor. He mounted an active campaign for the general election but lost to Jimmy Carter, the Democratic nominee.

In 1980 Republicans elected a congressman, Rep. Newt Gingrich of Carrollton, and Mack Mattingly to the U.S. Senate.

Although Mattingly lost in 1986, Republicans gained five more seats in the State Senate, giving them 10 of the 56 seats. In the state House of Representatives, the Republicans held 27 seats while the Democrats held 153 seats.

What suggests that Georgia is emerging as a two-party state?

All of these things suggest that Georgia is emerging as a two-party state.

Disappearance of County Unit Vote

Supporters of the county unit system believed that it balanced power between rural and urban sections. Its opponents pointed out that it violated the principle that no man's vote should count more than another's. A federal district court declared the system unconstitutional on May 18, 1962. The U.S. Supreme Court upheld the decision in an eight-to-one vote.

How was the county unit system abolished?

The disappearance of the county unit system meant that both primaries and general elections were on a "one man, one vote" basis. A vote in Fulton County is now worth just as much as a vote in Echols County.

Georgia took an additional step toward a more democratic system in 1970. Before 1970, if no candidate received a majority of the votes cast, the legislature elected the governor. The legislature passed a law providing that a run-off election be held instead. This type of election is between the two candidates receiving the largest number of votes. Since there are only two run-off candidates for each office, one will receive a majority unless there is a tie. A tie is unlikely.

Blacks Succeed in Georgia Politics

Many Georgia blacks have achieved outstanding success in the state. Some have become known far beyond Georgia.

Julian Bond, a key figure at the 1968 Democratic convention in Chicago, was elected to the Georgia State Senate. He has lectured on many of the nation's college campuses. *Life*

Julian Bond

magazine once said that he was perhaps the prototype of a whole new breed on the political scene: "Young, articulate, well-educated and determined young Negro politicians who must be included in planning the future." In 1986, there were 22 blacks in the 180-member House of Representatives. Six of the 56 state senators were black.

Maynard Jackson

In the spring of 1981 a federal court suit in Putnam County resulted in a decision which opens the way for more blacks to be elected to local offices. The court ruled that at-large voting for seats on the Putnam County Commission and school board was maintained for the specific purpose of preventing blacks from being elected to county offices. An at-large election is one where all voters in a city or county vote for candidates. The court held that such elections prevent blacks from public office by diluting black voting strength. The result is expected to be election in some counties and cities by district rather than at large. A district is a voting region within a city or county. If district lines were drawn so that a district had a large black population, it is likely that a black would be elected.

What is the problem in at-large elections?

Maynard Jackson, an attorney, began a successful career in politics by becoming vice mayor of Atlanta in 1970. In 1974, at age 35, he became the youngest person ever to hold the office of mayor of Atlanta. He was elected as mayor again in 1989.

Who are important black political leaders?

Rev. Andrew Young was once aide to Dr. Martin Luther King, Jr. In 1970 he became the first black nominated by Georgia Democrats as a candidate for Congress. Young lost to Republican Fletcher Thompson, the incumbent, but he evoked

Dr. Martin Luther King, Jr.

much interest and support. In 1972 he was victorious, defeating Thompson in the 5th Congressional District. The district was 62 percent white. He was the first black to serve in the Congress from Georgia since Reconstruction. Young was re-elected in 1974 and 1976. President Carter appointed him ambassador to the United Nations, a post to which he brought a fresh and sometimes controversial viewpoint. Young later resigned and returned to Georgia to become active in local and state politics. Elected mayor of Atlanta in 1981, Young was elected to a second term. He ran for governor in 1990.

King Awarded Nobel Peace Prize

Dr. Martin Luther King, Jr., began his career as co-pastor with his father of Ebenezer Baptist Church in Atlanta. He became a leader in the civil rights movement. King's belief was that blacks should seek equal rights through nonviolent means. The technique for doing this is called non-violent social change. Dr. King became head of the Southern Christian Leadership Conference and an important figure in national politics. As a result, he became known around the world.

What were Dr. King's ideas on social change?

Dr. King was awarded the Nobel Peace Prize in 1964. He is the only Georgian ever to have won the Nobel Peace Prize.

Dr. King's career was cut short when he was assassinated by James Earl Ray on April 4, 1968. The Martin Luther King, Jr., Center for Social Change was built in his honor and to carry on his work. A dream of his widow, Coretta Scott King, the Center is designed "to keep the dream of the Dreamer alive." There is a 100-foot-long reflecting pool which surrounds King's tomb. Directly behind the pool and running parallel to it is the beautiful arch-covered Freedom Walk. The eternal flame is encircled by a red brick walkway.

What makes up the Center for Social Change?

The Community Center is across the street. Constructed in the mid 1970's, the building has a library, a day care center, a gymnasium and other facilities. Nearby is a natatorium with an olympic-size swimming pool. Just up the street is the house where Dr. King was born. The administrative offices are in this area.

The latest and biggest project of the center is an $8.5 million Freedom Hall complex. It has an auditorium that seats 3,000, numerous conference rooms, the King Library and Archives, a translation facility. There is room for other projects to be pursued in future years.

In describing the center in 1980, *Ebony Magazine* said Mrs. King, in order to establish "a living monument to the peaceful warrior . . . has developed a number of programs: a Reading Academy which teaches adults how to read; a Day Care facility which serves children from six months to five years; a Scholars' Internship Program which brings together students from 25 of the nation's top colleges and universities to study the philosophy and workings of social change and to do field work in social activism; and the President's Program through which Mrs. King works with various organizations, particularly labor." All in all, the Center is an imposing array of modern buildings and landscaped grounds.

Georgia Gets More Involved in National Politics

In 1972, as a result of rules changes adopted at the 1968 national convention, the Democratic voters began to choose their own national convention delegates. Before this, the governor or party officials chose them. Georgia had a long allegiance to the Democratic Party but things were changing.

How do Georgians vote in presidential elections?

The newly emerging Republicans were able to carry Georgia in 1964 for Barry Goldwater over Lyndon B. Johnson. However, in 1968, neither the Democrats nor the Republicans won. Georgia's vote went to the Independent candidate, George Wallace of Alabama, who got 535,550 votes to Republican Nixon's 390,111 and Democrat Humphrey's 334,440. In 1972 Georgia voted for Richard Nixon, the Republican candidate for President.

Jimmy Carter was able to keep Georgia voting Democratic

Andrew Young

in the 1976 and 1980 presidential elections. After that, Georgia's electoral votes went to President Reagan in both of his terms and for President Bush in the 1990 election.

The emerging two-party system and the federal laws giving more voting right to blacks had the good effect of raising the registration rolls in Georgia. The number of registered voters increased from 733,349 in 1960 to 2,178,623 in 1976. There were specific efforts to encourage blacks to register to vote. This increase in registered voters is an important step toward wide citizen participation in government.

The Political Opinions of Georgians

What are Georgians' political opinions?

Most Georgians are moderates, though political beliefs range from extremely conservative to very liberal. A contemporary liberal in America is a citizen who believes that government can be used in some instances for solving many of society's problems. A liberal is sympathetic to government action to protect disadvantaged members of society (children, the elderly, the poor, for example).

A contemporary conservative in America views government as a source of many problems, not as their solution. Conservatives are generally opposed to government regulation of business. They argue for individual initiative as the best way to create and distribute wealth.

Not many Americans and not many Georgians are consistently liberal or conservative. They are moderates. That is, like Aristotle, they look for balance in public policy. They want government, if possible, to find a way to serve all people at the same time. That doesn't mean that they want government to do everything. It means, in Lincoln's phrase, that Americans want government to be "for the people."

What are your political beliefs? You need to think carefully about what you believe to be the proper role of government in American society.

For Extended Thinking

1. How did the integration of Georgia's public schools take place?
2. Evaluate the men who emerged as political leaders in post-WorldWar II Georgia.
3. What was Carter's strategy for winning the presidency?
4. How would you evaluate Jimmy Carter's performance as president?
5. What were the major factors in the emergence of a two-party system in Georgia?
6. Who are some of the most successful black political leaders in Georgia?
7. What were the high points in the career of Dr. Martin Luther King,Jr.?

Names, Terms and Concepts

Minimum Foundation Program
Solid South
Brown vs. Board of Education
Mack Mattingly
1964 Civil Rights Act
run-off election
Ernest Vandiver
at-large election
Lester Maddox
district election
the Carter Center
Maynard Jackson
civic obligation
Andrew Young

Names, Terms and Concepts (continued)

non-violent social change
Center for Social Change
liberal
conservative
moderate

To Help You Study

1. What was one of the important things Herman Talmadge did as governor?
2. What did Samuel Ernest Vandiver's father say when he was born? Did it come true?
3. Do you think Lester Maddox was a good governor or a bad governor?
4. Is Georgia becoming a two-party state? If so, why?
5. What was important about the disappearance of the county unit system?
6. What did the decision in Brown vs. Board of Education mean to Georgia? How did Georgia approach complying with the ruling?
7. What were the features of national politics that led Jimmy Carter to decide to run for president?
8. How did Iran affect the 1980 re-election campaign of Carter?
9. What were some of the problems Carter faced as president?
10. What was probably the greatest achievement of the Carter presidency?

11. Who is Julian Bond and why is he important?
12. Who was the first black U. S. ambassador to the United Nations? Tell about him.
13. Briefly outline the career of Martin Luther King, Jr. How was he honored before and after his death?
14. Describe the mission of the Martin Luther King, Jr., Center for Social Change.
15. Why is the question of at-large elections important?
16. What word best describes the political opinions of most modern Georgians?

CHAPTER 15

STATE GOVERNMENT IN MODERN GEORGIA

Abraham Lincoln said that government is "of the people, by the people and for the people." The Georgia Constitution states the idea this way: "All government, of right, originates with the people, is found on their will only, and is instituted solely for the good of the whole." This makes the people especially important in a government like ours. The word **citizen** takes on a special meaning. A citizen is an individual who pledges loyalty to a particular government. In return the government extends to that person certain rights and privileges. The protection of our rights as citizens is highly dependent on the acceptance of our responsibilities as citizens.

What does the Georgia Constitution say about government?

In the United States a person is a citizen of both the state and the nation. If a person is born in this country, he or she is referred to as a natural-born citizen. If the individual immigrates to the United States and acquires citizenship through residency and passing a test, the individual is referred to as a naturalized citizen. These are the ways an individual acquires citizenship in the United States.

What is the difference between a natural-born and a naturalized citizen?

How do they acquire citizenship in a state? State practice differs in this regard. The Georgia Constitution provides for state citizenship this way: "All citizens of the United States, resident in this State, are hereby declared citizens of this State, and it shall be the duty of the General Assembly to enact such laws as will protect them in the full enjoyment of the rights, privileges and immunities due such citizenship." What that last phrase means is that the state legislature passes laws

How do you acquire Georgia citizenship?

defining what we call the responsibilities and privileges of citizenship. For example, the legislature has passed laws saying how long a person has to live in the state to be eligible to vote. There is a rather complex law defining who is a citizen for the purposes of paying in-state tuition rather than out-of-state tuition at our public colleges and universities.

GEORGIA'S MANY CONSTITUTIONS

Georgia is now functioning under its tenth constitution. We have described all but the last three of them. The eight, ninth and tenth constitutions came in rapid-fire succession. The eight constitution was adopted in 1945 during the Arnall administration. It soon became a patchwork of amendments, with more than 700 having been added by 1976. Those amendments had been made necessary because of the length and detail of the 1945 constitution.

Experts point out that a constitution should include only the basic law of the state. It should not concern itself with local needs, specific regulations, or details. These should be left up to legislation. But much of that kind of thing had been in the 1945 constitution.

What should a constitution do?

Thus, Georgia was in need of a simpler constitution. In 1976 a new one was voted on and adopted by the people. It was ratified in the form of an amendment to the 1945 constitution. It reduced the number of General Articles and rearranged them in a more practical sequence. Other articles were brought into harmony with each other. One notable change was that the 1976 constitution allowed the governor to succeed himself.

What did the 1976 constitution do?

Many people in the state believed that the 1976 constitution, while an improvement, was still too lengthy and complicated. They believed that it contained too much that was local in nature. In 1977, a Select Committee on Constitutional Revision was established. This committee proposed a new constitution.

This document was approved by the House and Senate in a special session of the legislature in 1981. It was adopted by the people in 1982 and took effect on July 1, 1983.

How are the U.S. and Georgia constitutions similar?

In many respects, the constitution of the United States and the constitution of Georgia are similar. Both have a Bill of Rights. Georgia's Bill of Rights is the first article of the constitution. The Bill of Rights was added to the national constitution as the first ten amendments. Both constitutions provide for the organization of government. Both devote a separate article to the legislative, executive and judicial branches. Both assume that the base of all government is the people. Both provide for limited government by stating that there are some things that the government cannot do.

How are they different?

There are also some significant differences between the two documents. No amendments may be added to the Georgia constitution that are not voted on and approved by the people. The people do not vote on amendments to the United States constitution. State legislatures or conventions in the states do. The Georgia constitution has to provide for some things that the national constitution does not have to deal with. For example, the Georgia constitution has provisions defining the status of cities and counties. This can be different between states. Georgia's constitution also contains more detail than the national constitution. There is an article on education, another on retirement systems and educational scholarships, and a separate article on taxes. All of these things mean that the 1983 constitution will probably be amended often just like the earlier constitutions.

THE FEDERAL SYSTEM OF GOVERNMENT

One of the most important features of the national constitution is that it establishes a federal system of government. A **federal system** of government is one in which a national government and state governments exist side by side and derive their powers separately from the constitution. The national government is not dependent on the states, as ours was under the Articles of Confederation immediately after the Declaration of Independence. And the states are not dependent on the national government, as subnational governments are in Great Britain, for example.

What is a federal system?

The manner in which the U.S. constitution divides powers between the nation and states is important. The national government is given **delegated powers**. These are the powers that are listed in Article 1, Section 8 of the U.S. constitution. If the national government exercises powers not delegated to it that action is deemed unconstitutional. Since the case of Marbury vs. Madison, the U.S. Supreme Court has exercised the power to declare acts of Congress unconstitutional. States have **reserved powers**. Here is how the constitution defines reserved powers: "The powers not delegated to the United States by this Constitution, nor prohibited by it to the States, are reserved to the states respectively, or to the people." (Amendment 10). What this means is that if the constitution does not prohibit states from doing something it is generally presumed that the states have power. Notice again, though, there are some things no government can do and some powers that are reserved to the people.

What is the division of powers between the nation and the states?

GEORGIANS PARTICIPATE IN GOVERNMENT

There are many ways that individuals fulfill their responsibilities as citizens. One of the most important is through participation in government. You can participate in government through voting, by running for public office, by being an active member of a political party, or through organizations to which you belong.

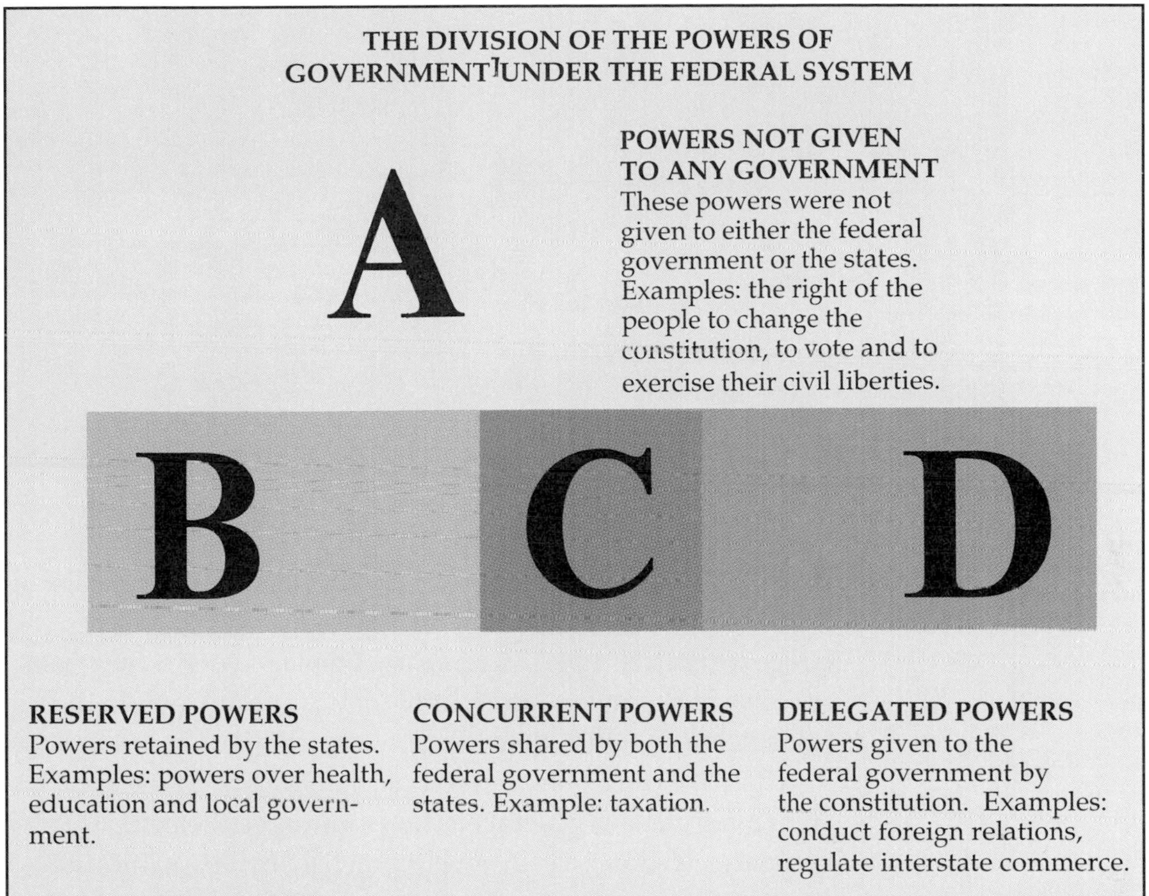

THE DIVISION OF THE POWERS OF GOVERNMENT UNDER THE FEDERAL SYSTEM

POWERS NOT GIVEN TO ANY GOVERNMENT
These powers were not given to either the federal government or the states. Examples: the right of the people to change the constitution, to vote and to exercise their civil liberties.

RESERVED POWERS
Powers retained by the states. Examples: powers over health, education and local government.

CONCURRENT POWERS
Powers shared by both the federal government and the states. Example: taxation.

DELEGATED POWERS
Powers given to the federal government by the constitution. Examples: conduct foreign relations, regulate interstate commerce.

This chart shows how the powers of government are shared by the federal government, the states and the people. The large, light block (A) represents the powers not given to any government. The smaller, slightly darker block (B) represents the powers retained by the states, while the darker block (D) represents those powers given to the federal government. Where the two blocks B and D overlap, we find an area of governmental power (C) shared by both the states and the federal government.

The right to vote is one of the most important privileges citizens have. Voting is one of the primary symbols of democracy. In Georgia, a person may vote if he or she is a citizen of the United States, a legal resident of the state and of the county in which he or she lives, and is 18 years of age. If a person is at least 17 1/2 years old and will be 18 by the election, the individual may go to the Voter Registrar's office and register to

Who can vote in Georgia?

Waiting in line to vote.

What are primary, general and special elections?

vote. This means that his or her name will appear on the list of qualified voters that election officials use on election day. Once registered, a person remains eligible to vote, if they vote as often as the law requires, until they die or move from the jurisdiction in which they live.

There are three types of elections in Georgia. These are primary elections, general elections, and special elections. A **primary election** is really an election held by the political party. Its purpose is to select the party's candidates for the general election. In Georgia, both the Democratic Party and the Republican Party will hold primary elections. A person can vote in either party's primary but they cannot vote in both primaries. If no candidate gets a majority of the vote, a second primary, or run-off primary, will be held between the top two vote-getters in the regular primary.

The **general election** is the election that finally decides who will hold the public offices involved. In other words, voters chose from the parties' candidates the individual they want to serve in each office. In Georgia, a general election usually is a contest between a candidate from the Democratic Party who is facing a candidate from the Republican Party. Occasionally, however, candidates from minor parties will appear on the ballot.

A third type of election is called a **special election**. In Georgia, there are many types of special elections. Perhaps your school has had a bond election. That is a special election where the voters approve or disapprove of a school district's plans to issue bonds to raise money for construction purposes. A special election can also be held when an official dies in office or resigns.

Why does Georgia schedule elections to separate state from national politics?

The scheduling of elections in Georgia is designed to separate state politics from national politics. This separation is accomplished by electing most state officials in the non-presidential election years. For example, the election of Georgia's governor occurs in 1994; election of the president occurs in 1992. This arrangement means that national issues will not tend to dominate state politics. Most state officials are pleased with it too, since it eliminates the possibility of a coattail effect. When there is a coattail effect, a very popular presidential candidate influences a state election.

Georgia policy makes it very easy for a citizen to run for a public office. The City of Whitesburg once elected a mayor who was 19 years old, so you are not far from the time when you can run for public office. So let us engage in a thought experiment. Suppose you wished to run for the position of representative from your district to the Georgia House of Representatives. What would you do?

How can a person run for public office in Georgia?

The first thing that you would have to do is to qualify. You would qualify by filing forms that show that you meet the requirements for the office. In addition, you would have to pay a filing fee to the political party whose nomination you will seek. The filing fee amount differs between offices, but in this instance it would be $400. The party will send 75% of the fee to the state to be used to pay election expenses and it will keep 25%. The party will then certify to the secretary of state that you are qualified to run for its nomination for the General

Assembly. The secretary of state will place your name on the primary ballot for that jurisdiction. If you win your party's nomination, you will then be on the general election ballot. If you beat the other party's candidate, you will become the next representative from your district to the Georgia House of Representatives.

In addition to voting and running for offices, citizens can have influence over government through their political party or through an interest group. While political parties are not mentioned in either the national or Georgia constitution, they are important links between a citizen and government. The remarkable thing about political parties in this country is that they do not have well-defined rules of membership like political parties in some other countries.

How does a person become a member of a political party?

At a practical level, a person becomes a member of a political party simply by declaring themselves to be such. For example, when you participate in a primary election, the election clerk will ask you which party's ballot you wish to be given. If you answer "Republican," for voting purposes you are a Republican and will be given a Republican primary ballot. If you answer "Democrat," for voting purposes you are a Democrat and will be given a Democratic primary ballot. A responsible citizen should go further than this, however. To be really effective in a political party, an individual should join the county organization of the party of his or her choice. The principle is most often stated like this: Be active at the local level in the political party of your choice.

What is an interest group?

Interest groups include all organizations that are interested in influencing what government does. If a farm group, for example, attempts to influence Georgia state government to increase its research on peanuts, then that farm group becomes an interest group. If a teacher group encourages the state to reduce the student-to-teacher ratio in class, then that organization becomes an interest group. Nearly every organized group has some interest in what government does. So at some point, nearly every organized group acts like an interest group.

Interest groups use a number of tactics to influence what government does. Some of them employ individuals, known as **lobbyists**, to represent them. Lobbyists become experts in their field of policy and are sources of information for legislators. Georgia requires that persons who will lobby the legislature register as such and pay a small fee. This is true whether the person plans to lobby on behalf of their own self- interest or that of an organization. Interest groups also engage in public relations activities. These are designed to create a favorable public opinion among the people of the state.

What tactics do interest groups use?

The more highly organized interest groups also contribute money to the campaigns of persons seeking public office. Georgia has tried to keep this activity from getting out of hand. It has placed limitations on the amount of the contribution. Most recently, the state has passed a financial disclosure law. This law means that a person seeking public office must disclose how much money has been contributed to the campaign and how that money has been spent. Tactics used by interest groups can be effective. Most scholars agree that interest groups have been growing in power and influence.

THE STRUCTURES OF GOVERNMENT IN GEORGIA

The Georgia constitution, like the national constitution, provides for separation of powers. **Separation of powers** means that the power exercised by government is divided among three branches. These branches are called the legislative, executive and judicial branches. Each has very important responsibilities under the Georgia constitution.

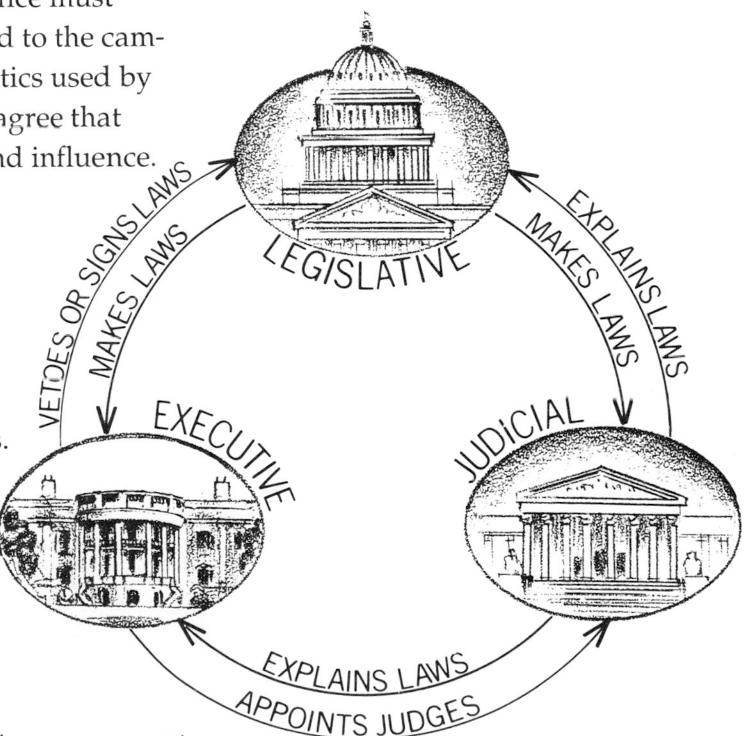

Checks and balances in our government.

The Executive Branch

How is the executive power in Georgia shared?

Unlike the national government, where executive power is almost exclusively in the president, Georgia's constitution provides for several elected executive officials. In addition to the governor, the secretary of state, the attorney general, the commissioner of agriculture, the commissioner of labor and the superintendent of schools are elected. Thus, while the governor is the chief executive of the state, he is required to share executive power with other elected officials.

What do governors do?

We have mentioned a number of governors throughout the book. What is it that governors do? One way to visualize the role of governors is to say that it is their responsibility to get things done. The governor is to enforce the law and to implement policy. Thus the governor is to execute, or carry out, those things the constitution and the legislature say are in the state's interest.

What power does the governor have?

In order to get things done, the governor has a number of **formal** and **informal powers**. Formal powers are defined in the constitution or in laws. For example, the constitution gives the governor the power to issue pardons for crimes and makes him or her the commander-in-chief of the state militia. Other powers are informal and are derived from custom and usage. The governor's position as chief politician is an example of informal powers.

The Greek Revival Governor's Mansion, built during the administration of Governor Carl Sanders.

At base, the power of a governor in Georgia depends to a great extent on the individual's political skills. If a governor is to be successful in this state, he or she must possess the ability to persuade other individuals, political leaders and legislators to the governor's point of view. A successful governor must understand how the legislature functions. He or she must know how to keep a small group of legislators from blocking a proposal from becoming law. The effective governor must be able to get a large number of differing groups to compromise and accept positions different from what they might want ideally. Certainly in the modern era of the mass media, a successful governor must know how to relate to the media.

How important are political skills to the governor?

The executive departments are the agencies responsible for carrying out programs and policies. Georgia at one time had 107 separate state agencies. This number was reduced to 18 in 1931 when Richard Russell was governor. However, more and more agencies were created so that by 1971 there were over 200 agencies, departments and boards. This caused substantial confusion, duplication of effort and blurring of responsibility. Gov. Jimmy Carter proposed a reorganization plan designed to group agencies by function. The plan reduced the number of budgeted agencies to 22. Some of these departments and agencies are headed by an elected official or by a director elected by a board. Others are appointed by the governor. The presence of so many executive officials who are not appointed by the governor is important. It makes it difficult for the governor to provide overall direction to the executive branch of Georgia's government.

What is the role of executive departments?

The Legislative Branch

The legislature in Georgia is known as the **General Assembly**. As with the national Congress and all other states except Nebraska, the General Assembly is a bicameral body. A bicameral legislature is one which has two houses. This means

What is a bicameral legislature?

STEPS IN THE LEGISLATIVE PROCESS

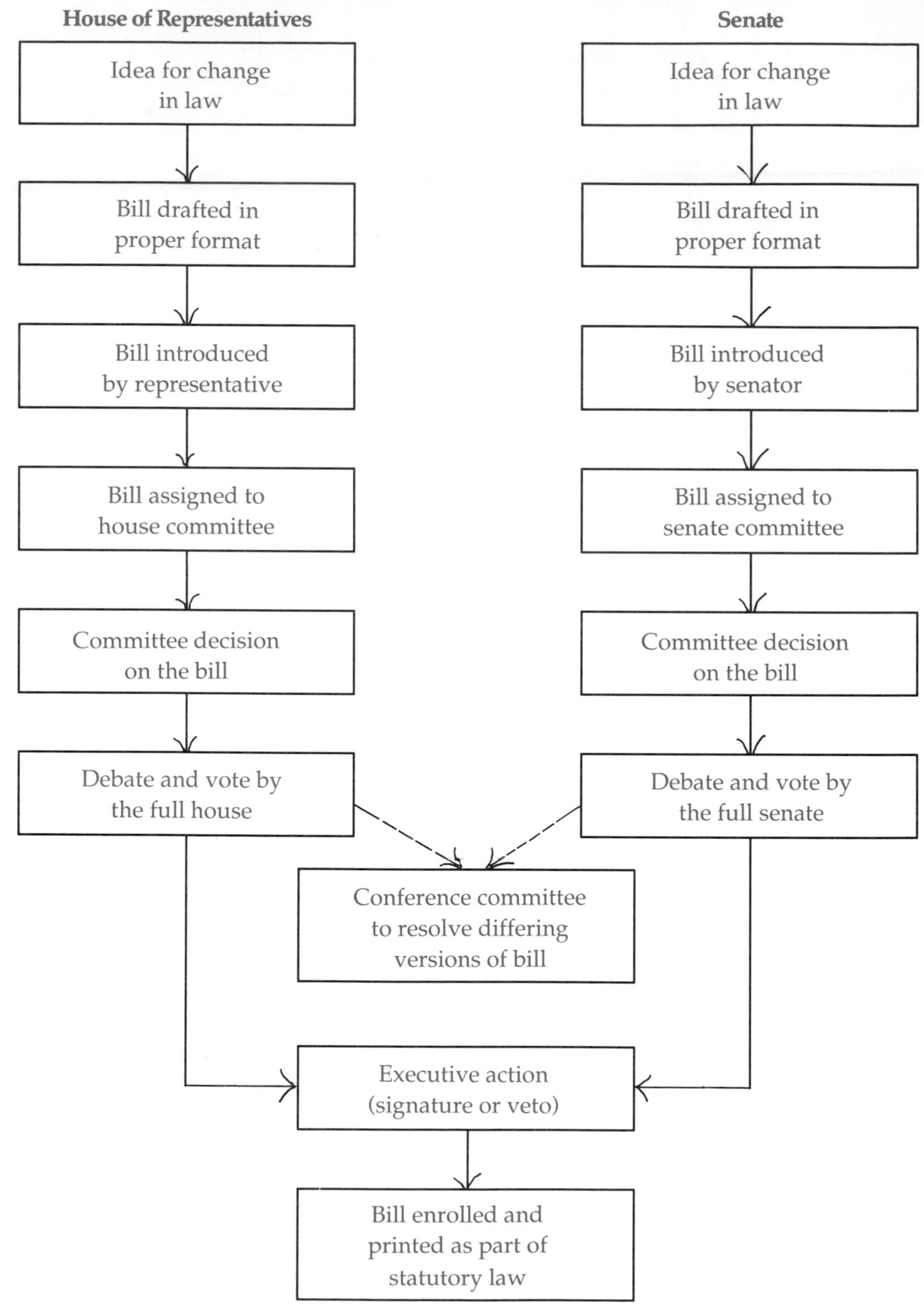

that the constitution takes legislative powers and further divides them between a Senate and a House of Representatives. In Georgia, the General Assembly has power to decide how many members each house will have and from what districts they will be elected.

The Georgia Senate consists of 56 members. Each senator is elected from and represents one district. Some Senate districts consists of only a part of a county while others include several counties. The Sixth Senatorial District has parts of eight different counties. The House of Representatives has 180 members. They also are elected from districts. Some House districts, however, elect only one member, while others may elect six or more representatives. In both the House and the Senate, the question of drawing the district lines is extremely important. Georgia, along with the other states, has to redraw its district lines every 10 years. This is to assure that the districts are equal in population. In this way, each person's vote counts the same as every other person's vote.

Who are the officers of the legislature?

The legislature elects its own officers. In the Senate, the lieutenant governor is the president of the Senate. That means he presides over the Senate. He also serves as the chairman of the Committee on Committees. This important committee selects all Senate committee members. The Senate elects a president pro tempore to serve if the lieutenant governor is absent. It also selects a non-senator as its secretary. The secretary of the Senate is the chief administrative officer of that body. The House of Representatives elects a speaker and a speaker pro tempore to preside if the speaker is absent. The speaker is a very influential person. Since the Democrats have had a majority of the members of the House, a Democrat has always been elected as speaker. Each house also has a majority leader and a minority leader to help mobilize their party's members for or against a particular bill. Members known as party whips help in this effort too.

The basic work of the legislature is done in committees. The

Senate has 24 committees and the House has 28. They are created in each house according to the rules of that house. They are called **standing committees** because they are permanent and continue from session to session. They are sometimes referred to as subject matter committees because they are organized on the basis of the subject of legislation. For example, there is an agricultural committee, an insurance committee and so forth. These committees do the basic work on a bill. They will hold public hearings, study and analyze it and debate its provisions. Most importantly, they recommend that the bill either pass or not pass when considered by the full house. A "Do Not Pass" recommendation for a bill is the kiss of death for all practical purposes.

Why are committees important?

A bill is considered by both the House and the Senate. To become law, it must be passed by both houses. Often the bill passed in the House does not contain the same wording or have exactly the same provisions as the bill passed in the Senate. In this instance, the bill goes to a Conference Committee made up of three representatives and three senators. This committee works out the differences in the bill and sends it back to the two houses. If it is passed this time, the bill is sent to the governor. The governor may veto the bill, thus preventing it from becoming law. He may sign the bill. In this case it becomes law and is printed in the *Official Code of Georgia Annotated*. If you want to find a law of Georgia, the Official Code is the place to look.

The Judicial Branch

How does a bill pass?

In both the nation and the states, the courts are responsible for interpreting and applying the law when there is a case or controversy. The power to hear cases is called jurisdiction. The court that first hears a case is called the court of original jurisdiction, or the trial court. If a court is responsible for reviewing a case which has been tried in another court, that court is called an appellate court. Georgia's court system experienced a significant reorganization effective in July 1988.

The easiest way to understand the court system is to begin with the courts of original jurisdiction. These are the courts that will first try a case. Georgia's primary trial court is known as the **Superior Court**. This court can try practically all kinds of civil and criminal cases. A feature of the Superior Court that makes it somewhat confusing is that this court can also exercise appellate jurisdiction. It can accept cases from courts of limited jurisdiction (state court, probate court, etc.) and review and correct errors made in those courts. Georgia is divided into 45 circuits or judicial regions, with a Superior Court in each circuit.

How is the Georgia court system organized?

In addition to the Superior Courts, Georgia has a number of **courts of limited jurisdiction**. These are courts that concern themselves with specific types of cases. The juvenile court is the trial court in matters involving individuals under 17 years of age. A delinquent juvenile is one who has committed a criminal offense. An unruly juvenile is one who is unmanageable or has run away from home. A deprived juvenile is one who is neglected by parents and needs the special assistance of the court.

What are the courts of limited jurisdiction?

There are several other courts of limited jurisdiction. The state courts try misdemeanor and civil cases. Probate courts handle wills. Magistrate courts issue warrants and handle civil cases under $2,500 in claims.

There are two levels of appellate courts in Georgia. The first level is known as the **Court of Appeals**. It has appellate jurisdiction over most cases from lower courts. In other words, if a case is appealed, the Court of Appeals will be the first court in which the appeal is heard. The **Supreme Court** is the court of final jurisdiction. It consists of seven judges elected by the people to staggered six-year terms. The constitution designates the type cases that can be appealed to it. In addition, the court has developed a number of rules that

What appellate courts exist in Georgia?

enable it to decide which cases it will hear and which cases it will not hear. If the Supreme Court decides not to hear a case, the decision of the lower court stands as the final decision.

How are jury members selected?

The **jury** is an important component of the courts. The Superior Court judge or judges appoints a jury commission in each county of their circuit. This commission prepares a jury list from a number of sources, primarily the voter registration lists. Both the grand jury and the petit (traverse) juries will be drawn from that list. The grand jury, consisting of from 18 to 23 persons, investigates criminal charges and the public affairs of the county. It is the body that determines if there is sufficient evidence to bring an accused person to trial. If a true bill is returned the individual is brought to trial. If the grand jury returns a no bill, the person is released and not tried. The petit jury is the trial jury and will decide questions of fact in both civil and criminal cases. In criminal cases, a jury of twelve must reach a unanimous verdict in order to convict an accused person of a crime.

What does a grand jury do?

What does a trial jury do?

Along with many other states, Georgia faces a serious problem with the prison system. Among the most serious is the fact that the national courts have ordered many states to reduce overcrowding in the prisons. Georgia began working on the problem in 1943 when Gov. Ellis Arnall called a special legislative session to deal with the prison problem. The level of activity in this reform effort increased beginning in 1977. Since 1977, Georgia has led the nation in attempting to find solutions to the prison problem.

What are problems in the prison system?

Among the most visible of Georgia's efforts has been the program known as **alternatives to sentencing**. The best known of these alternatives is probation. In probation, a person convicted of a crime is not sent to prison but is placed under the supervision of a probation officer. Between 1971 and 1987, the number of persons on probation in Georgia increased from 60,000 to 102,000.

What is meant by alternatives to sentencing?

Probation is not the only alternative to sentencing. Home confinement means that the individual is confined to his or her home, but is allowed to leave home to work or to receive medical treatment. Electronic surveillance is used to monitor certain high-risk offenders more closely. In this instance, the person is required to wear an ankle device that is tied into a computer at a central location. The individual's whereabouts can be detected at any time.

How does the special residential program work?

Several alternative-to-sentencing programs place the offender in a special residential program. **Detention centers** are used in some cases for persons who have violated their probation requirements. Instead of being sent back to prison, the individual will be confined in a detention center. He or she is often required to work and pay the costs of the detention. **Special Alternative Incarceration** is a military boot camp that attempts to shock the individual back into normal behavior. It is based on the "scared straight" idea.

A final alternative sentencing is **community service**. In this program, an individual is required to work in some way that benefits the community. By 1988, this program was estimated to have resulted in over one million hours of community service—all the way from picking up trash on the highways to counseling other individuals who are having problems.

WHAT STATE GOVERNMENT DOES IN MODERN GEORGIA

Because of the nature of our federal system, what states do will vary a great deal between states. One state may have a very active government, another a very inactive one. One state may emphasize one set of programs and services, another state may emphasize quite a different set. All of this is possible because states have reserved powers under the constitution and can make those sorts of decisions.

One way of understanding what a state does is to look at the money it spends. Georgia's annual budget is around $7 billion. Here is how the state allocated that money among programs in 1987:

How does Georgia spend its money?

Distribution of State Funds by Program

Program	% of total funds
Educational development	53.5%
Human development	19.5%
Transportation	8.5%
Protection of persons and property	7.4%
Issued debt service	4.8%
General government	2.2%
Natural environment	1.7%
Legislative-judicial branches	1.3%
Economic development	1.1%

Notice that over half of Georgia's state budget is committed to education.

How does Georgia raise its money?

How does the state raise its money? The usual way to answer this question is to think in terms of two types of state revenue. These are "own source" revenues and federal aid revenues. Federal aid is an important source of revenue for state and local governments. In 1984, federal aid was 21.9% of Georgia state and local revenue. **Own source** revenues refer to those taxes, charges, fines and the like that the state imposes on its citizens. Here are Georgia's own source revenues in 1986:

Source of Tax Dollars

Tax	% of total tax dollars
Income tax	47.3%
Sales tax	32.5%
Motor fuel tax	7.8%
Fees and sales	3.9%
All other	8.5%

Georgia, then, obtains most of its own source revenue from either the income tax or the sales tax.

YOU AND YOUR GOVERNMENT

Our thought experiment for this chapter has to do with the way government affects you individually and personally. The objective of this experiment is to determine how many ways government affects you in a normal or regular day. This will help to answer the question, "How important is government to me?"

We will get you started by identifying the ways government affects you in the very first thing you do and the way it affects you in the very last thing you do on a normal day. Your objective in the thought experiment is to fill in the rest of the day.

When you wake up in the morning, what is the first thing you do? For most people, the first thing they do is turn on a light. What does government have to do with that simple act? The electricity for that light is generated and delivered to your home by a utility company. A lot of people refer to utility companies as "public utilities" for an important reason. The utility company is either a part of a local government (the city operates it) or it is a private company regulated closely by government agencies. In Georgia, the electric companies are regulated by the Georgia Public Service Commission, an agency of the state. Among other very important regulations the commission places on electric utilities is a control on the price they can charge for electricity. In addition, local governments have building codes that specify the kind of wire that can be installed in a house and how it is to be installed. In many ways, then, both state and local governments are involved in that simple first act of turning the light on in the morning.

The last thing a person will do in a day varies a great deal among individuals. Let us suppose that it is to take a bath, brush your teeth and use the bathroom. There are a very large number of ways these activities involve government. Take the very last one of them—using the bathroom. The water necessary to flush the toilet, if you live in a city, came from a municipal water department. And in most rural areas in Georgia, individually-owned wells have to be approved by the local health department to make sure they are safe for home use.

So a department of local government is responsible for an adequate and clean supply of an absolutely necessary resource—water. When the toilet is flushed, where does the water go? Suppose the waste was dumped from bathrooms into yards or city streets. Can you imagine how bad the area would smell or how many flies and rats would be around, with all the diseases they spread? For these reasons, local governments either have a sanitation department for city residents or require a septic tank which has been inspected and approved for rural residents.

So from getting out of bed in the morning to getting back in bed that night, government directly and personally affects your life. Actually, the mattress and pillows on which you sleep are also regulated by government for content, flammability and such things.

The thought experiment is for you to think of the ways government affects your lives as you go about that normal day. What about the clothes you wear to school? How did you get to school? What about the activities in which you engaged in school? Does government affect your after-school activities? In thinking through these questions, you will come to realize how important government is to your life. And you should come to realize how important it is for you to be informed about your government and to join with other citizens in making it the kind of government you want it to be.

For Extended Thinking

1. Why is a citizen so important in a democracy?
2. How are the United States and Georgia constitutions similar to each other? In what ways do they differ?
3. In a democracy, what are the most important ways a citizen can participate in government?
4. What does separation of powers mean?
5. What programs are emphasized in Georgia state government?

Names, Terms and Concepts

citizen
special election
veto
natural-born citizen
coattail effect
jurisdiction
naturalized citizen
filing fee
trial court
federal system
interest group
appellate court
delegated powers
lobbyist
jury commission
reserved powers
financial disclosure laws
grand jury

Names, Terms and Concepts (continued)

voter registration
separation of powers
petit jury
primary election
bicameral legislature
probation
general election
standing committee
own source revenue

To Help You Study

1. What do we mean by the word "citizen"?
2. How do you acquire citizenship in the United States? How do you acquire citizenship in Georgia?
3. What do we mean by a federal system?
4. Explain separation of powers.
5. What is the difference between a primary election and a general election?
6. Why does Georgia schedule election of state officers on different years than national elections?
7. How do interest groups try to influence government officials?
8. How can a person run for public office in Georgia?
9. How does a person become a member of a political party in Georgia?
10. In Georgia, how is the executive power shared between the governor and other executive officials?

11. What power does the governor have?
12. What is a bicameral legislature?
13. Describe how the legislature passes a bill.
14. How is the Georgia court system organized?
15. How are members of a trial jury selected?
16. What are the alternatives to sentencing found in Georgia?
17. Where does Georgia get most of the revenue that the state spends?
18. On what programs does Georgia spend most of the money it raises?

CHAPTER 16

LOCAL GOVERNMENT IN MODERN GEORGIA

The U.S. constitution determines the powers that the national and state governments can have. The national government has delegated powers. State governments have reserved powers. But where does all this leave local governments?

Local governments were strong and active at the time the U.S. constitution was written. Yet there is no mention of them in that document. This is a surprising fact, especially since there are over 80,000 units of local government in existence today. If they are not mentioned in the constitution, where do they fit in our system? The existence and powers of local governments depend on the states.

How did the law on local governments emerge?

For the most part, the legal nature of local government simply evolved over time. Much of that development occurred in court rulings, both in national and state courts. In those rulings, local governments were defined as **creatures of the state** where they are located. The state brings local governments into being. It determines how they will be organized. The state decides what powers they can and cannot exercise. This is one of the most important things to remember about local government.

What does "creature of the state" mean?

We need first to understand what is meant by the term local government. These are governments that exist within the state. The most important of them are called by the names counties, cities and special districts.

Counties are the traditional units of local governments. Their use goes back to early English history. After the Norman conquest, all of England was divided into smaller districts. A count was placed over each of the districts. Thus the area was called the county. The county, then, is simply a way of dividing up a state. There is an important consequence of this fact, however. Counties are viewed as agencies or arms of the state. One of the basic purposes of counties is to carry out programs and services of the state. Georgia has 159 counties, more than any state except Texas.

What is a county?

A **city** is a municipal corporation for a defined and limited geographical area. Cities, too, are creatures of the state. The state must bring them into being. The basic document creating a city is called the incorporation charter. It is from this term that we get the terms, an incorporated place and an unincorporated place. An incorporated place is the area inside the defined limits of a city. Unincorporated places are all areas of a county except those that are in a city.

What is a city?

You have heard the term **urban** also. This is a term that is used mostly for census purposes. The U.S. Bureau of the Census says that an urban area is any incorporated place with 2,500 or more population. The term **metropolitan area** is also a census term. It refers to an area with a central city of 50,000 or more and surrounding cities that have close ties to the central city. For example, people in Pooler who work in Savannah have close ties to Savannah as the central city. The most difficult term to give a common meaning is **suburb**. The word can refer to a housing development which may or may not be a part of a city. Suburb can refer to the entire area surrounding a large city. Many Georgians refer to the "Atlanta suburban area." Finally, it has been used to refer to incorporated cities adjacent to a central city. In this usage, Pooler would be a suburb of Savannah although Pooler is a separate city. The 1987 Census of Governments counted 532 cities in Georgia.

What does "urban" mean?

What does the term "metropolitan area" mean?

What is meant by the word "suburb"?

The local government that is not well known to Georgians is the **special district**. A special district is often referred to as a single purpose government. This is because special districts

The Atlanta skyline.

are local governments set up by the state to accomplish a single purpose. There are some special districts that perform two or more functions. The usual pattern is the single function district. In Georgia, most school districts are special district governments. If you attend a public school it is probable that you are attending a school operated by a special district government. Unfortunately for understanding them, school districts are usually named for the city or county in which they are located—the Atlanta School System, for example.

What is a special district?

Authorities are a type of special district government. They take on the character of a public corporation. They are usually created to operate projects, such as a water system or an airport. In addition, Georgia has provided for downtown development authorities. These seek to encourage economic development in their particular city. Georgia allows cities to organize development authorities under conditions set by the state. Since some authorities are organized by cities and counties, it is hard to determine just how many of them there are in Georgia. The 1987 Census of Governments counted 410 special district governments in Georgia. Most people believe

What is an authority?

that there are more special districts than that in the state.

How many local governments does Georgia have?

It is clear that Georgia has a large number of local governments. As of January 1987, the U.S. Bureau of the Census counted 1,286 in total. Georgia ranks 24th among the states in number of local governments. More important than their number is the fact that these are the governments that are closest to the people. In smaller cities and counties in particular, officials in them are our friends and neighbors. Also, local governments tend to perform those services that are most personal to us—providing the water that we drink, picking up the garbage at our driveway, or patrolling the street in front of our house. Georgians see these services so frequently that they become a part of their everyday life. As a result, we sometimes take our local governments for granted. We think of local services as routine. As a result, we cannot understand why our city has to ration water during a dry summer. So it is very important that we understand local governments and participate in them.

Why is it important to understand local governments?

COUNTY GOVERNMENT IN GEORGIA

Counties are "creatures of the state." Their organization and powers are determined by the state constitution and state laws. Here is how the Georgia constitution states this principle: "Each county shall be a body corporate and politic with such governing authority and with such powers and limitations as are provided in this Constitution and as provided by law" (Article IX). Notice several important things about this provision. First, counties do have governing authority. Each one is a "body corporate and politic." Second, the governing authority of the county is determined by the constitution and state law. The more common way to refer to "governing authority" is to use the words "the organization of the county." Thus how counties are organized depends on the state. Third, counties

What does the Georgia constitution say about counties?

only have those powers the state grants to them. Just because the citizens in a county might want to do something does not mean that they are empowered to do it. Fourth, counties are under limitations that are stated in the constitution and state laws. That means that there are a lot of things that counties cannot do.

Given these things, how are counties organized? The **governing authority** in most Georgia counties is the Board of Commissioners. This type of organization is almost government by committee. The size of the board will vary between counties. Some counties in Georgia have only one member on their Board of Commissioners. That means that the governing authority of the county is given to one person. There is one county with 11 members on its board. Actually, that one is the Muscogee-Columbus council. It governs a city and county which consolidated into one government. The most common number of county commissioners is five. Members of the Board of Commissioners are elected by the people.

What is a Board of Commissioners?

There are other county officials who are elected by the people. This is the list found in the Georgia constitution: clerk of the superior court, judge of the probate court, sheriff, tax receiver, tax collector, and tax commissioner. Actually, some counties elect more officials than these. You might find that your county elects its coroner, treasurer or surveyor, for example. All of these elected county officers perform important functions. An interesting project for you would be to find out who these people are in your county.

What county officials are elected?

In addition to these elected county officials, there are a number who are appointed. Some counties have a county manager or administrator. This person functions much like the chief executive officer of the county. The manager is responsible to the commissioners. How many appointed officials a county has depends on each county and the programs that it provides. Nearly all counties will have a county clerk, a county attorney, and a voter registrar. Most will have

Who are the appointed county officials?

zoning commissioners and building inspectors. These county officials will be very important to you when you are building a home or want to construct a business. Counties provide for managers of all of their programs by appointment.

What do counties do?

An important question, then, is what do counties do? The answer is that they do some very important things. What they do will vary between counties. Georgia's constitution lists fourteen things that counties *may* do. Notice that the constitution permits counties to do these things. It does not require counties to do them. This is the list of the things counties may do and the services they may provide:

- police and fire protection
- garbage and solid waste collection and disposal
- public health facilities and services, including hospitals, ambulance and emergency rescue services, and animal control
- street and road construction and maintenance, including curbs, sidewalks, street lights, and devices to control the flow of traffic
- parks and recreational areas, programs, and facilities
- storm water and sewage collection and disposal systems
- development, storage, treatment, purification, and distribution of water
- public housing
- public transportation
- libraries, archives, and arts and sciences programs and facilities
- terminal and dock facilities and parking facilities
- codes, including building, housing, plumbing, and electrical codes
- air quality control
- maintain and modify existing retirement or pension systems

This is an impressive list of things that counties may do. How many of them does your county do?

Counties spend considerable sums of money in providing these services. How much do counties spend and where do they get the money? Both of these things will vary between counties. In other words, each county will spend a different amount on each program than will every other county. And as we have indicated, counties do not necessarily perform all the functions that the state constitution permits them to do. Revenues that counties raise will vary also between counties. For example, the amount that a county collects from the property tax will depend on the kind of property found in that county. Statewide, however, county finances in 1984 took the patterns shown in the following pie charts:

What sources of revenue are important to counties?

How do counties spend their money?

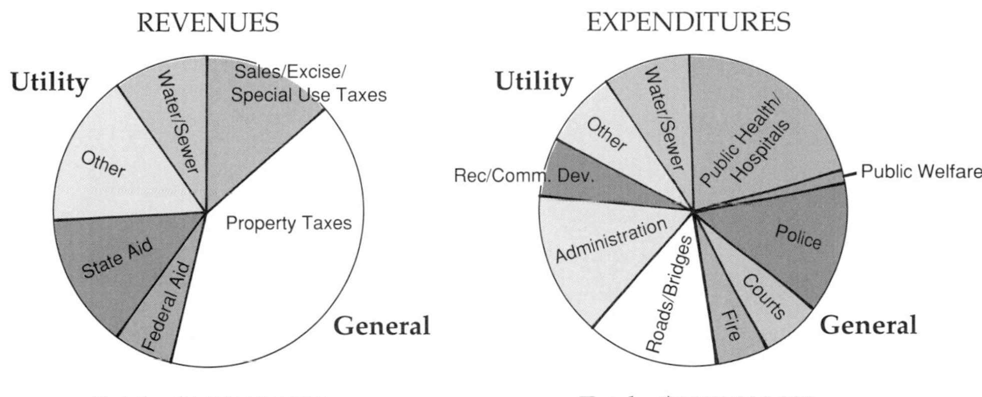

Source: The Atlas of Georgia, p. 231.

Examine those charts carefully. The entire pie is 100%. So the part of the pie taken by each individual factor shows you the importance of that factor in the counties' revenues and expenditures.

Some individuals find it easier to understand data when it is in table form. The following is essentially the same data as in the pie charts but in table form.

County Finances

	Amount in Millions of $	Percent of Total
Revenues		
Property tax	$567	41.4%
Intergovernmental revenue	$288	21.0%
Sales, excise, special use taxes	$174	12.7%
Utility revenues	$143	10.4%
Other revenues	$199	14.5%
Expenditures		
Health/human services	$288	22.6%
Public safety	$245	19.2%
Administration	$185	14.5%
Highways	$179	14.1%
Utilities	$118	9.2%
Courts	$95	7.4%
Leisure services	$52	4.1%
Public works	$36	2.8%
Housing/community development	$20	1.6%
Other	$57	4.5%

Source: Georgia Local Government Finance, 1984. Georgia Department of Community Affairs.

What is important about the way we present data?

You should study both ways of presenting data. Notice also that the data are organized slightly differently. In the pie chart, fire and police are shown separately. In the table they are lumped together under public safety. This suggests that you should ask some very important questions about any data that you see. How is that data presented? What is the table or chart trying to show? Does the table deliberately lump some things together? Does it deliberately show some data separately? What all this means is that the way data is presented can make a point or emphasize some things over others.

CITY GOVERNMENT IN GEORGIA

Surprisingly, the constitution of Georgia does not define what a city is. It refers to municipalities, defines their powers and sets limits on them. But it is left up to the legislature to determine the legal nature of a city. As indicated earlier, a city is a municipal corporation for a defined and limited geographical area. As such, it is also a "creature of the state."

In order to explain some important things about a city, engage in another thought experiment. Assume that you are living in an unincorporated place. A beautiful stream runs through the area. The residents of your community do not believe that county and state laws are adequate to protect the stream from pollution. Someone suggests that you become a city. Their argument is that the city could then pass laws protecting the stream. How can they make their unincorporated community a city?

Remember that the state must create a city. So the first thing our residents would seek to do is to obtain a **charter** from the state. State law establishes certain requirements before a charter is granted. The community must have at least 200 people living in it. It must be at least three miles from the boundary of any other city. Finally, at least 60 percent of the area must be developed. So the residents who want their area to become a city try to determine whether it meets the requirements for becoming a city. What would they do then?

How is a city created?

The charter must be granted by the state legislature. The residents of the community would talk with the **local delegation** to the state legislature. The local delegation consists of the representatives and senators who represent the area in which the community is located. To become a city, the residents convince the local delegation that the community should become a city. The delegation would then introduce a bill in the legislature providing for the city's charter. Other legislators are likely to vote for the charter if the local delegation supports it.

They say that they are showing "courtesy" to those members who make up that local delegation. Actually, they want other legislators to vote for similar bills that they introduce.

If sponsored by the local delegation, the bill will be passed and the charter will be granted. The community has become a city. The charter is very important. It will provide for many aspects of the organization and powers of the city. It will certainly define the city's boundaries and specify its name. It is on the basis of the charter that the offices of the city will be established and its officers elected.

How are cities organized?

TYPICAL ORGANIZATION OF A GEORGIA MAYOR-COUNCIL CITY

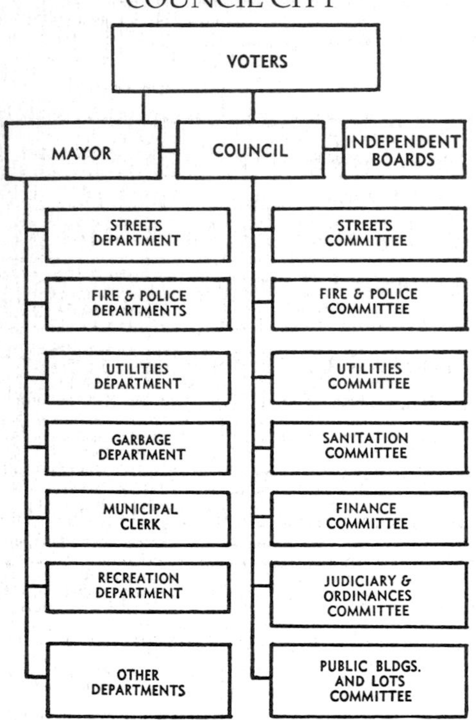

There are several ways that cities can be organized. The most important of these are the mayor-council form, the council-manager form, and the commission form.

Most cities in Georgia use the **mayor-council** form. The key element in this form is that both the mayor and council members are elected directly by the voters. The council functions as the legislative, or policy-making, body. It passes laws, called ordinances at the city level, that provide for the general direction of the city. The council will also adopt the annual budget of the city. The mayor is the chief executive officer of the city. He or she oversees the major departments of the city. The mayor usually appoints the department heads with consent of the council.

The relationship between the mayor and the council differs considerably between cities in Georgia. These differences give rise to two subtypes of mayor-council forms. The first is called the strong-mayor form. As its name suggests, the mayor has strong executive powers and has substantial independence from the council. The second type is the weak-mayor form. In this form, the mayor has less executive power and is dependent on the approval of the council for a number of things.

The **council-manager** form is the second way that a city could be organized. In this form, the council is responsible for the overall operation of the city. There will be a mayor. The mayor has what are known as ceremonial powers, and presides over the council. The council employs a professional administrator who oversees the executive departments. This person is called the city manager. The objective in this form is to get professional management of the city's affairs. The manager is responsible to the elected council.

What powers do cities have?

The **commission** form of organizing cities is much like the commission form used by counties. Not many cities in Georgia use the commission form. In fact, its use is declining among cities nationally.

Georgia's constitution grants to cities the same powers that it does to counties. So, to see what cities may do, review the list of fourteen powers and services granted to counties. The constitution is very clear that the city is to exercise those powers within its boundaries. The county is to exercise its powers within its boundaries.

Where does the city get its money and how does it spend it? As with counties, revenues and expenditures will vary between cities. One city's revenues and expenditures may be quite different from another's. Statewide, city finances in 1984 took the patterns shown in the following pie charts:

TYPICAL ORGANIZATION OF A GEORGIA COUNCIL-MANAGER CITY

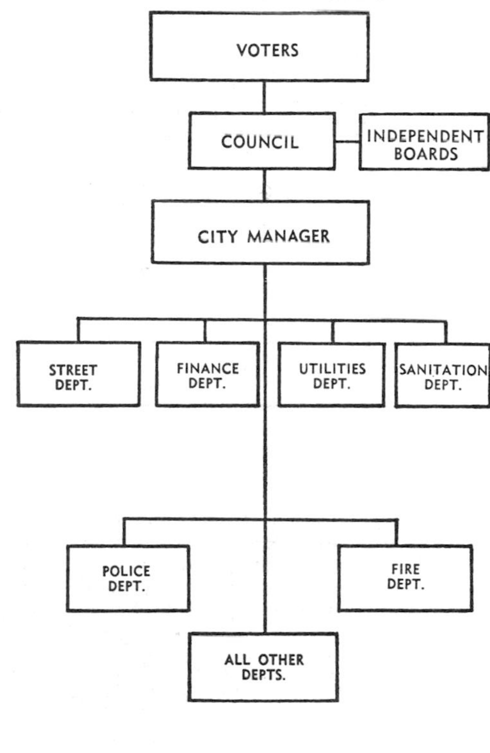

MUNICIPAL GOVERNMENT FINANCES

REVENUES

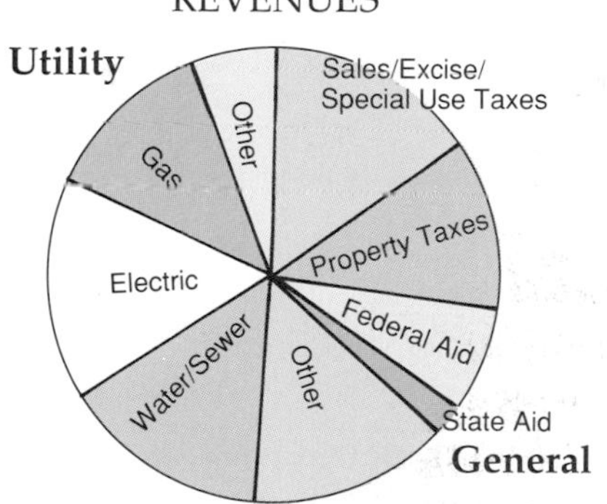

Total = $1,934,000,000

EXPENDITURES

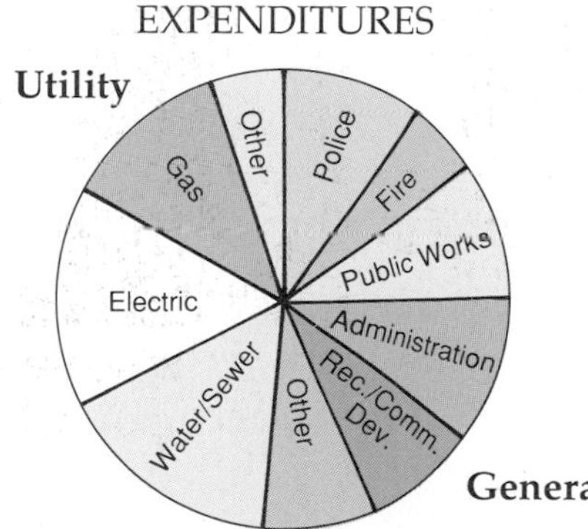

Total = $1,690,000,000

Source: The Atlas of Georgia, p. 231.

What are the sources of revenue for cities?

How do cities spend their money?

You should compare these pie charts with the ones on the counties. There are significant differences in how cities and counties raise money and in how they spend it. What are some of those differences?

The following table may allow you to compare those differences a little more closely:

City Finances

	Amount in Millions of $	**Percent of Total**
Revenues		
Utility revenues	$943	48.8%
Sales, excise, special use taxes	$287	14.9%
Property tax	$224	11.6%
Intergovernmental revenues	$223	11.5%
Other revenues	$257	13.3%
Expenditures		
Utilities	$815	48.2%
Public safety	$271	16.1%
Administration	$179	10.8%
Public works	$168	9.9%
Housing/community development	$66	3.9%
Leisure services	$66	3.9%
Health	$15	.9%
Education	$14	.9%
Courts	$ 5	.3%
Miscellaneous	$91	5.4%

Source: Georgia Local Government Finance, 1984. Georgia Department of Community Affairs.

Like counties, Georgia cities collect and spend considerable amounts of money.

In order to spend this money as wisely as possible, cities and counties use what is known as a budget. A budget is the plan by which a city or county will raise and spend its money. For the city, the budget will be prepared either by the mayor or manager and approved by the council. If the county has a manager, the budget will be prepared by the manager and approved by the board of commissioners. If there is no manager, the budget will be prepared by the chairman of the board or committee of the board formed for that purpose. The budget process is very important since it determines how much support the city or county will give to a particular program.

What is a budget and how is it prepared?

SPECIAL DISTRICT GOVERNMENTS IN GEORGIA

Special district governments have been referred to as shadow governments. This is because they are not very well known by the public. For that matter, they have not been studied very closely by scholars either. It is hard to obtain even the most basic facts about them. For example, how many special district governments are there in Georgia? The Census of Government lists 410. Most people believe that there are many more than that. There may be over 700 authorities in Georgia. And authorities are a subtype of special districts.

Why are special districts called shadow governments?

Special districts may be created in several ways. The state may create a special district for a statewide purpose. The Georgia Port Authority would be an example of such a special district government. Second, the state may create a special district for a local or regional purpose. MARTA, or the Metropolitan Atlanta Rapid Transit Authority, is an example of this type. Third, the state has passed legislation allowing cities and counties to create special districts. Your city may have a

Who creates special district governments?

downtown development authority. If it does, it probably is an example of this third type of special district government.

How are special districts organized?

Special district governments are usually governed by a board. For the school districts, there will be the Board of Education. These boards are elected by the voters in that district. Sometimes special district boards will be appointed. The most common practice is to allow the mayors of the cities and commissioners of the counties in which the special district is located to appoint the members. The board is responsible for all aspects of the special district government. It will appoint a director and hire what staff is needed to carry out its purpose.

What do special districts do?

What do special district governments do? They do a wide range of things. In Georgia, one type of special district is responsible for providing education in its area. This is the school district. There are 159 school districts in Georgia. The number keeps changing because of **consolidation**. This action merges two school districts, usually districts with small enrollments, into one district. But special district governments do many other things. Here is a list of the kinds of special districts other than education: cemeteries, school buildings, fire protection, highways, health, hospitals, housing, urban renewal, libraries, drainage, flood control, irrigation, water conservation, soil conservation, natural resources, parks, recreation, sewers, water supply, gas supply, electric power, transit, and mosquito control. There are some districts that provide two or more services. Those are usually a combination of two or more on our list. Do you know of other types of special district governments?

How much money do special districts spend and where do they get it? It is easy to answer the last half of that question and almost impossible to answer the first half. Special districts get their money either through taxes (school districts and the property tax), through special charges (a water district) or through borrowing. One of the reasons some areas use special districts is because they can borrow money. The Georgia constitution places severe restrictions on cities and counties so far as borrowing money is concerned. So special districts have some advantage there.

Where do special districts get their money?

It is hard to say how much money special district governments spend in Georgia. There is no data that enable us to draw pie charts or construct tables of expenditures and revenues. One study did find an authority which spent around $250,000,000 per year. It reported having 3,400 employees. But not all special districts are large. Some have only a part-time director and very small budgets.

How do special districts spend their money?

Whether large or small, special district governments are very important units of government in Georgia. We need to know more about them.

For Extended Thinking

1. What is the legal nature of local governments?
2. Why are local governments important to us?
3. How are counties organized?
4. How important are county programs to our everyday life?
5. How are cities organized?
6. What powers do cities have?
7. What are the differences between how counties and cities raise and spend money?
8. Why are special district governments called shadow governments?
9. Why are special districts important to us?

Names, Terms and Concepts

creatures of the state
suburb
mayor-council
county
special district
council-manager
city
authorities
ordinances
incorporation charter
county manager
budget
urban
pie chart

Names, Terms and Concepts (continued)

consolidation
metropolitan area
local delegation

To Help You Study

1. How did the law on local governments come into existence?
2. What does creature of the state mean?
3. What is an authority? Who creates them?
4. How many local governments does Georgia have?
5. What does the Georgia constitution say about counties?
6. What is a board of commissioners?
7. What do counties do?
8. How is a city created?
9. What powers do cities have?
10. Where do cities get their money? How do they spend it?
11. Who creates special district governments?
12. Why are special districts important to us?

CHAPTER 17

THREE PUBLIC PROGRAMS IN MODERN GEORGIA

EDUCATION, HEALTH AND WELFARE

Modern Georgians experience a very different environment from that of earlier residents. There are now a number of things that the state does to improve the well-being of its citizens. This chapter will look at three of those important state programs. There are many other important public programs.

EDUCATION MEETS MODERN NEEDS

Rip Van Winkle was astonished at the changes he found. Georgia's early schoolmasters would be even more astonished at changes that have come about in Georgia education.

Once, each community had only such schools as it could support. Many had a three-month school term. Teachers' salaries were around $20 a month. They often boarded around in pupils' homes as part of their pay. Since young people often helped harvest crops, school terms were short. There were recesses for picking cotton or working the crops. It was 1937 before the state guaranteed a seven-month school term and state salaries for teachers. As late as 1920, Georgia had 8,359 schoolhouses. Some were so bad that, as a wit once said, " The pupils could study geology through the floor, forestry through the walls, and astronomy through the roof." Now Georgians spend billions each year to educate their

What changes have occurred in education?

children. Georgia has built more new school buildings than any state except New York and California.

How is the school system organized?

The organization for education through high school in Georgia is a little complicated. The easiest way to understand it is to think in terms of two layers. The first layer consists of various state agencies and officials. The group that determines basic education policy is the **State Board of Education**. The ten-member board is appointed by the governor. One member is appointed from each of the ten districts from which we elect congressmen. Thus all of Georgia is represented on the board. That fact is significant since the board makes some very important decisions. The board determines the main outlines of what you will study. It sets the qualifications of the teachers in your classes. It determines the requirements you will have to fulfill in order to graduate. All public schools in the state must operate within the policies set by the State Board of Education.

The highest education official in Georgia is the **state superintendent of schools**. This official is elected by the people. The state superintendent is responsible for enforcing the policies issued by the Board of Education. He is also the head of the Georgia Department of Education.

What does the state Department of Education do?

The Georgia Department of Education is the state level agency responsible for administering all education laws, policies and regulations of the state. In so doing, it provides a number of services to local schools. It provides specialists to help teachers in many ways, including what textbooks to use. It has architects and engineers to assist local systems. It provides many different kinds of educational materials and resources. A list of all the activities of the State Department of Education would be very long.

How are local school systems organized?

The second layer in the organization for education in Georgia is the local level. Most of the state is divided into **school districts**. These are special district governments talked about in the preceding chapter. There are 187 local school districts in

Georgia. District organization consists of a school board and a local superintendent. The board is elected by the voters in the district. In some districts, the local superintendent is elected by the people. In others he or she is appointed by the board. The local board and superintendent are responsible for the day-to-day operation of the schools in that district. As such, they are very important officials.

The School Lunch Program, a boon to education, was launched nationally by Georgia's U.S. senators Richard B. Russell and Herman Talmadge. By the 1970's, Georgia, with other states, had begun to experiment with serving breakfast also. "Hungry children can't learn," said the teachers. The Georgia School Foods Service Association was invaluable in the school lunch program. About 10,000 people now work in Georgia's lunch program.

Four Big Laws Make a Difference in Education

Many people have struggled hard and long to promote education. The big breakthroughs were in 1937, 1949, 1963 and 1984.

The 1937 law was titled the **Education Equalization Bill**. It provided for a seven-month school and state salaries for teachers. The 1948 law was the **Minimum Foundation Law**. It brought about a 10-month teacher employment, more professional recognition for all teachers, and phased out the certification of teachers with only two years of college. This law began the gigantic school building program, too. The three-cent sales tax finally made these things possible. Programs for exceptional children—handicapped and unusually talented—were set up so that every Georgia child could be educationally included. The Department of Education was building the largest film and tape library in the world for Georgia schools.

Why is the Educational Equalization Bill important?

In 1963, the **Minimum Foundation Program for Education**

Why is MFPE important?

(MFPE) Law was extended. It established the vocational-technical schools. MFPE provided more building money and better salary and certification programs for teachers. It set up the Governor's Honors Program for gifted students. It authorized more visiting teachers, counselors and other specialists. The act extended educational television. It also contained state financial aid for lunchrooms and 12-month school programs.

Joe Frank Harris was elected governor in 1983. His platform called for education reform as its number one priority. His **Quality Basic Education Act** passed without a no vote in either the House or the Senate. It called for an increase in education spending by nearly $700 million. The program provided for a full-day statewide kindergarten, better teacher pay, leadership development, uniform subjects to be taught in schools, and accountability at all levels of education. It has provisions for rewarding the best educational professionals. All four of these laws have done much to make Georgia's education system a modern and effective one.

Why is QBE important?

Educational Television Widens the World for Students

Georgia is served by a network of 10 educational television stations. Eight are operated by the State Board of Education, one by the University of Georgia, and one by the Atlanta city school system. A $2 million production studio is located in Atlanta. Educational television offers courses that add to the classroom teacher's programs or that a local school might not have staff to teach. In the evening, the stations enrich the lives of Georgians in their homes with marvelous programs in art, public events, drama and science. They also provide what is known as an equivalency certificate. Through this program, Georgians who did not graduate from high school could study, take exams, and earn a high school diploma.

What contribution does educational television make?

Atlanta Area Technical School.

Vocational-Technical Schools and Junior Colleges Cover Georgia

Vocational education in public schools was started during the Wilson Administration by two Georgians in Congress: Rep. Dudley Hughes of Danville, and Sen. Hoke Smith of Atlanta. In recent years, vocational courses have been expanded in comprehensive high schools. There were 56,000 students enrolled in these schools in 1975.

Why are vo-tech schools and junior colleges important?

Junior colleges have put college within reach of all Georgians. Some are on the same campuses as the Vo-tech schools and others are nearby so students can take both humanities and technology courses. Scholarships have made it possible for Georgians to prepare themselves for skilled, well-paid trades or professions.

Fernbank Science Center

What does the Fernbank Science Center do?

World attention was focused on Georgia during the moon landings. The Fernbank Science Center in DeKalb County played an important part in the historic event. Fernbank, which is a part of the DeKalb School System, has the nation's third largest planetarium. It is the only one in the U.S. owned and operated by a school system. Nearly a half million visitors, from all 50 states and many foreign countries, have seen it. During the Apollo 12 moon mission the 36-inch reflector telescope (largest in the southeast) made the first visual observation of the Apollo space craft in orbit.

Higher Education and Space Age Changes

Why are private universities important?

Private colleges and universities are important components of higher education in Georgia. Wesleyan, in Macon, was the world's first chartered college that gave degrees to women. Among its well-known former students were Madame Chiang Kai-shek and Mrs. Sidney Lanier. Atlanta University is known all over the world as the largest complex for the education of blacks. In recent years a center for black studies has been developing as part of a memorial to Dr. Martin Luther King, Jr. Emory University in Atlanta is one of the nation's best private universities. The Berry Schools at Rome are three schools started originally for mountain children by Miss Martha Berry. At the Rabun Gap-Nacoochee School, journalism students attracted national attention with their series of *Foxfire* books. The books proudly portray old mountain lore and customs "before they die out and people forget them." In all, there are 18 four-year private colleges and universities and 8 private junior colleges. These institutions are active providers of higher education in Georgia.

The Woodruff Library at Emory University.

How is the university system of Georgia organized?

Public colleges and universities in the state are a part of the university system of Georgia, created in 1931. The system is composed of four comprehensive universities, one regional university, 14 senior colleges and 15 junior colleges. The university system is governed by a **Board of Regents** appointed by the governor. The board is composed of 15 members, one from each of the congressional districts and 5 appointed at large. The chancellor is elected by the board as the chief administrative officer of the university system. Each institution in the system has its separate president. He or she serves as chief administrative officer of that unit.

There were 161,783 students enrolled in university system institutions in the fall of 1988. Students came from all of the Georgia counties, all 50 states and from 152 foreign countries. In all, 89.1% of the enrollment was from Georgia. Blacks were 15.1% of the total enrollment.

The total budget of the system was $1.48 billion in 1989. The state appropriated $813 million to the system that year. Student fees accounted for 25% of the instruction budget. The typical cost to a student attending a system senior college in 1989 was estimated to be $3,619. The rest of the system's budget came from grants, gifts, endowment earnings and the like.

What type program does it offer?

In addition to resident instruction, the university system engages in a number of research and services activities. The universities in the system have 131 institutes and centers that conduct research and provide service. They received $246 million in 1989 in external grants and contracts. The senior colleges received $17.9 million and the two-year colleges received $4.3 million in external grants and contracts to support research and service.

Adult education and continued professional development are important parts of the university system's program. In all, 513,316 individuals enrolled in continuing education courses in 1989.

HEALTH SERVICES MEET MODERN NEEDS

Georgians have had concern for good health since their earliest days. The Trustees had provided medicines for the first settlers. Later, plantation owners built summer homes in the cool blue mountains, to escape the hot, malarial coastal lands. They believed that a "miasma" or fog caused malaria. When they realized that mosquitoes were responsible, they began to screen their houses.

What department is responsible for public health in Georgia?

State government was reorganized by Gov. Carter in 1972. The responsibility for the health and well-being of all Georgians was placed in the Georgia Department of Human Resources. It has six divisions: (1) Public Health, (2) Mental Health and Mental Retardation, (3) Family and Children Services, (4) Rehabilitation Services, (5) Youth Services and (6) Administrative Services. The department is the largest state agency. It has 28,000 employees working in its 100 human services programs. It has 1500 locations in all 159 counties. By the mid-1980's, the department's annual budget was about $1.3 billion, half of it from the national government.

The Division of Public Health

What are the functions of the Division of Public Health?

Each year over a million residents receive medical, health and educational help. Children are checked for some health problems. Many people are examined for heart disease, strokes, high blood pressure, lung problems, diabetes and arthritis. Many are examined for venereal diseases. Thousands, many of them teenagers, receive family planning services. Handicapped and disabled children are checked to try to improve their condition. Children receive vaccinations to keep them from suffering most of the old and well-known children's diseases.

Low-income individuals are able to be treated for cancer, tuberculosis, high blood pressure, kidney problems and other diseases. Tests are made for suspected infectious diseases.

Several cases of snakebite and rabies are recorded and treated each year. Entries of birth, death, abortion, marriage and divorce are recorded by the Vital Records Unit. In 1980, there were 255,000 entries.

Division of Mental Health and Retardation

This division is the largest one in the department. Problems of mental health are increased by the pressures of modern-day living. In 1980, more than 94,000 Georgians were treated in one of the mental health division's facilities. Centers are located all over the state. To make help more readily available there are eight state hospitals, four retardation centers, 34 community service facilities and 130 mental retardation programs. One of the main purposes of the program is to keep those with retardation problems out of an institution and in a home or a home-like atmosphere.

The administration building at the Georgia Retardation Center in Dekalb County.

There are centers available in several places for alcohol and drug abusers. These centers work closely with law enforcement officials to determine what to do with a person who has had too much alcohol or drugs to function properly. The Commission on Alcoholism was created by the General Assembly in 1951. Since then, 265,000 alcoholics have been studied and treated.

What does the Division of Mental Health and Retardation do?

When Mrs. Jimmy Carter became Georgia's First Lady in 1971, she chose mental retardation as her special interest. When she became the U.S.'s First Lady in 1977, her interest became nation-wide.

The CDC Studies the World's Health

The national government's Centers for Disease Control (CDC) is located in Atlanta. It provides research and epidemic aid for better health in the United States and throughout the world. Each year, CDC trains some 20,000 health workers and assists state health departments investigating more than 1,500 outbreaks of disease.

What is the Centers for Disease Control?

CDC works with governments of other nations and with the World Health Organization to help control diseases before they can spread from one country to another. CDC exchanges information with health authorities throughout the world, enabling them to take quick action as problems arise and are identified.

The CDC has conducted invaluable research. It assisted in the international eradication of smallpox. The CDC conducted the study of Legionnaire's disease. Much of the applied research related to the rare, newly defined illness toxic-shock syndrome has been done by the CDC. Through its many-faceted programs, the Centers for Disease Control offer a more abundant health future for all people.

Centers for Disease Control

Progress and Problems in the Health Story

Georgia's history of health has the light and dark of a Rembrandt painting: shining achievements and problems that still shadow the picture. Georgians believe that human health, good or bad, affects history. Reflecting that philosophy, Georgians are beginning to coordinate their efforts to insure that the effect will be good.

An example of this coordination is the effort to conquer tuberculosis. Tuberculosis has decreased spectacularly, but it is not yet conquered. In downtown Rome there is a monument to Dr. Robert Battey. Dr. Battey developed surgery for tuberculosis. His innovations were so daring that the medical association once summoned him to explain his activities. Later he became their president and edited their magazine. He received many other honors, both in America and in Europe. Battey State Hospital in Rome was named for him. The hospital is now known as the Northwest Regional Hospital.

What efforts are being made to improve health?

Drug abuse is a problem. Drug abuse centers have been set up all over Georgia. Toll-free lines are in operation for anyone who wants help or information. Officials have pointed out that it is better to help addicts before their health is ruined and they resort to crime to buy drugs. It costs the state only half as much to keep a drug patient in a treatment center for a year as it does to keep a person in prison for a year. More importantly, many bright talents can be salvaged if drug users are reached in time and helped.

What are some health problems in Georgia?

The three biggest killers of Georgians aged one to 44 are accidents, heart disease and cancer. A national survey disclosed that more residents of the southeast have strokes than of any other region. Alcoholism still plagues Georgians. Infant deaths are a problem too. Some babies still die before their first birthday.

Rural Areas Need Doctors

By 1980 almost half of Georgia's doctors were concentrated in the greater Atlanta area. Fifteen counties in the state had no doctors at all and many had only one. Many counties had no dentist. Some rural areas and small towns were making great efforts to attract doctors by making their communities pleasant places to live and by providing clinics.

Pollution Is a Concern For Georgia

What efforts has Georgia made to protect the environment?

In Georgia there is much concern over the problems of pollution, both air and water. Some rivers are becoming polluted to the detriment of both fishing and water sports. The seafood industry on the coast was damaged by pollution. In 1967 the Georgia legislature enacted the state's first air quality control law. A clean water act soon followed. Another important statute attempts to control the disposal of toxic chemical substances. The Environmental Protection Division of the Department of Natural Resources is the state agency responsible for carrying out the state's laws on clean air, clean water and toxic chemicals.

WELFARE IN MODERN GEORGIA

Georgia's view of helping others has changed somewhat. Two ideas helped. One was research and information which helped the public to understand that their funds help the helpless and not just "lazy bums who refuse to work." The other is job training, education, and inspiration to move from welfare rolls to payrolls.

The Division of Family and Children Services

What programs are provided by the Department of Family and Children Services?

The Division of Family and Children Services is responsible for two basic types of programs. The first is called targeted assistance. These programs help specifically defined groups, like the blind or otherwise handicapped. The other type is general assistance. The idea here is to assist persons temporarily down on their luck.

There are caseworkers for each program in each county. One aim of the division's social service is to try to keep families together and out of costly institutions. Keeping children out of foster care and the elderly out of nursing homes is better for the individuals involved. It also saves Georgians millions of dollars each year.

The division makes an effort to locate runaway parents, mostly fathers. Cases of people getting Aid to Families with Dependent Children payments and food stamps illegally are checked closely.

Division of Vocational Rehabilitation

Vocational rehabilitation was transferred from the Department of Education to the Department of Human Resources. The division's purpose is to train physically and mentally handicapped Georgians so that they can enjoy productive lives. State rehabilitation centers at Augusta, Cave Spring, Atlanta, Alto and Milledgeville offer training in various ways. The Warm Springs Rehabilitation Hospital and Center, now owned by the state, offers specialized training to disabled Georgians. The objective is to help the handicapped to be able to care for themselves financially and physically as much as possible. A 1985 study found that the average annual earnings of a disabled person rose from about $800 to over $8,200 after rehabilitation.

What is the purpose of the Division of Vocational Rehabilitation?

Division of Youth Services

In 1985 the Division of Youth Services worked with about 20,000 young people from 9 to 18 years of age. The division counsels young people and their families. It also works with the courts. The purpose is to try to keep juveniles out of jail and have them live a productive life. An effort is made to see if parents of juveniles charged with breaking the law can supervise them until the courts decide what to do. The program is successful. Since 1975, the number of youths held in Georgia jails over 18 hours has decreased by 98 per cent. The number held for serious offenses has decreased by 82 per cent.

How does the Division of Youth Services do its work?

NEW DIRECTIONS FOR AN OLD CONCERN

The founding of Georgia occurred, at least in part, because of the desire to help the truly helpless (persons imprisoned for debt in England). There was a time when one generation after another stayed on welfare rolls. This was called the cycle of poverty. The idea now is to break that cycle of poverty. Through education, public health and welfare programs, an attempt is made to help each individual who is physically and mentally able to prepare for a self-supporting life. This new direction brings new hope to many.

How does Georgia try to break the cycle of poverty?

The new hope throws a happier light on the recipient's situation. A former housing project director said he never forgot what he heard a slum-dwelling Georgian once say: "People need pride, and these here ain't got nothing to be proud of, and no hope of ever gittin' anything to be proud of. And you know, mister, when folks ain't got no hope, they got less than nothing."

Now for our thought experiment. Remember to think analytically and systematically. Assume for purposes of the experiment that the man who made that statement is honest, religious, and willing to work. If he can make the kind of observation he made to the director, he must also be observant and capable of thinking well. Now put yourself in that man's shoes. How would you go about getting something "to be proud of"? What would that something be? Would you try to obtain some material possession like a car or a house? Would you try to finish high school through the GED program so that you would take pride in your education? Robert Frost, the poet, once said that among the most miserable people in the world are those who "have nothing to look backward to with pride and nothing to look forward to with hope." Is having something to be proud of a necessary element before you have hope?

How can all Georgians have pride in themselves, pride in their state and hope for the future?

For Extended Thinking

1. Why would Georgia's early teachers be surprised at the changes in education in the state?
2. How is the higher education system organized in Georgia?
3. How is the Department of Human Resources organized?
4. What efforts are made to improve public health in the state?
5. What are the primary programs of the Division of Family and Children Services?
6. How can all Georgians have "some thing to look backward to with pride and something to look forward to with hope"?

Names, Terms and Concepts

State Board of Education
Foxfire books
University System of Georgia
school board
targeted assistance
Minimum Foundation Law
general assistance
Quality Basic Education Act
Department of Human Resources
cycle of poverty
Fernbank Science Center
Robert Battey

To Help You Study

1. How is the local school system organized?
2. What does the State Department of Education do?
3. Why is the Educational Equalization Bill important?
4. What contribution does educational television make?
5. What does the Fernbank Science Center do? Why did it receive national attention?
6. What type programs does the university system of Georgia offer?
7. What department is responsible for public health programs in Georgia?
8. Why is the work of the Centers for Disease Control important?
9. What are some health problems still faced by Georgians?
10. What efforts has Georgia made to protect the environment?
11. What is the purpose of the Division of Vocational Rehabilitation?
12. How does the Division of Youth Services do its work?
13. How does Georgia attempt to break the cycle of poverty?

CHAPTER 18

ECONOMIC ACTIVITIES IN MODERN GEORGIA

INDUSTRY, AGRICULTURE, TOURISM AND TRANSPORTATION

Georgians once made their living in agriculture. Modern Georgians have seen their state's economy gradually achieve a balance between agriculture and industry. In 1910, fewer than one-eighth of all Georgia workers worked in manufacturing. By 1940, one-fourth did. By mid-century, industry outpaced agriculture as an employer. The products of factories brought more money to Georgia than the products of the farm.

What changes are taking place in agriculture and industry?

DOWN ON THE FARM

The old ballad said, "The old gray mare she ain't what she used to be . . . many long years ago." The old gray mare has not merely changed. She has practically vanished from the Georgia scene. Many other things vanished too—the one-crop farm, the one-room school, and one-party politics. In 1930, 60 per cent of all Georgians lived in rural areas. Now fewer than 10 per cent live in rural areas. But with rural Georgia developing small manufacturing and native crafts, many are moving back into country quietness and beauty—but not to farm.

What are the major changes in agriculture?

Farming Has "Gone Dramatic"

Big machinery came to Georgia farms. As a result, thousands of people who worked on farms moved to the cities.

Mechanization meant there were no longer jobs for them on the farms. Yet Georgia farms produced more than ever. A single modern machine could do the work once done by many human hands. Georgia farm output increased 92 per cent between 1950 and 1966, while that of the nation increased only 52 per cent. Georgia's annual income from agriculture in 1980 was about $3 billion. Georgia has a good climate for farming. There are 230 frost-free days in north Georgia and 260 in south Georgia. The state receives an average rainfall of 48.41 inches. Its average temperature is 61.5 degrees. Georgia has a warm, moist climate well suited to farming.

What are the major crops grown in Georgia?

By 1987 the five top producers of income for Georgia farmers were broilers, peanuts, soybeans, eggs and cattle. The tiny, devastating boll weevil had moved Georgia away from its dependence on one crop: cotton.

The peanut center of the world is southwest Georgia. There is a monument to the peanut in Early County. Georgia produces 43 per cent of all the peanuts in the U.S. In 1987 the state produced 787,500 tons of peanuts, three times that of any other state. Like many other crops in Georgia, most peanuts are processed outside the state. This loses money that should jingle in Georgia pockets. The pecan also grows profitably here, on 1.4 million trees.

Corn is grown in every Georgia county. It has been a favorite Georgia crop since the Indians grew it and called it maize. De Soto saw one Georgia corn field six miles long!

Tobacco was the third highest money crop in Georgia in 1975. Cancer warnings and less cigarette advertising have begun to affect this somewhat. The colorful tobacco fields, the drying barns, the auctions, and the curious chant of the auctioneer made tobacco farming interesting as well as profitable.

Soybeans formerly were planted primarily as a cover crop. But they are rich in protein, minerals and vitamins. Many uses have been found for them in the soybean processing industry. In 1987, Georgia farmers received over $83 million from soybeans, over twice as much as in 1975.

Cotton was once the main crop grown in Georgia. Farmers could not grow enough. The three million bales produced in 1916 shrank to fewer than a half million in 1921. But cotton is still a moneymaker. Synthetics and other fabrics have made some inroads. Cotton—first grown in India thousands of years ago—is still used for about 40 per cent of all fabrics.

The broiler-chicken industry has had unbelievable growth. Gainesville is the broiler capital of the world. In 1987 Georgia's 733 million broilers sold for $835 million. In 1987 Georgia's hens laid 4.4 billion eggs that sold for $255 million. By comparison, in 1979 Georgia raised 561 million broilers that sold for $534 million. The chicken business employs engineers, geneticists, home economists, nutritionists, journalists, pathologists, physiologists, salesmen, and market researchers.

One product sold nationally is the Claxton fruit cake produced in Claxton. The cakes appear in stores over much of the nation during the Thanksgiving and Christmas seasons. Some civic groups sell Claxton fruit cakes to make money.

The World's Biggest Farmers Market

The big, sprawling, city-like, 146-acre Farmers Market near Atlanta is a money maker for farmers and a sight for tourists. It does more than $100 million of business a year. Besides farm produce from Georgia, there are often such produce as onions from Italy, tomatoes and cantaloupes from Mexico, melons from Chile, and bananas from South America.

How important is the Farmers Market to Georgia's economy?

Before sunrise every morning, big trucks roll in from everywhere. People come to buy and to see the colorful scene: red tomatoes and pimentos, purple eggplants, rosy peaches, green beans and watermelons, and all the other rainbow-hued products in huge piles. A Watermelon Festival is held at the market each Fourth of July. A Pumpkin Art Show is held later in the fall.

"Agribusiness" is Something New in Georgia

The idea was old: that farmers and businessmen needed each other. The **Georgia Agribusiness Council** was formed to encourage farmers and businessmen to work together. The council identified several things that needed to be done. They pointed out that the production of some crops is still needed. The state now has to buy from other states much of its livestock feed. That amounts to a quarter of a billion dollar market a year.

What is the purpose of the Agribusiness Council?

There is need for processing, too. Why should Georgia housewives have to put California peaches on their tables? Georgia is the Peach State. Benet wrote, "Wherever the winds of Georgia run, they smell of peaches long in the sun." Why does Georgia sell its peanuts to other states to turn out peanut candy and peanut butter? Turkeys could be processed here. The council found only 15 to 20 per cent of Georgia's products were being processed in the state.

There have been other efforts to make rural living profitable and pleasant. The **Rural Development Center** at Tifton and Abraham Baldwin College have done much through the years to enrich farm life. Regional planning councils have been set up. Better schools, more jobs, good housing, clean water, adequate roads, and recreation and cultural opportunities are being developed. These provide powerful magnets for city dwellers who prefer to live in the quiet, green, uncrowded rural areas of Georgia.

The Georgia Agrirama

At Tifton, the Georgia Agrirama recreates a typical south Georgia village and farm of the late 1800's. Its official name is the State Museum of Agriculture. It fills a unique and interesting educational role for thousands of students who attend

What is the purpose of the Agrirama?

Agrirama, in Tifton, is a living historical museum honoring the farming pioneers of the 19th century. Above left: *Farmhouse and outbuildings.* Above right: *Grist mill.* Left: *Country store.*

special "Living History Workshops." The students live and work for a day learning 19th-century skills and chores.

The Agrirama has steam-powered sawmills, sugar cane grinders, typical houses of the period, smokehouses, a restored chapel, a blacksmith shop, a cotton gin, a grits and corn meal gristmill and a print shop which produces an Agrirama newspaper. All of these were designed as they were in the late 1800's.

The Vidalia Onion

Another crop has gained nation-wide recognition. It is the yellow granex type F hybrid onion. It grows to a sweeter taste in the soil around Vidalia than it does anywhere else.

The taste of the Vidalia sweet onion is limited to those grown in the Vidalia area. This includes Toombs, Tattnall and portions of Montgomery counties. No other area of the nation has been able to duplicate it. Vidalia onion growers once went to court to determine the onions that could be labeled Vidalia Onions. Today all bags of Vidalia onions carry a tag, changed each year, guaranteeing that the contents are from the Vidalia area of Georgia.

Why is the Vidalia onion different?

Agriculture in Georgia's Future

What agencies and organizations promote Georgia agriculture?

A number of government agencies and private organizations attempt to promote agriculture in Georgia. The Department of Agriculture was established in the state government in 1874. Georgia was the first state in the nation to organize such an agency. The head of the department is known as the Commissioner of Agriculture and is elected by the people. The department does many things to promote Georgia agriculture in addition to operating the Farmers Market. For example, it inspects farm production facilities. It regulates and inspects dairies, meat processing plants, and even soft drink bottlers. The Department of Agriculture is the agency that controls the use of insecticides and pesticides in food production. Most people know that certain chemicals stay on food—DDT, for example. When the food is eaten, the poison gets into the human body. Georgia attempts to prevent harmful chemicals on food through regulations issued by the Department of Agriculture.

The University of Georgia is the **land grant** college in the state. This means that it receives special funding to operate the College of Agriculture. Agriculture is a big and complicated business in today's world. The College of Agriculture educates farmers to be effective in that business. It also conducts research designed to improve farming and farm products. An Agriculture Research Center is named for Richard B. Russell, who was a senator from Georgia at the time it was built.

The **Extension Service** is a part of the College of Agriculture. Extension offices are located in every county in the state. They provide assistance to farmers in many ways. They also engage in a number of educational programs. If you are a member of the 4-H Club you are participating in an extension-sponsored program.

Several private organizations promote the interests of farmers. The Cotton Producers Association was formed to promote the marketing of cotton. It has expanded to help market many other Georgia farm products throughout the world.

The numbers on Georgia agriculture are impressive. In 1980 there were 54,000 farms growing some kind of crop, 39,000 cattle farms, 24,000 hog farms and 3,400 dairy farms. Agriculture officials estimate that there are 16 million acres in farm land. The average size of farms is 296 acres. By contrast, the average Georgia farm was 230 acres in 1975. Georgia farm income for 1980 exceeded $3 billion. In spite of these numbers, fewer than one in every 10 Georgians worked on farms in 1980.

How is Georgia trying to attract people back to the rural areas?

To get more Georgians back into the rural areas is a goal for the decades ahead. A better urban-rural balance is being worked on by a number of groups. Since the vanished farm jobs will not return, the objectives are to attract small industries to the farm areas, to develop tourist sites and to provide good schools and other public services in rural areas.

INDUSTRY'S NEW IMAGE

Georgia's oldest industry, textiles, started about 1811 on Upton Creek in Wilkes County. It was natural for this industry to develop in Georgia, as this was a great cotton-producing area. Today when research and technology have produced many man-made fibers, Georgia still has very favorable conditions for the textile industry. It has a good climate, water power, and sources of electricity for spinning and weaving. It offers good transportation necessary for a great textile center. Textiles became the state's largest employer, 114,300 people in 1980. Georgia is the third largest textile state, trailing North Carolina and South Carolina.

Why is Georgia a favorable location for the textile industry?

One of the most interesting phases of the textile industry was that of tufted textiles. This type of textile began with bedspreads. It rapidly expanded to many other products.

Making tufted textiles.

Tufted Textiles' Strange Beginning

Tufted textiles, now very important to Georgia, started with a wedding present. Katherine Evans, a 15-year-old Georgian, had seen an old tufted bedspread. She decided to make one like it for a friend who was getting married. When other people saw it, they asked her to make bedspreads for them. She sold the first one in 1901. The demand grew. She hired neighbors to help her. But hand work was slow.

With the advent of machines, the industry grew rapidly. In addition to bedspreads, rugs, carpeting, tapestries, and other products are made through the tufted process. All these products bring greater prosperity to Georgia. Katherine Evans Whitener said, "That wedding present gave work to a lot of people, didn't it?"

Cotton thread manufactured in Georgia has an interesting history. Once all sewing thread was silk or linen. When Napoleon's 1806 embargo cut off silk shipments to Britain, the Clarks began to make cotton thread. Now they have plants in Georgia. When Elias Howe invented the sewing machine in 1846, this increased the demand for sewing thread.

Textiles grew into a mighty industry that brought more money into Georgia than any other manufacturing industry. Second was forestry, with its lumber and naval stores, pulpwood products and furniture.

Minerals are Important to Georgia's Economy

How important are minerals to Georgia's economy?

Georgia has some 300 mining operations in 100 of its 159 counties. It ranks fifth in the nation in producing minerals. Georgia leads all other states in the mining of kaolin, granite and marble.

Mining has been important in Georgia since its early days when kaolin was shipped to England to go into the widely known Wedgewood dishes. Georgia marble has gone into many of the world's outstanding structures. Georgia marble was first used for a public memorial in Lawrenceville in 1840.

Many other minerals are mined in Georgia. Most of them can be seen in the Capitol Museum in Atlanta. Mining means millions to the Georgia economy.

Georgia's Manufacturing Goes From A to Z

From automobiles to zippers, Georgia plants turn out products that add billions to the state's economy. In 1915, Henry Ford opened an assembly plant in Atlanta. It is now one of the major automobile assembly plants in the nation.

General Motors was also assembling cars in Atlanta by 1927. Chrysler set up a $2 million Training Center for its employees from 13 southeastern states. Many supporting industries, such as U.S. Rubber, have come in the wake of these industries.

Georgia's "Colas"

Somewhere in the world somebody is always drinking a Georgia-originated drink, Coca-Cola.

The drink was first made by a druggist named John S. Pemberton, born in Knoxville, Ga. He brewed the first Coca-Cola in a three-legged pot in his back yard. Pemberton soon sold out to Asa Candler. First, Candler bought a two-thirds interest for $1200; then the rest for $500. Candler gave most of his interest to his family. In 1919 they sold it for $25 million.

With Coca-Cola being so widely consumed, most people forget that Georgia is the home of another cola. Royal Crown Cola originated in Columbus.

Who invented Coca-Cola?

The New Image of Industry

A new idea has added interest to the Georgia industrial picture. Business has begun to commission artists to beautify buildings, offices, and downtown streets in many Georgia communities. Trees and plants growing in business sections, good paintings on the walls, crystal fountains sparkling and sculpture gardens make happier places in which to work. Small towns began to enlist university art departments to brighten their business centers. Hamilton-on-the-Square, not far from Columbus, painted its old stores to emphasize the picturesque quaintness of days long gone. Stores began to do more business. In the Georgia mountains, communities have joined to market the picturesque crafts and arts of the mountain people: cornshuck dolls, bonnets, quilts, dried apple dolls, splint chairs, pottery, baskets—and corncob backscratchers!

Modern sculpture on Peachtree Street in downtown Atlanta.

The most extensive "business and beauty" combination is Atlanta.

What is Georgia doing to beautify its cities and towns?

John Portman and Peachtree Center

The dramatic change in the Atlanta skyline was sparked by a Georgia-born architect, John Portman. The Merchandise Mart was the first of the fabulous Portman structures. Then there were two remarkable hotels.

What is Portman's idea of how cities should be developed?

The Hyatt Regency, a hotel unique in the nation, has a lobby 22 stories high. A revolving restaurant on top turns every 44 minutes. A bridge 22 stories above Peachtree Street connects with other buildings. The Peachtree Plaza Hotel is a shining glass tower which soars 73 stories high. The lobby is a seven-story atrium that contains a half-acre lake, more than 100 trees, live (caged) birds, sculptures, tapestries, and hundreds of boxes of trailing ivy.

Portman explained it this way: "We are planning gardens and galleries, restaurants, museums and theatres here, places to live and work—everything! This is what cities are all about. In Peachtree Center in the future, a person will be able to live, work, shop, play and worship without leaving it, and do it all on foot without walking more than 7 1/2 minutes at a time from one unit to another."

The Peachtree Plaza

Industry and Commerce in Georgia's Future

The magazine *Venture* said, "Atlanta is the boom city of the South, the commercial, transportation, governmental center of the Southeast. It bubbles with optimism and aspiration. And do not let the slow Southern drawl fool you; brains are clicking at top speed."

It is said there is more black wealth in Atlanta than in New York and Chicago put together. Blacks own newspapers, banks, insurance companies and other business enterprises.

The state was not really late getting interested in industry. There was more industry in the south than in New England when the 19th century began. Then the cotton gin made cotton profitable. The south turned back to farming. After the Civil War, Henry Grady and others sought valiantly, with expositions and speeches, to interest northern money in coming south for industrial investment. Today Georgia is one of the most industrialized states in the southeast.

TOURISM

New Money and Visitors

There was a time when tourists sped right on through Georgia on their way to Florida. But by the summer of 1980 the 53rd millionth tourist stopped at one of Georgia's 12 welcome stations. In 1979 recreation-seekers spent an estimated $2.2 billion in Georgia.

The folklore of the tourist business has a teaser: "Tourists are a better crop than cotton—and a darn sight easier to pick!" Actually, however, tourism is a natural for the warm south where hospitality is a long tradition. Georgia was simply a little late discovering how many interesting sites and services it had to offer people. Historic sights, beautiful scenery, courteous services, comfortable lodging, good food, delightful recreation, and better roads have all combined to promote tourism. So have the Chamber of Commerce's "Stay and See Georgia" campaign and the Department of Industry and Trade with its widely-advertised "Georgia, This Way to Fun" campaign.

Why is tourism a natural for Georgia?

A Welcome Center in Sylvania

Why is Savannah so attractive to tourists?

The gentle charm of Savannah, with its historic colonial buildings and modern hotels, is a typical magnet for tourists. *Holiday Magazine* in 1969 reported, "There is not another town like Savannah in all America. You feel the richness of its heritage as you read the many bronze plaques bolted to the old walls." Oglethorpe and his architect friend would be pleased at the comment of a modern city planner, Edmond Bacon. He called Savannah "the best planned city in America." The Historic Savannah Foundation has led in the movement to restore Savannah's most interesting old buildings.

Those interested in Indians often go to New Echota, where Cherokees now gather for an annual Cherokee Spring Festival. New Echota, once the capitol of the Cherokee nation, has been restored.

The perpetual attractions in Georgia are still FDR's Little White House, Callaway Gardens, Anna Ruby Falls, Stone Mountain, the weird and wonderful Okefenokee, Six Flags

Left: *An example of beautiful architecture found in the restored areas of Savannah.* Right: *The Owens-Thomas House.*

near Atlanta, Rock City and fabulous Jekyll Island. In addition, the Atlanta area has many attractions. The city itself has many great restaurants, theatres, a world renown orchestra and fine art galleries. In addition, there are the Stone Mountain Memorial, Atlanta University Center, the Martin Luther King Memorial, the Hyatt Regency and Peachtree Plaza Hotels, and the Memorial Arts Center. Underground Atlanta, which portrays the old city as it used to be beneath the railroad tracks, has been renovated and is a great attraction. Plains, former President Carter's hometown, draws many visitors.

What are the perpetual tourist attractions in Georgia?

Rock City atop Lookout Mountain in Georgia.

Tourism in Georgia's Future

Georgia has so many things that are attractive to tourists. Did you notice that the perpetual attractions list did not mention Georgia's Seven Wonders? Of course, they are great attractions. But how do you list them all?

Given all those things, this is where we want you to do another thought experiment. Suppose that you are the individual in the Department of Industry and Trade who is responsible for promoting tourism in Georgia. How would you start thinking systematically and analytically about your responsibility? What target groups of individuals would you try to interest in spending their vacations and leisure time in Georgia? What attractions would you promote? How would you promote Atlanta as one of the world's great urban areas? How would you promote the Okefenokee swamp with all its uniqueness and beauty? How would you promote the mountains and how would you promote the beaches? What slogans would you use?

Tourism is now very important to Georgia's economy. It is likely to become even more important in the future.

TRANSPORTATION IN MODERN GEORGIA

Georgia travel has grown immensely, by highway, air, water, and rapid transit city systems. Railroad travel has declined.

Georgians have been concerned about roads since the days when Oglethorpe built roads for troops and trade. Later on, U.S. Postmaster General Benjamin Franklin set up post roads for mail delivery. These were designed for the horse and wagon, since the automobile did not appear until around 1900. These early highways were not suited for automobiles and trucks.

How did Georgia's highway system develop?

In order to improve its highways, the legislature provided for a State Highway Commission. The main responsibility given to the commission was to build hard-surfaced roads which would "get Georgia out of the mud." But this was more than simply a program decision. It was a political decision also. Who would get the roads? What would their routes be? These questions were very important to local communities since the answers to them affected economic growth.

In order to take road building out of politics, Georgia estab-

The Blue Star Memorial Highway.

lished the **Department of Transportation** in 1950. The department is governed by a board that is appointed by the General Assembly. The Commissioner of Transportation is the chief executive of the department and is appointed by the board. In 1981, there were a total of 103,680 miles of public roads in the state. As Georgia has developed an adequate highway system, the department has turned its attention increasingly to other forms of transportation. There is even some discussion of high speed trains that would connect Georgia's major cities with each other.

The Interstate Highway System

The Interstate Highway System was begun in 1959. It was designed to link the great cities of the nation together and make faster, safer travel possible. At first the planners expected to have the entire 42,500-mile network finished by 1972. Delays pushed completion well into the 1980's. The total mileage assigned to Georgia was 1,207. Georgia paid 10 per cent of the interstate cost and the federal government 90 per cent.

What was Georgia's share of the cost of the interstate highway system?

Georgia transportation officials have stated that by the time the nation-wide system is completed, it will have saved motorists $107 billion—$37 billion more than the system cost to build. This savings occurs because of fewer accidents and lower property damage and hospital costs.

Air Transportation in Georgia

Why is Atlanta an important hub for air travel?

The beginning of the 1980 decade saw the opening of Atlanta's new airline passenger terminal. Named the Hartsfield-Atlanta International Airport, it is one of the busiest airports in the world. The Atlanta airport and O'Hare Airport in Chicago compete for the title of busiest. The new airport terminal building covers nearly 60 acres. It has 144 gates where planes can park. Six of them are for international travel, where luggage can be inspected and passports checked. The airport cost almost $700 million. It was one of the major construction projects of all time in the south.

Delta Air Lines first started passenger service in Atlanta in 1929. The changes and progress since then have been varied and rewarding for Georgia.

Although some airlines are moving their hubs to other cities, Atlanta remains a major connecting point in every direction. A favorite saying of airline passengers in the south is "When I go to heaven, I'll have to go through Atlanta."

Railroads

How did Congress try to save railroad passenger service?

Railroad travel decreased after plane and automobile travel began to serve most passengers. Atlanta's growth had been due largely to its being a railroad center in early days. Congress set up a corporation, Amtrak, to save passenger service when the railroads experienced financial difficulties. This corporation took over most of the nation's rail passenger service on May 1, 1971. The idea was to keep passenger trains running between points where there was most demand for them.

Amtrak continues to serve Atlanta. Yet passenger service on

A MARTA train crossing over two Interstate Highways in Atlanta

railroads is still low. However, railroads continue to be a major mover of freight in the United States and in Georgia.

The Atlanta Area Mass Transit System

A rapid transportation system, known as MARTA because it is run by the Metropolitan Atlanta Rapid Transit Authority, is being built to serve the Atlanta area. When completed, MARTA will cover 53 rail miles and eight miles of bus routes. Many hope that MARTA will reduce traffic congestion in the Atlanta area.

Transportation in Georgia's Future

Some people are predicting great changes in transportation in the future. People envision electric cars guided by automation on computer-controlled highways. They dream of parking areas at the city's edge, keeping wheels out of the downtown walking plazas beautified by greenery, parks, statues, fountains and quietness. Many foresee trucks moving by underground tunnels to service stores and offices. We have mentioned high speed trains, rolling in protected shells on compressed air at 350 miles an hour. On land, air, and water an almost unbelievable revolution in transportation is under way. Georgia will be a part of that revolution.

What are some changes that are predicted for transportation?

For Extended Thinking

1. What changes have occurred in Georgia agriculture?
2. How important is agriculture to Georgia's economy?
3. What changes have occurred in industry in Georgia?
4. How important is the textile industry to Georgia today? What other industries are important to Georgia's economy?
5. How important is tourism to Georgia's economy?
6. Why is Atlanta the connecting point for so many airline flights?

Names, Terms and Concepts

mechanization
land grant college
Underground Atlanta
agribusiness
Extension Service
Department of Transportation
Rural Development Center
tufted textiles
MARTA
John Portman
Amtrak
Department of Agriculture
Agrirama

To Help You Study

1. What are the major crops grown in Georgia?
2. How important is the Farmers Market to Georgia's economy?
3. What is the purpose of the Georgia Agribusiness Council?
4. Why is the Vidalia onion different?
5. What agencies and organizations promote Georgia agriculture?
6. How is Georgia trying to attract more people back into the rural areas?
7. Why is Georgia a favorable location for the textile industry?
8. How important are minerals to Georgia's economy?
9. What is John Portman's idea of how cities should develop?
10. Why is tourism a natural for Georgia?
11. How did Georgia's highways develop?
12. How did Congress try to save passenger service on the railroads?
13. How is the Department of Transportation organized?
14. What are some changes that are pre dicted for transportation?

CHAPTER 19

CULTURE AND RELIGION IN MODERN GEORGIA

Those things associated with the word culture have taken on new vigor in modern Georgia.

A society's **culture** is its customary beliefs, social practices and art forms. Most people think of culture as appreciation of art, music, drama and literature. And certainly those things are parts of culture. Most people believe that appreciation for art forms should be cultivated. We will review the great range of cultural activities that exist in modern Georgia.

COMMUNICATION

The Media

How has communication changed?

Two important developments have occurred in communication. First, communication has grown less personal. Once communication consisted of a speaker and a listener. Now radio and television remove the personal contact. Second, the media have increased their influence in Georgia. It is said that a young person spends more time watching television than they spend in the classroom.

How many newspapers and TV stations are there in the state?

Georgia has some 40 daily and about 200 weekly newspapers. A number of organizations sponsor education, scholarships, and internships for bright young journalists. Your high school, for example, might offer journalism classes.

In 1981 the Georgia Association of Broadcasters listed 20 commercial television stations, 10 educational television stations, 191 AM radio stations and 108 FM radio stations. WSB Radio in Atlanta went on the air in 1922, the first in the south. The call letters WSB stood for "Welcome South, Brother." Television and radio stations cover the state.

Georgia's most unusual weekly newspaper editor may have been W. B. Townsend, editor of the *Dahlonega Nugget*. His paper printed frank opinions and news of people. He wrote the articles and set the type. He refused to have more than 1,000 subscriptions.

What Georgians have been successful in journalism?

Many Georgians have achieved distinction in the national media. Jessica Daves, of Cartersville, became editor-in-chief of *Vogue*, the fashion magazine. Miss Daves once taught school in Cartersville. Bill Emerson, former *Newsweek* regional bureau manager in Atlanta, was the last editor of the *Saturday Evening Post*. Mark and Willie Snow Ethridge, formerly with the *Macon Telegraph*, both became famous for newspaper editing and books. Some Georgia news reporters went on to national network jobs. Among them are George Page, Kenley Jones and John Palmer. A Georgia woman, Martha Rountree, originated *Meet the Press*. Douglas Edwards was once a reporter in Georgia. Roger Mudd taught school in Rome.

One of the most significant events in Georgia's sports and communication history has been the rapid rise of Ted Turner and his various enterprises. Turner owns the Atlanta Braves and the Atlanta Hawks. He is also one of the world's finest sailboat skippers.

What was Ted Turner's major achievement?

Turner's major accomplishment may have been his foresight in recognizing the impact cable systems would have on television broadcasting. Turner quickly made Channel 17 in Atlanta a station seen on nearly all cable systems around the nation. Soon it rivaled the major networks and became WTBS, the Super Station. Still not content, Turner, in 1980, established a 24-hour, round-the-clock news station known as Cable News Network. CNN propelled Turner's stations into an even more competitive position with ABC, CBS and NBC. Cable TV continues to grow throughout the nation. Georgia's Turner is the leader in using it to build a communication empire.

FINE ARTS ACROSS THE STATE

From the Apple Tree Theater in Habersham County to the $13 million Memorial Arts Center in Atlanta and southward to the Florida line, the fine arts have involved more and more Georgians. Shakespeare festivals in the mountains, seminars on art at the colleges, and original plays everywhere give life and beauty to Georgia's cultural life.

The beautiful Memorial Arts Center in Atlanta was built in memory of 122 Georgians who died in a flaming plane crash at Orly Field near Paris in June 1962. It houses the Atlanta Symphony, an art school, the High Museum of Art, theaters, the ballet, a children's theater, and other things. France, in sympathy for the tragedy, gave Atlanta a cast of Rodin's statue *L'Ombre* ("The Shadow"). Back of the statue are these words: "Dedicated to all who truly believe the arts are a continuing effort of the human spirit to find new meaning in existence. Orly, France, June 3, 1962." Great plays, famous music, and immortal painting and sculpture make the Memorial Arts Center great. It is the home of much creative talent.

What arts are produced at the Memorial Arts Center?

Above: *The monument to the apple in Habersham County.*

Left: *The Atlanta Memorial Arts Center.*

Theaters Help Georgians Appreciate Drama

What are some of Georgia's most important theater groups?

There are many theater groups doing interesting work in many parts of Georgia. Among them are the Alliance Theater, the Springer Theater and the Academy Theater.

The Alliance Theater is located in the Memorial Arts Center. It has a permanent troup of actors and invites special guest stars for various performances. A children's theater is an important part of its activities. The Center for Puppetry Arts is a unique component of Atlanta's theater activity.

The Academy Theater is housed in an old church building on Roswell Road in Atlanta. It is widely known and has a great reputation. Its purpose is to present fine drama. The group has presented great classics as well as original plays of young moderns. The group took productions into the high schools, and stayed to talk with the students about drama. This had a major impact on encouraging interest in drama.

The old Springer Theater in Columbus was started in 1856 by Francis J. Springer. Many historic personages have appeared on its stage. They include Edwin Booth as Hamlet, Oscar Wilde, P.T. Barnum, Joseph Jefferson, Will Rogers, Harry Lauder, Martha Graham, the dancer Geraldine Farrar and many others. The old theater was restored in 1964. The theatre won an international award as an outstanding example of what can be achieved by a hard-working local citizenry.

Art Flourishes in Georgia

Who are some of Georgia's best known artists?

As with the theatre, there is substantial creative energy in art in Georgia. There are many examples of fine artists doing great work. We can mention only a few of them.

George Beattie is a widely known artist. He was also executive director of the Georgia Art Commission, now known as the Georgia Council for the Arts and Humanities. Among his works is the mural in the federal building in Macon. The mural depicts the phases of middle Georgia's history. Its many scenes include the Emperor Brim, de Soto, Alexander Stephens and Wesleyan College.

The Phoenix is a bronze sculpture by Francesco Somaini of Italy. It is in a reflecting pool at the First Atlanta Bank in Atlanta and adds to the beauty of the inner city. In mythology, the phoenix is a bird that rose again from its own ashes. It is often seen as the symbol of Atlanta, which rose again from the ashes of Sherman's burning during the Civil War.

A triptych mural—the only one in the world made of egg-shells—is on the wall of the C & S Emory Bank in DeKalb County. This old 15th-century art form was revived by Athos Menaboni, a native of Italy who became a Georgia artist.

Along with individuals, art galleries and academies play a major role in giving vitality to art in Georgia. The High Museum of Art in the Memorial Arts Center brings some of the world's greatest art to Atlanta. An art gallery and school are a part of Savannah's Telfair Academy of the Arts and Sciences. The academy is built on the site of the residence of Georgia's royal governors. The Piedmont Art Festival in Atlanta, sidewalk art shows throughout Georgia and college art galleries all combine to create interest in the arts. The art school and the art museum at the University of Georgia are housed in attractive buildings. About 20,000 people a year visit them. The Plum Nelly clothesline art show continues to draw bumper-to-bumper traffic each autumn to the north Georgia mountains.

The Phoenix, a bronze sculpture, represents the rise of Atlanta out of the ashes of the Civil War.

A mural made of eggshells can be found in the C&S Emory Bank in Dekalb County.

Music in Georgia: From Ballads to Symphony

How has music been important to Georgia life?

Music has been an important part of Georgia life since before Charles Wesley, the great Methodist hymn writer. Beautiful spirituals rose from the sorrow of slavery. Hymns echoed from little country churches where gathered hard-working people. The music of great symphonies, sophisticated church choirs, rock-and-roll singers and country music groups have been among the sounds of Georgia.

Georgia has had a number of talented musical groups and individuals. The Emory Glee Club was one of the first groups to carry its music on tour in America and Europe. The A Cappella Choir from Milledgeville presented concerts over the south. Unusual groups like the Bell Ringers of Atlanta varied the musical range. Johnny Mercer of Savannah became one of the most famous American song writers. He wrote such songs as *Moon River, Old Black Magic, I'm An Old Cowhand,* and many others. He played them when he returned to Savannah in 1972 for the opening of the $10 million, 2,566-seat Civic Center theater.

Every spring since 1910, the Metropolitan Opera has come to Atlanta for a week. Georgia music lovers flocked to hear Caruso, Geraldine Farrar, Rosa Ponselle and other great performers. Farrar did the first (moderate) strip tease in Atlanta and was so offended by audience disapproval that she never returned! Once an opera singer was killed in the train station in Atlanta. A tenor, already entrained and ready to depart, left the train on some errand and was found dead the next morning. The mystery has never been solved. Blanche Thebom, a former Met star, came to Atlanta to live in recent years to promote interest in opera. The late James Melton of Dawson was an early star at the Metropolitan Opera.

Robert Shaw

The 90-member Atlanta Symphony Orchestra, directed for many years by Robert Shaw, is one of the great symphony orchestras of the nation. Directed since 1988 by Yoel Levi, it works for the education of youth as well as the entertainment of the public. The only major orchestra within a radius of 500 miles, it grew out of a youth orchestra organized by Henry Sopkin. It became the Atlanta Symphony in 1947.

How did the Atlanta Symphony Orchestra start?

Shaw, the son of a minister, studied theology but changed to choral directing. He worked with Koussevitsky at Tanglewood, directed the NBC choral group under Toscanini, and developed the famous Robert Shaw Chorale. He went into symphony work and came to Atlanta from Cleveland.

Music was another field of high achievement for Georgia blacks. Roland Hayes, born in Curryville, sang at Buckingham Palace. "I love Georgia," he said, "my roots are there." Ray Charles, a blind pianist and singer, has achieved world fame. Frank Sinatra once called him the "only genius in our profession." His rendition of the song *Georgia On My Mind* moves many residents to tears. James Brown had such success with his music that he bought the building in Augusta in front of which he once shined shoes. Miss Mattewilda Dobbs of Atlanta became an opera star with the Metropolitan Opera in New York.

The Poets and Storytellers

The great surge of writing by Georgia authors mentioned earlier continues. Three examples will give you a flavor of their work.

Who are some of Georgia's best-known modern authors?

A Georgian who won fame for both poetry and prose was the former Atlanta advertising man, James Dickey. *Life* magazine termed him "the best poet in the U.S. today." In 1970, he made the best-seller list with his first novel, *Deliverance*. The book was made into a movie and filmed in north Georgia. It is a story of survival, and as one critic described it, "of how decent men kill when they have to."

Conrad Aiken, a Georgia-born poet and prose writer of world-wide fame, won many prizes, including the Pulitzer. At age 11, he had gone to New England to live after the tragic death of his parents. He moved back to Savannah. Aiken was described by *Time* as "a cosmic spirit that outsoars Eliot and Pound." Aiken had told his own life story in his third-person prose book entitled *Ushant*.

Frank Yerby, a black novelist from Augusta, became a best-selling novelist. His many novels have sold more than 20 million copies. Yerby once lived on the Riviera and later in Spain.

Architectural Triumphs

Architecture has been an art form in Georgia since colonial times. During that period, the English architect William Jay and his associates designed beautiful houses in the Savannah area. Imaginative buildings span the centuries, from the Herb House in Oglethorpe's old Savannah to John Portman's Hyatt Regency Hotel in Atlanta.

What are good examples of imaginative architecture in Georgia?

The two Governor's Mansions—the new one in Atlanta and the old one in Milledgeville—are gems of architecture that draw many visitors. Old houses in such places as Madison, LaGrange, Birdville, Milledgeville, Savannah, Athens, Washington and Atlanta are often shown on tours.

Savannah's restoration of many of its oldest homes and Oglethorpe's 20 original squares has drawn national attention. *Newsweek* reported, "Architecturally what makes Savannah so different . . . is Oglethorpe's masterful plan." Conrad Aiken, the poet, became actively involved in the restoration.

The World Congress Center in Atlanta was approved in 1974 by the legislature and Gov. Carter. It had its grand opening on Dec. 1, 1976, with Gov. Busbee officiating. A parade, complete with bands and floats, was held entirely within the building. The Center's cost of $90 million is proving to be a good investment.

The facility now contains 650,000 square feet of exhibition

The old Telfair home in Savannah.

space. There are 91 meeting rooms and eight of them hold over 1,000 people. There are three permanent restaurants. The ballroom contains 40,000 square feet. One of the meeting rooms is a 2,000 square-foot auditorium with audio equipment that can translate speeches into six languages at the same time. So foreign businesses use the center for a variety of purposes.

GEORGIANS AND THEIR SPIRITUAL CONCERNS

How active have religious groups been?

The late Howard Odum, famous Georgia-born sociologist, said, "It is impossible to explain the religion of the South, but it is impossible to understand the South without its religion." Georgia has some 10,000 churches, synagogues, and chapels with over 8,000 ministers. They have over three million members, or 75 per cent of Georgia's people. Leading in membership are Baptists, Methodists, Catholics and Presbyterians.

The Episcopal Church evolved from the Church of England and was once the colony's official church. The Church of God, the Seventh Day Adventists, Christian Science, and others have strong adherents.

What are some of the historically interesting churches?

There are many interesting churches architecturally or historically. Faith Chapel is the Tiffany-windowed, brown-shingled place of worship of the millionaires who once owned Jekyll Island. Waiters formed the choir in this church. There is a tiny country church which is now a chapel inside Thompson's Methodist Church. Christ Church on St. Simon's Island is where the Wesleys once preached. St. Stephens Episcopal Church in Milledgeville is where Sherman stabled horses and soldiers poured syrup in the organ "to make the music sweeter." The 1848 Zion Church in Talbotton has a hand-pumped organ. Wooden pegs and handmade nails were used in its construction. Ahavath Achim Synagogue in Atlanta is adorned with contemporary art. Midway Church along the coast was the church of the Puritans. Old Jerusalem Church of the Salzburgers in Effingham County has Luther's symbol, the swan, on its steeple. Big Bethel in Atlanta is famous for its

The Salzburgers' Jerusalem Church.

Ida Cason Calloway Chapel at Calloway Gardens in Pine Mountain.

annual *Heaven Bound* musical. The musical has been performed more than 1,000 times. Atlanta's Greek Orthodox Church, a gem of Byzantine art by Italian artist Sirio Tonelli, has a Creation picture made of three and one-half million pieces of mosaic glass in its 60-foot dome. The mosaic is the second largest in the world. Old Christ Church in Savannah displays an 1819 bell. It is one of the 400 made by Paul Revere and Son and the only one not in New England. Savannah's Mickvah Israel Synagogue, organized by the Jews who came over July 11, 1733, has the scroll of the *Torah* they brought with them on the boat. The jewel-like Ida Cason Callaway Chapel has stained glass windows depicting the four seasons. Its beauty is reflected in a quiet lake. The Westville Church has a mysterious painting on its ceiling. There are many more historic and beautiful churches in Georgia. These are only a few of them.

One of Georgia's most famous preachers was Rev. Peter Marshall. He was once pastor of the Westminster Presbyterian Church in Atlanta. During his Georgia pastorate, he married a girl from Agnes Scott College. After his death in Washington, D.C., Catherine Marshall became famous as a writer. Many of her books were about her husband and his work.

AN IMPOSSIBLE, BUT IMPORTANT, THOUGHT EXPERIMENT

Now for our last thought experiment. It probably is impossible to accomplish. But just because we cannot fully understand some things does not mean that we should cease to think about them. Just the opposite is true. We should think especially carefully and systematically about things that cannot be fully understood.

What we want you to do is to think carefully about the importance of art, literature, music, drama, architecture and religion to a society. In how many ways do these things enrich a society? How do they add meaning to our lives? What would our understanding of beauty, honor, love, trust and joy be without them?

In a very personal way, we want you to think about how art, music and literature affect your life. Do you expose yourself enough to them? How much good literature do you read? How much of the world's best music do you enjoy? Do you know the great artists of Georgia and the world? What will your life be like if you do not come to know, enjoy and appreciate these things?

Ralph Waldo Emerson once said that "Nature and books belong to the eyes that see them." Art, literature, drama and architecture belong to the eyes that see them. Music belongs to the ear that hears it. Keep your eyes and ears attuned to the best in our culture.

For Extended Thinking

1. How active are the mass media in Georgia?
2. Why was the Memorial Arts Center built? What activities go on there?
3. What theater groups are important in Georgia?
4. Who are some of the Georgia artists whose work is best known?
5. What music activities and groups are important in Georgia?
6. What structures in Georgia reflect an imaginative architecture?
7. How important is it to understand religion in Georgia?

Names, Terms and Concepts

culture
Academy Theater
Robert Shaw
Ted Turner
George Beattie
Ray Charles
Memorial Arts Center
High Museum of Art
James Dickey
Alliance Theater
Johnny Mercer
World Congress Center
Springer Theater

To Help You Study

1. How has communication changed in Georgia?
2. What Georgians have been successful in the mass media?
3. What was Ted Turner's idea about television? How successful was it?
4. What arts are produced at the Memorial Arts Center?
5. How has music been important to Georgia's life?
6. When did the Atlanta Symphony Orchestra start? Who is its conductor now?
7. What modern Georgia authors are widely known?
8. Describe some of the work of John Portman.
9. What are the largest religious groups in Georgia?
10. Name three churches in Georgia and tell why they are historically or architecturally interesting.

WHAT A STATE YOU ARE IN

Here's your Georgia. Cherish what is brave and worthy out of its past. Involve yourself in its present. Help plan its future.

Georgia has completely rural places in a crowded world. It has great cities rising toward the sky. There is a sun-splashed, history-haunted coast with marine industry and research labs. There are farms producing more and more food and fiber, and industries manufacturing goods sold around the world. Great art and music, wider communication, better schools and colleges are here.

Along with its beauty and wealth, Georgia has problems. Some people have bad housing, inadequate education, insufficient food, and no jobs. Most importantly, they do not have a chance to develop their talents to be somebody. Per capita income of Georgians is below the national average.

We live in a democracy. We can vote. We can choose good and wise leaders—or bad ones. From the people, voting in their local communities, power flows to Atlanta and Washington. Yet thousands of Georgians who could vote do not bother to do so.

Drug abuse, alcoholism, and mental illness thwart the talents of young and old. There is crime in the street. Many old are lonely, and many young are neglected. There is much to be done. The job is for all Georgians, working together, planning intelligently, voting wise-ly for leaders of honor and purpose. Democracy works best when it works for all. That idea does not change, though the state does change.

There are many roads but not one leads back to yesterday. Learning how to cope with the swift change that the future is bringing us is the only way for Georgia. Somewhere among you right now are our future governors, congressmen, legislators, judges, maybe another president. Most importantly, all of you will be voters. What are you thinking, learning, doing that will make a difference in the kind of Georgia we have tomorrow?

Georgia Studies tells you about Georgia's past. Only you can write Georgia's future. You *are* Georgia's future!

GOVERNORS OF GEORGIA

Name	Term
COLONIAL	
James Edward Oglethorpe	1733-1743
William Stephens	1743-1751
Henry Parker	1751-1753
Patrick Graham	1753-1754
PROVINCIAL	
John Reynolds	1754-1757
Henry Ellis	1757-1760
James Wright	1760-1776
PROVISIONAL	
Archibald Bulloch	1776-1777
Button Gwinnett	1777
STATE	
John Adams Treutlen	1777-1778
John Houstoun	1778-1779
John Wereat	1779-1780
George Walton	1779-1780
Richard Howley	1780
Stephen Heard	1780-1781
Nathan Brownson	1781-1782
John Martin	1782-1783
Lyman Hall	1783-1784
John Houstoun	1784-1785
Samuel Elbert	1785-1786
Edward Telfair	1786-1787
George Mathews	1787-1788
George Handley	1788-1789
George Walton	1789
Edward Telfair	1789-1793
George Mathews	1793-1796
Jared Irwin	1796-1798
James Jackson	1798-1801
David Emanuel	1801
Josiah Tattnall, Jr.	1801-1802
John Milledge	1802-1806
Jared Irwin	1806-1809
David B. Mitchell	1809-1813
Peter Early	1813-1815
David B. Mitchell	1815-1817
William Rabun	1817-1819
Matthew Talbot	1819
John Clark	1819-1823
George M. Troup	1823-1827
John Forsyth	1827-1829
George R. Gilmer	1829-1831
Wilson Lumpkin	1831-1835
William Schley	1835-1837
George R. Gilmer	1837-1839
Charles J. McDonald	1839-1843
George W. Crawford	1843-1847
George W. Towns	1847-1851
Howell Cobb	1851-1853
Herschel V. Johnson	1853-1857
Joseph E. Brown	1857-1865
James Johnson	1865
Charles J. Jenkins	1865-1868
Gen. Thomas H. Ruger	1868
Rufus B. Bullock	1868-1871
Benjamin Conley	1871-1872
James M. Smith	1872-1877
Alfred H. Colquitt	1877-1882
Alexander H. Stephens	1882-1883
James S. Boynton	1883
Henry D. McDaniel	1883-1886
John B. Gordon	1886-1890
William J. Northen	1890-1894
William Y. Atkinson	1894-1898
Allen D. Candler	1898-1902
Joseph M. Terrell	1902-1907
Hoke Smith	1907-1909
Joseph M. Brown	1909-1911
Hoke Smith	1911
John M. Slaton	1911-1912
Joseph M. Brown	1912-1913
John M. Slaton	1913-1915
Nathaniel E. Harris	1915-1917
Hugh M. Dorsey	1917-1921
Thomas W. Hardwick	1921-1923
Clifford Walker	1923-1927

Continued

Name	*Term*	*Name*	*Term*
Lamartine G. Hardman, M.D.	1927-1931	Herman E. Talmadge	1951-1954
Richard B. Russell, Jr.	1931-1933	S. Marvin Griffin	1955-1959
Eugene Talmadge	1933-1937	S. Ernest Vandiver	1959-1963
Eurith D. Rivers	1937-1941	Carl E. Sanders	1963-1967
Eugene Talmadge	1941-1943	Lester Maddox	1967-1971
Ellis G. Arnall	1943-1947	Jimmy Carter	1971-1975
Eugene Talmadge (died before taking office)		George Busbee	1975-1983
Melvin E. Thompson	1947-1948	Joe Frank Harris	1983 -1991
Herman E. Talmadge	1948-1950	Zell Bryan Miller	1991

COUNTIES OF GEORGIA

County Name	*Named For*	*County Seat*	*Date Formed*	*1990 Population*
Appling	Col. Daniel Appling	Baxley	1818	15,744
Atkinson	Gov. William Y. Atkinson	Pearson	1917	6,213
Bacon	Augustus O. Bacon	Alma	1914	9,566
Baker	Col. John Baker	Newton	1825	3,615
Baldwin	Abraham Baldwin	Milledgeville	1803	39,530
Banks	Dr. Richard E. Banks	Homer	1858	10,308
Barrow	Chanc. David C. Barrow	Winder	1914	29,721
Bartow	Gen. Francis S. Bartow	Cartersville	1832	55,911
Ben Hill	Benjamin H. Hill	Fitzgerald	1906	16,245
Berrien	John M. Berrien	Nashville	1856	14,153
Bibb	Dr. W. W. Bibb	Macon	1822	149,967
Bleckley	Logan E. Bleckley	Cochran	1912	10,430
Brantley	Benjamin D. Brantley	Nahunta	1920	11,077
Brooks	Preston L. Brooks	Quitman	1858	15,398
Bryan	Jonathan Bryan	Pembroke	1793	15,438
Bulloch	Archibald Bulloch	Statesboro	1796	43,125
Burke	Edmund Burke	Waynesboro	1777	20,579
Butts	Capt. Sam Butts	Jackson	1825	15,326
Calhoun	John C. Calhoun	Morgan	1854	5,013
Camden	Earl of Camden	Woodbine	1777	30,167
Candler	Gov. Allen D. Candler	Metter	1914	7,744
Carroll	Charles Carroll	Carrollton	1826	71,422
Catoosa	Catoosa (an Indian name)	Ringgold	1853	42,464
Charlton	Robert M. Charlton	Folkston	1854	8,496
Chatham	Earl of Chatham	Savannah	1777	216,935
Chattahoochee	Chattahoochee River	Cusseta	1854	16,934
Chattooga	Chattooga River	Summerville	1838	22,242

Continued County Name	Named For	County Seat	Date Formed	1990 Population
Cherokee	Cherokee Indians	Canton	1831	90,204
Clarke	Gen. Elijah Clark	Athens	1801	87,594
Clay	Henry Clay	Fort Gaines	1854	3,364
Clayton	Augustine S. Clayton	Jonesboro	1858	182,052
Clinch	Gen. Duncan L. Clinch	Homerville	1850	6,160
Cobb	Thomas W. Cobb	Marietta	1832	447,745
Coffee	Gen. John E. Coffee	Douglas	1854	29,592
Colquitt	Walter T. Colquitt	Moultrie	1856	36,645
Columbia	Christopher Columbus	Appling	1790	66,031
Cook	Gen. Philip Cook	Adel	1918	13,456
Coweta	Coweta (an Indian chief)	Newnan	1826	53,853
Crawford	William Crawford	Knoxville	1822	8,991
Crisp	Charles Crisp	Cordele	1905	20,011
Dade	Maj. Francis L. Dade	Trenton	1837	13,147
Dawson	William C. Dawson	Dawsonville	1857	9,429
Decatur	Comdr. Stephen Decatur	Bainbridge	1823	25,511
De Kalb	Baron De Kalb	Decatur	1822	545,837
Dodge	William E. Dodge	Eastman	1870	17,607
Dooly	Col. John Dooly	Vienna	1821	9,901
Dougherty	Charles Dougherty	Albany	1853	96,311
Douglas	Stephen A. Douglas	Douglasville	1870	71,120
Early	Gov. Peter Early	Blakely	1818	11,854
Echols	Col. Robert M. Echols	Statenville	1858	2,334
Effingham	Lord Effingham	Springfield	1777	25,687
Elbert	Gen. Sam Elbert	Elberton	1790	18,949
Emanuel	Gov. David Emanuel	Swainsboro	1812	20,546
Evans	Gen. Clement A. Evans	Claxton	1914	8,724
Fannin	Col. James W. Fannin	Blue Ridge	1854	15,992
Fayette	Gen. LaFayette	Fayetteville	1821	62,415
Floyd	Gen. John Floyd	Rome	1832	81,251
Forsyth	Gov. John Forsyth	Cumming	1832	44,083
Franklin	Benjamin Franklin	Carnesville	1784	16,650
Fulton	Robert Fulton	Atlanta	1853	648,951
Gilmer	Gov. George R. Gilmer	Ellijay	1832	13,368
Glascock	Gen. Thomas Glascock	Gibson	1857	2,357
Glynn	John Glynn	Brunswick	1777	62,496
Gordon	William W. Gordon	Calhoun	1850	35,072
Grady	Henry W. Grady	Cairo	1905	20,279
Greene	Gen. Nathaniel Greene	Greensboro	1786	11,793
Gwinnett	Gov. Button Gwinnett	Lawrenceville	1818	352,910
Habersham	Maj. Joseph Habersham	Clarkesville	1818	27,621
Hall	Gov. Lyman Hall	Gainesville	1818	95,428
Hancock	John Hancock	Sparta	1793	8,908
Haralson	Hugh A. Haralson	Buchanan	1856	21,966

Continued County Name	Named For	County Seat	Date Formed	1990 Population
Harris	Charles Harris	Hamilton	1827	17,788
Hart	Nancy Hart	Hartwell	1853	19,712
Heard	Gov. Stephen Heard	Franklin	1830	8,628
Henry	Patrick Henry	McDonough	1821	58,741
Houston	Gov. John Houstoun	Perry	1821	89,208
Irwin	Gov. Jared Irwin	Ocilla	1818	8,649
Jackson	Gov. James Jackson	Jefferson	1796	30,005
Jasper	Sgt. William Jasper	Monticello	1807	8,453
Jeff Davis	Jefferson Davis	Hazelhurst	1905	12,032
Jefferson	Thomas Jefferson	Louisville	1796	17,408
Jenkins	Gov. Charles J. Jenkins	Millen	1905	8,247
Johnson	Gov. Herschel V. Johnson	Wrightsville	1858	8,329
Jones	James Jones	Gray	1807	20,739
Lamar	L. Q. C. Lamar	Barnesville	1920	13,038
Lanier	Sidney Lanier	Lakeland	1919	5,531
Laurens	Col. John Laurens	Dublin	1807	39,988
Lee	Gen. Richard Henry lee	Leesburg	1826	16,250
Liberty	American Independence	Hinesville	1777	52,745
Lincoln	Gen. Benjamin Lincoln	Lincolnton	1796	7,442
Long	Dr. Crawford W. Long	Ludowici	1920	6,202
Lowndes	William J. Lowndes	Valdosta	1825	75,981
Lumpkin	Gov. Wilson Lumpkin	Dahlonega	1832	14,573
McDuffie	George McDuffie	Thomson	1870	20,119
McIntosh	McIntosh family	Darien	1793	8,634
Macon	Nathaniel Macon	Oglethorpe	1837	13,114
Madison	Pres. James Madison	Danielsville	1811	21,050
Marion	Gen. Francis Marion	Buena Vista	1827	5,590
Meriwether	Gen David Meriwether	Greenville	1827	22,411
Miller	Andrew J. Miller	Colquitt	1856	6,280
Mitchell	Gen. Henry Mitchell	Camilla	1857	20,275
Monroe	Pres. James Monroe	Forsyth	1821	17,113
Montgomery	Gen. Richard Montgomery	Mt. Vernon	1793	7,163
Morgan	Gen. Daniel Morgan	Madison	1807	12,883
Murray	Thomas W. Murray	Chatsworth	1832	26,147
Muscogee	Muscogee Indians	Columbus	1826	179,278
Newton	Sgt. John Newton	Covington	1821	41,808
Oconee	Oconee River	Watkinsville	1875	17,618
Oglethorpe	Gen. James E. Oglethorpe	Lexington	1793	9,763
Paulding	John Paulding	Dallas	1832	41,611
Peach	Georgia peach	Fort Valley	1924	21,189
Pickens	Gen. Andrew Pickens	Jasper	1853	14,432
Pierce	Pres. Franklin Pierce	Blackshear	1857	13,328
Pike	Gen. Zebulon M. Pike	Zebulon	1822	10,224
Polk	Pres. James K. Polk	Cedartown	1851	33,815

Continued County Name	Named For	County Seat	Date Formed	1990 Population
Pulaski	Count Casimir Pulaski	Hawkinsville	1808	8,108
Putnam	Gen. Israel Putnam	Eatonton	1807	14,137
Quitman	Gen. John A. Quitman	Georgetown	1858	2,209
Rabun	Gov. William Rabun	Clayton	1819	11,648
Randolph	John Randolph	Cuthbert	1828	8,023
Richmond	Duke of Richmond	Augusta	1777	189,719
Rockdale	Rockdale Church	Conyers	1870	54,091
Schley	Gov. William Schley	Ellaville	1857	3,588
Screven	Gen. James Screven	Sylvania	1793	13,842
Seminole	Seminole Indians	Donalsonville	1920	9,010
Spalding	Hon. Thomas Spalding	Griffin	1851	54,457
Stephens	Gov. Alexander H. Stephens	Toccoa	1905	23,257
Stewart	Gen. Daniel Stewart	Lumpkin	1830	5,654
Sumter	Gen. Thomas Sumter	Americus	1831	30,228
Talbot	Gov. Matthew Talbot	Talbotton	1827	6,524
Taliaferro	Col. Benjamin Taliaferro	Crawfordville	1825	1,915
Tattnall	Gov. Josiah Tattnall	Reidsville	1801	17,722
Taylor	Pres. Zachary Taylor	Butler	1852	7,642
Telfair	Gov. Edward Telfair	McRae	1807	11,000
Terrell	Dr. William Terrell	Dawson	1856	10,653
Thomas	Gen. Jett Thomas	Thomasville	1825	38,986
Tift	Nelson Tift	Tifton	1905	34,998
Toombs	Gen. Robert Toombs	Lyons	1905	24,072
Towns	Gov. George W. Towns	Hiawassee	1856	6,754
Treutlen	Gov. John A. Treutlen	Soperton	1917	5,994
Troup	Gov. George M. Troup	La Grange	1826	55,536
Turner	Henry G. Turner	Ashburn	1905	8,703
Twiggs	Gen. John Twiggs	Jefferson	1809	9,806
Union	the Union	Blairsville	1832	11,993
Upson	Stephen Upson	Thomaston	1824	26,300
Walker	Maj. Freeman Walker	La Fayette	1833	58,340
Walton	Gov. George Walton	Monroe	1818	38,586
Ware	Nicholas Ware	Waycross	1824	35,471
Warren	Gen. Joseph Warren	Warrenton	1793	6,078
Washington	George Washington	Sandersville	1784	19,112
Wayne	Gen. Anthony Wayne	Jesup	1803	22,356
Webster	Daniel Webster	Preston	1853	2,263
Wheeler	Gen. Joseph Wheeler	Alamo	1912	4,903
White	David T. White	Cleveland	1857	13,006
Whitfield	Rev. George Whitefield	Dalton	1851	72,462
Wilcox	Capt. John Wilcox	Abbeville	1857	7,008
Wilkes	John Wilkes	Washington	1777	10,597
Wilkinson	Gen. James Wilkinson	Irwinton	1803	10,228
Worth	Gen. William J. Worth	Sylvester	1853	19,745

Index